SOURCE MATERIALS ON KOREAN
POLITICS AND IDEOLOGIES

Compiled by

DONALD G. TEWKSBURY

VOLUME II
of the Series, Source Books on
Far Eastern Political Ideologies

International Secretariat
INSTITUTE OF PACIFIC RELATIONS
1 East 54th St. New York

1950

Price: $2.50

THE INSTITUTE OF PACIFIC RELATIONS

The Institute of Pacific Relations is an unofficial and non-partisan organization, founded in 1925 to facilitate the scientific study of the peoples of the Pacific area. It is composed of autonomous National Councils in the principal countries having important interests in the Pacific area, together with an International Secretariat. It is privately financed by contributions from National Councils, corporations and foundations. It is governed by a Pacific Council composed of members appointed by each of the National Councils.

In addition to the independent activities of its National Councils, the Institute organizes private international conferences every two or three years. Such conferences have been held at Honolulu (1925 and 1927), Kyoto (1929), Shanghai (1931), Banff, Canada (1933), Yosemite Park California (1936), Virginia Beach, Virginia (1939), Mont Tremblant, Quebec (1942), Hot Springs, Virginia (1945), Stratford, England (1947). The Institute conducts an extensive program of research on the political, economic and social problems of the Pacific area and the Far East. It also publishes the proceedings of its conferences, a quarterly journal, Pacific Affairs, and a large number of scholarly books embodying the results of its studies.

Neither the International Secretariat nor the National Councils of the Institute advocate policies or express opinions on national or international affairs. Responsibility for statements of fact or opinion in Institute publications rests solely with the authors.

NATIONAL COUNCILS

American Institute of Pacific Relations, Inc.
Australian Institute of International Affairs
Canadian Institute of International Affairs
Comite d'Etudes des Problemes du Pacifique
Indian Council of World Affairs
Japan Institute of Pacific Relations
New Zealand Institute of International Affairs
Pakistan Institute of International Affairs
Philippine Council, Institute of Pacific Relations
Royal Institute of International Affairs
U.S.S.R. Council, Institute of Pacific Relations

IPR INTERNATIONAL SECRETARIAT   1 East 54 St., New York 22, N. Y.

Copies of the two volumes thus far published in this series may be purchased from Professor D. G. Tewksbury, Teachers College, Columbia University, New York City, or from the IPR Publications Office, 1 East 54th St., New York 22, N. Y.

PREFACE

Recent events in Korea lend special significance to the documents included in this volume. It is hoped that selection of source materials here presented will prove valuable to students of Far Eastern history and of the present crisis in Korea. It serves as a useful supplement to George M. McCune's excellent book Korea Today, recently published for the Institute of Pacific Relations by the Harvard University Press.

This volume is the second in a series of volumes designed to provide a preliminary collection of key ideological documents essential to an understanding of Far Eastern political ideologies during the modern period. Volume I on China and Japan was the first of the series published under the general title of a Source Book on Far Eastern Political Ideologies. Volume III on Southeast Asia, and Volume IV on India, Pakistan, and Ceylon, will be published shortly to complete the series.

Suggestions for improvements and additions to the materials included in the present volume will be welcomed. Acknowledgement of sources used is indicated in every instance. In the preparation of this volume, many Korean friends and friends of the Korean people have been most helpful. Special acknowledgement is made of the advice received during publication from Mr. William L. Holland and Miss Mary F. Healy of the Institute of Pacific Relations. Responsibility for the selection of the documents and for the footnotes given at the end of each document rests solely with the compiler.

Teachers College
New York
September 15, 1950

Donald G. Tewksbury

CONTENTS

CONTENTS

PART II. FROM ANNEXATION BY JAPAN TO WORLD WAR II

PART I. FROM ISOLATION TO ANNEXATION BY JAPAN

1871

KOREAN REPLY TO JAPANESE POST-RESTORATION PROPOSAL

We have received your letter and have given it very deep consideration, comparing your dispatch with other dispatches. It is a long time
since there has been any intercourse between our two countries. Your
dispatch demands payment of tribute. We will show how this affair
stands. Taiko Sama (Hideyoshi) without provocation or cause of any kind,
invaded Korea 1592 , and made Korea sign a document agreeing to pay
tribute. In those days Korea was unprepared for war, and had not even
been informed of the intention of Japan. But it is very different now.
The invasion by Taiko was a crime committed against Korea by Japan,
which is not yet punished. Your demand is so unreasonable, that instead of Korea paying you tribute, it is for you to return the money
paid by Korea. In your dispatch you have made many insinuations of
your having adopted foreign customs; we can assure you that Japan is
Japan, Korea is Korea -- but Korea has its own customs. Some years
back we had a difference with a country called France, which is, among
barbarians, considered to be very powerful and very large, whilst Korea
is very small -- but we defeated that great country. We assembled all
our warriors, every one of them was ready to die. According to our old
treaty of friendship, whenever either is attacked by barbarians, the
other is to help. To show our honesty, when the barbarians went to your
country, we immediately wrote to you that we had made every preparation
to help you. During the French attack on Korea we day and night expected
that you would come with your forces to our aid; but not having received
your assistance we wrote and informed you of our distress, informing you
of our position, and asking for immediate help. You have neither sent
us aid, nor any answer to our dispatch. From that day our treaty of
friendship was at an end. We no longer consider each other friends but
enemies. The tone of your dispatch is so friendly that we look upon it
as treachery; and after having been so friendly with Japan and being re-
paid by treachery, we never can be friendly again. Not only have you
broken the treaty as above described, but you have also broken another
very chief point of treaty in adopting the manners and customs of the
Western barbarians. Our information is, that you have adopted French
drill; and whenever you want money you go to England; and if you wish to
tax your own people or impose duties you take advice from America. But
you have never consulted us, as agreed in our old treaty. You think the
Western barbarians are great people. We, Koreans, are a very small country, but yet we have the courage to put in writing to you, that Western
barbarians are beasts. The above we intend as a direct insult to you and
your allies -- the barbarians. We desire that you should join them and
bring your great ships and your army here. Fusan is the nearest part of
Korea to Japan. To make your attack as inexpensive as possible to you
and your friends, we will send and clear Fusan for a battlefield, and will
appoint the battle. It is useless to go into any correspondence, because
the wrong you have done to us is so great, that your apologies will not
avail. The only alternative is a bloody war -- a war that will cost
Japan all its warriors; and then we will bring you to terms.

2.

This is our intention. You must not attempt to write us again; and the above is a notice to you to make all preparation, for either Japan must invade Korea, or Korea will invade Japan.

From: The Story of Korea, Longford, Joseph H., Scribner, New York, 1911, pp.297-298.

(The above document is reported by Longford to be the Korean reply to a letter sent by Japan to Korea after the Meiji Restoration of 1868 suggesting that the old tributary relations between the two countries be renewed. Although some assert that this version of the reply is not a true copy, there is no doubt, according to Longford and other scholars, that the Tai Won Kun (("Lord of the Great Court")) made a reply that was regarded by the Japanese as insulting and contemptuous. The Tai Won Kun was the Regent of Korea, who at that time was acting for the young king.)

\#　　　\#　　　\#

February 26, 1876

JAPANESE KOREAN-TREATY OF 1876

(The Kangwha Treaty)

The Governments of Japan and Chosen, being desirous to resume the amicable relations that of yore existed between them, and to promote the friendly feelings of both nations to a still firmer basis, have for this purpose appointed their Plenipotentiaries, that is to say: The Government of Japan, Kuroda Kiyotaka, High Commissioner Extraordinary to Chosen, Lieutenant-General and Member of the Privy Council, Minister of the Colonisation Department, and Inouye Kaoru, Associate High Commissioner Extraordinary to Chosen, Member of the Genro In; and the Government of Chosen, Shin Ken, Han-Choo-Su-Fu, and In-Jisho, Fu-So-Fu, Fuku-So-Kwan, who, according to the powers received from their respective Governments, have agreed upon and concluded the following Articles:

ARTICLE I

Chosen being an independent state enjoys the same sovereign rights as does Japan.

In order to prove the sincerity of the friendship existing between the two nations, their intercourse shall henceforward be carried on in terms of equality and courtesy, each avoiding the giving of offense by arrogance or manifestations of suspicion.

In the first instance, all rules and precedents that are apt to obstruct friendly intercourse shall be totally abrogated and, in their stead, rules, liberal and in general usage fit to secure a firm and perpetual peace, shall be established.

ARTICLES II - XI

ARTICLE XII

The foregoing eleven Articles are binding from the date of the signing thereof, and shall be observed by the two contracting parties, faithfully and invariably, whereby perpetual friendship shall be secured to the two countries.

The present Treaty is executed in duplicate, and copies will be exchanged between the two contracting parties.

In faith whereof we, the respective Plenipotentiaries of Japan and Chosen, have affixed our seals thereto, this twenty-sixth day of the second month of the ninth year of Meiji, and the two thousand five hundred and thirty-sixth since the accession of Jimmu Tenno; and, in the era of Chosen, the second day of the second moon of the year Heishi, and of the founding of Chosen the four hundred and eighty-fifth.

(signed)

KURODA KIYOTAKA
INOUYE KAORU
SHIN KEN
IN JI-SHO

From: British and Foreign State Papers, Vol. LXVII, pp.530 - 533.

(This was the first treaty entered into by Korea that was negotiated and framed on the basis of Western concepts of international law. Japan hoped by this treaty to separate Korea from her "Confucian" dependency on China.)

\#   \#   \#

May 22, 1882

U.S.-KOREAN TREATY OF 1882

The United States of America and the Kingdom of Chosen, being sincerely desirous of establishing permanent relations of amity and friendship between their respective peoples, have to this end appointed, that is to say: the President of the United States, R.W. Shufeldt, Commodore, U.S. Navy, as his Commissioner Plenipotentiary; and His Majesty the King of Chosen, Shin Chen, President of the Royal Cabinet, Chin Hong-Chi, Member of the Royal Cabinet, as his Commissioners Plenipotentiary; who, having reciprocally examined their respective full powers, which have been found to be in due form, have agreed upon the several following articles:

ARTICLE I

There shall be perpetual peace and friendship between the President of the United States and the King of Chosen and the citizens and subjects of their respective Governments.

If other Powers deal unjustly or oppressively with either Government, the other will exert their good offices, on being informed of the case, to bring about an amicable arrangement, thus showing their friendly feelings.

ARTICLE II - XIII

ARTICLE XIV

The high contracting Powers hereby agree that should at any time the King of Chosen grant to any nation, or to the merchants or citizens of any nation, any right, privilege, or favour, connected either with navigation, commerce, political or other intercourse, which is not conferred by this treaty, such right, privilege, and favour shall freely inure to the benefit of the United States, its public officers, merchants, and citizens; provided always, that whenever such right, privilege, or favour is accompanied by any condition or equivalent concession granted by the other nation interested, the United States, its officers and people, shall only be entitled to the benefit of such right, privilege, or favour upon complying with the conditions or concessions connected therewith.

In faith whereof, the respective Commissioners Plenipotentiary have signed and sealed the foregoing at Yin-chuen, in English and Chinese, being three originals of each text, of even tenor and date, the ratifications of which shall be exchanged at Yin-chuen within one year from the date of its execution, and immediately thereafter this treaty shall be in all its provisions publicly proclaimed and made known by both governments in their respective countries, in order that it may be obeyed by their citizens and subjects respectively.

Chosen, May the 22nd, A.D. 1882.

(l.s.) (Signed) R.W. Shufeldt, Commodore, U.S.N., Envoy of the U.S. to Chosen.
(l.s.) (Signed) Shin Chen   In
(l.s.) (Signed) Chin Hong-Chi   Chinese

From: Treaties, Conventions, etc., Malloy, W.M.- Editor, Washington, D.C., 1910, Vol. I - 1776-1909, pp.334-339.

(Underlining not in original text.)

(Ratified by the U.S. Senate on January 9, 1883, and proclaimed by President Arthur on June 4, 1883. The second clause in Article I was later the subject of considerable discussion between Korea and the United States. Because of this clause, Korea came to regard the United States as her "Elder Brother".)

# # #

PROCLAMATION OF THE KING OF KOREA ON FOREIGN RELATIONS

Our country is situated far away to the east in a nook of the sea, and hitherto we have had no relations or dealings with foreigners; for which reason we have neither seen nor heard very much. We have pursued this policy of jealous seclusion now for five hundred years, during which time we have never swerved from the customs of the days of old. Now, the countries of the West, say, England, France, America and Russia, have invented appliances of the most ingenious and beneficial description, by virtue of which they have attained to great wealth and political power. Their railways and their steamboats pervade the whole face of the land, and all the countries of the world are connected with others by treaty; their balance of power is preserved by standing armies, and their relations are maintained intact by adherence to the principles of international law, just as was the case among the states in the time of the "Chun Tsin." For this reason, China, although she stands alone and pre-eminent among the nations of the world, still makes treaties with them on equal terms, while Japan, which repelled all the advances of foreigners with such austerity, has now formed compacts of friendship with them all. Thus have they both done that which was directly opposed to their own original ideas; in truth, not even their strength was sufficient to withstand the pressure of the times. Well, then, our country, in the spring of 1876, ratified the friendly agreement come to between ourselves and Japan, and promised her to open three ports to trade, and now we have established new treaties with America, England and Germany. This is an innovation, certainly, and there is nothing to be astonished at in the dissatisfaction expressed by our people. But international relations are now of general prevalence; so there is no difficulty in bringing about friendly associations by the employment of right principles and good faith. The object of a resident minister in any country is primarily to watch over the interests of the merchants who may be settled there; there is no cause for suspicion of any ulterior motives on his part. There is no law or principle in the matter of international relationship, and this is found written in the classics and their commentaries. But there exist certain doltish and stupid scholars, who bear in mind how, in olden days, a feudal state would be ruined by making a compact with another, recklessly setting up this as an illustration, and then urging that Japan should be kept at a distance. Why do not such persons consider that if other people come to our shores in all friendliness, and we receive them as enemies and fight them, all the world would cry, What sort of a nation can that be? If one nation stands isolated and alone, it will be bereft of all assistance, and give rise to enmity on the part of all other countries. It will become the object of general attack, and then it will be defeated, and at last ruined, and then its repentance will be great indeed. And what virtue will there be in it?

Those who reason about these matters condemn treaty-making on the ground that foreign nations will contaminate us with their depraved religions. This is because they have pondered so long and so deeply upon the religion of their ancestors. But as regards entering into treaty relations, of course we shall enter into them, and as regards prohibiting the foreign religion, of course, we can prohibit it, and in establishing

treaties of amity and commerce, we shall do so in accordance with the
principles of international law. According to the rules of propriety,
it cannot be permitted that religion shall be promulgated in the interi-
or; besides, how can you, who have for so long practiced the teachings
of Confucius and Mencius, and bathed yourself in decorum and rectitude
all your lives, suddenly abandon the true and embrace the false and
bad? Supposing, for instance, there were to be some stupid fellow, some
uneducated lout, secretly attempting to diffuse his teachings (in our
country); then we have the law of our state, by which all such shall be
exterminated and destroyed without mercy; what reason, then, is there for
sorrow on account of our (alleged) inability to deal with such abuses?
Moreover, when (these malcontents) see even so little adoption of foreign
methods in the direction of mechanism and machinery, they immediately regard that as contamination with foreign heresies. This, indeed, is the
ne plus ultra of obtuseness! If the (foreign) doctrine is to be regarded as a doctrine of lechery and sensuality, then it can be kept at
a distance; if a foreign mechanism is advantageous, then we can reap
advantage from it and use it to increase our wealth. Why fear, instead
of having recourse to, such things as agriculture, sericulture, medical
science, medicines, military weapons, ships and carriages? Let us repel
their doctrines, but learn to use or imitate their machinery; both these
courses of policy can be carried out; and thus no outrage will be done to
propriety. Besides, the strength of foreign nations and the weakness of
our own are as far removed asunder as heaven from earth. If we do not
learn to use their machinery, how can we withstand the contempt they feel
for us, or prevent their covetousness (being directed against our land)?
Most certainly are we able to cultivate their principles of government
in regard to our domestic legislation, and enter into friendly relations
with our neighbors; maintain the integrity and decorum of our own nation
while emulating the strength and riches of those outside, so that all,
from the highest to the lowest, may enjoy prosperity and peace. How
can we delay about it any longer? At present, it is difficult to change
those institutions which have existed from time immemorial. The popular
will is not fixed. The rising which took place in the sixth moon caused
the neighboring country (Japan) to lose faith in us, and has bequeathed
a legacy of ridicule of us to the entire world. The prestige of our
country has declined from day to day. The indemnity we owe to Japan
amounts to myriads of taels. Does not this reflection make you shudder
(literally, give you a cold heart)? Was the entrance of the Japanese
into our country attended with any results or breach of friendly relations towards ourselves? Yet our soldiers, prompted by unworthy suspi-
cions, sought to oppose them; and their breasts becoming fuller and fuller (of such thoughts), their anger at last burst forth. Thus, without
any reason, they themselves were the first to rebel. Think, then, all of
you, on whose side was the fault? Now, happily, our arrangements are
very nearly finished, and our former good relations stand on a better
footing than ever; America, England, and other countries are following
on each other's heels (in resorting to our shores), and making treaties
of amity and commerce with us, a custom which is prevalent among all the
nations of the world, and by no means an innovation of our own. There is,
indeed, no ground whatever for any apprehension on this score, and you may
may, all of you, rest perfectly tranquil and undisturbed.

Let scholars attend diligently to their studies, and the people to

their agricultural pursuits; let there be no more talk about "European"
and "Japanese" or any further stirring up of sedition and trouble. Although there be foreigners moving about in the open ports, let everybody
continue just as quiet as usual, and see to it that you are not the first
to make a disturbance. If they begin to insult or annoy you in any way,
they will be dealt with in strict accordance with the provisions of the
treaty, so that our own people will not be unfairly treated, and foreigners too will be protected. Alas! the use of a stupid person of his own
stupidity is deprecated by the Holy Man; scoffing at high authorities by
those under them is a punishable offense according to the laws of the
land. To punish without instructing the people is to do them wrong; for
which reason I now make this distinct and public declaration. Moreover,
now that friendly relationships are being cultivated with Western nations, (I order that) all roadside obelisks, outside the capital, no-
tifying that foreigners are not allowed to pass, be forthwith taken up
and removed, as being unsuitable to the new orders of things. You,
scholars and people, now understand this perfectly. This order is now
promulgated under authority of the Government, and is to be placarded
in prominent places over the length and breadth of the entire country.

From: Papers Relating to the Foreign Relations of
the United States, 1883, Government Printing
Office, 1884, pp.170-172, Document No. 78.

(This proclamation, attributed by the U.S. Legation in Peking
to the King of Korea and forwarded by the Legation to the
State Department in Washington for its information, first
appeared in a Japanese journal, and afterwards in a Shanghai
English paper. Treaties with the U.S., Great Britain, Germany,
Italy, Russia, and France were made by Korea in 1882, 1883,
1883, 1884, 1884, and 1886 respectively. These treaties
finally ended the period of Korean "isolation".)

#   #   #

August 1, 1894
JAPAN'S DECLARATION OF WAR AGAINST CHINA

Imperial Rescript

We, by the Grace of Heaven, Emperor of Japan, seated on a Throne
occupied by the same dynasty from time immemorial, do hereby make proclamation to all our loyal and brave subjects as follows:

We hereby declare war against China and We command each and all of
Our competent authorities, in obedience to Our wish and with a view to
the attainment of the national aim, to carry on hostilities by sea and by
land against China, with all the means at their disposal consistently
with the Law of Nations.

During the past three decades of Our reign, our constant aim has been to further the peaceful progress of the country in civilization; and being sensible of the evils inseparable from complications with foreign States, it has always been our pleasure to instruct our Ministers of State to labor for the promotion of friendly relations with our Treaty Powers. We are gratified to know that the relations of Our Empire with those Powers have yearly increased in good will and in friendship. Under the circumstances we were unprepared for such a conspicuous want of amity and of good faith as has been manifested by China in her conduct towards this country in connection with Korean affair.

Korea is an independent State. She was first introduced into the family of nations by the advice and under the guidance of Japan. It has, however, been China's habit to designate Korea as her dependency, and openly and secretly to interfere with her domestic affairs. At the time of the recent civil insurrection in Korea, China dispatched troops thither, alleging that her purpose was to afford succour to her dependent State. We, in virture of the treaty concluded in 1882, and looking to possible emergencies, caused a military force to be sent to that country.

Wishing to procure for Korea freedom from the calamity of perpetual disturbance, and thereby to maintain the peace of the East in general, Japan invited China's cooperation for the accomplishment of that object. But China, advancing various pretexts, declined Japan's proposal. Thereupon, Japan advised Korea to reform her administration so that order and tranquility might be preserved at home, and so that the country might be able to discharge the responsibilities and duties of an independent State abroad. Korea has already consented to undertake the task. But China has secretly and insidiously endeavoured to circumvent and to thwart Japan's purpose. She has, further procrastinated, and endeavoured to make warlike preparations both on land and at sea. When those preparations were completed, she not only sent large reenforcements to Korea, with a view to the forcible attainment of her ambitious designs, even carried her arbitrariness to the extent of opening fire upon Our ships in Korean waters. China's plain object is to make it uncertain where the responsibility resides of preserving peace and order in Korea, and not only to weaken the position of that State in the family of nations -- a position obtained for Korea through Japan's efforts -- but also to obscure the significance of the treaties recognizing and confirming that position. Such conduct on the part of China is not only a direct injury to the rights and interests of this Empire; but also a menace to the permanent peace and tranquility of the Orient. Judging from her actions, it must be concluded that China, from the beginning, has been bent upon sacrificing peace to the attainment of her sinister object. In this situation, ardent as Our wish is to promote the prestige of the country abroad by strictly peaceful methods, We find it impossible to avoid a formal declaration of war against China. It is Our earnest wish that, by the loyalty and valor of our faithful subjects, peace may soon be permanently restored and the glory of the Empire augmented and completed.

Given this 1st day of the eighth month of the 27th year of the Meiji.

(Sign Manual).

(Countersignatures
of Minister President of
State and other Ministers).

From: <u>Korea Treaties and Agreements</u>, Carnegie Endowment for International Peace, Washington, D.C.,
Pamphlet No. 43, 1921, pp.8-10.

(The Sino-Japanese War was declared on August 1, 1894, the
date of the above document, and hostilities were legally ended
on April 17, 1895, with the signing of the Treaty of Shimonoseki.
From this time on, Japan influence on Korea became more direct
and powerful in opposition to the claims of Russia and China,
and culminated in the establishment of a Japanese protectorate
over Korea in 1905.)

\#   \#   \#

January 8, 1895

<u>THE KING'S OATH OF INDEPENDENCE FROM CHINA</u>

On this 12th day of the 12th moon of the 503rd year of the founding
of the Dynasty, we presume to announce clearly to the Spirits of all our
Sacred Imperial Ancestors that we, their lowly descendant, received in
early childhood, now thiry and one years ago, the mighty heritage of our
ancestors, and that in reverent awe towards Heaven, and following in the
rule and pattern of our ancestors, we, though we have encountered many
troubles, have not loosed hold of the thread. How dare we, your lowly
descendant, aver that we are acceptable to the heart of Heaven? It is
only that our ancestors have graciously looked down upon us and benignly
protected us. Splendidly did our ancestor lay the foundation of our
Royal House, opening a way for us his descendants through five hundred
years and three. Now, in our generation, the times are mightily changed,
and men and matters are expanding. A friendly Power, designing to prove
faithful, and the deliberations of our Council aiding thereto, show that
only as an independent ruler can we make our country strong. How can we,
your lowly descendant, not conform to the spirit of the time and thus
guard the domain bequeathed by our ancestors? How venture not to strenuously exert ourselves and stiffen and anneal us in order to add lustre
to the virtues of our predecessors? For all time from now no other
State will we lean upon, but will make broad the steps of our country
towards prosperity, building up the happiness of our people in order to
strengthen the foundations of our independence. When we ponder on this
course, let there be no sticking in the old ways, no practice of ease or
of dalliance; but docilely let us carry out the great designs of our ancestors, watching and observing sublunary conditions, reforming our internal administration, remedying there accumulated abuses.

10.

We, your lowly descendant, do now take the fourteen clauses of the Great Charter and swear before the Spirits of our Ancestors in Heaven that we, reverently trusting in the merits bequeathed by our ancestors, will bring these to a successful issue, nor will we dare to go back on our word. Do you, bright Spirits, descend and behold!

1. All thoughts of dependence on China shall be cut away, and a firm foundation for independence secured.

2. A rule and ordinance for the Royal House shall be established, in order to make clear the line of succession and precedence among the Royal Family.

3. The King shall attend at the Great Hall for the inspection of affairs, where, after personally interrogating his Ministers, he shall decide upon matters of State. The Queen and the Royal family are not allowed to interfere.

4. Palace matters and the government of the country must be kept separate, and may not be mixed up together.

5. The duties and powers of the Cabinet and of the various Ministers shall be clearly defined.

6. The payment of taxes by the people shall be regulated by law. Wrongful additions may not be made to the list, and no excess collected.

7. The assessment and collection of the land tax, and the disbursement of expenditure, shall be under the charge and control of the Finance Department.

8. The expenses of the Royal household shall be the first to be reduced, by way of setting an example to the various Ministries and local officials.

9. An estimate shall be drawn up in advance each year of the expenditure of the Royal household and the various official establishments, putting on a firm foundation the management of the revenue.

10. The regulations of the local officers must be revised in order to discriminate the functions of the local officials.

11. Young men of intelligence in the country shall be sent abroad in order to study foreign science and industries.

12. The instruction of army officers, and the practice of the methods of enlistment, to secure the foundation of a military system.

13. Civil law and criminal law must be strictly and clearly laid down; none must be imprisoned or fined in excess, so that security of life and property may be ensured for all alike.

14. Men shall be employed without regard to their origin, and in seeking for officials, recourse shall be had to capital and country alike in order to widen the avenues for ability.

From: Bishop, I.L., Korea and Her Neighbours, London, 1898, Vol. II., pp.35-37. (The author was an eye-witness of the ceremony.)

(Official translation of the text of the oath taken by His
Majesty the King of Korea, at the Altar of Heaven, Seoul, on
January 8, 1895. This historic oath was taken by the King
under pressure from the Japanese ((Count Inouye)) during the
Sino-Japanese War.)

#   #   #

February 11, 1896

ROYAL PROCLAMATION   (FROM THE RUSSIAN LEGATION)

Alas! Alas! on account of Our unworthiness and mal-administra-
tion the wicked advanced and the wise retired. Of the last ten years,
none has passed without troubles. Some were brought on by those We had
trusted as the members of the body, while others, by those of Our own
bone and flesh. Our dynasty of five centuries has thereby been often
endangered, and millions of Our subjects have thereby been gradually
impoverished. These facts make Us blush and sweat for shame. But these
troubles have been brought about through Our partiality and self-will,
giving rise to rascality and blunders leading to calamities. All have
been Our own fault from the first to the last.

Fortunately, through loyal and faithful subjects rising up in
righteous efforts to remove the wicked, there is a hope that the tribu-
lations experienced may invigorate the State, and that calm may return
after the storm. This accords with the principle that human nature will
have freedom after a long pressure, and that the ways of Heaven bring
success after reverses. We shall endeavour to be merciful. No pardon,
however, shall be extended to the principal traitors concerned in the
affairs of July 1894 and of October 1895. Capital punishment should be
their due, thus venting the indignation of men and gods alike. But to all
the rest, officials or soldiers, citizens or coolies, a general amnesty,
free and full, is granted, irrespective of the degree of their offenses.
Reform your hearts; ease your minds; go about your business, public or
private, as in times past.

As to the cutting of the Top-Knots -- what can We say? Is it such
an urgent matter? The traitors, by using force and coercion, brought
about the affair. That this measure was taken against Our will is, no
doubt, well known to all. Nor is it Our wish that the conservative subjects throughout the country, moved to righteous indignation, should rise
up, as they have, circulating false rumours, causing death and injury to
one another, until the regular troops had to be sent to suppress the disturbances by force. The traitors indulged their poisonous nature in
everything. Fingers and hairs would fail to count their crimes. The
soldiers are Our children. So are the insurgents. Cut any of the ten
fingers, and one would cause as much pain as another. Fighting long continued would pour out blood and heap up corpses, hindering communications
and traffic. Alas! if this continues the people will all die. The mere
contemplation of such consequences provokes Our tears and chills Our
heart. We desire that as soon as orders arrive the soldiers should return

to Seoul and the insurgents to their respective places and occupations.

As to the cutting of Top-Knots, no one shall be forced as to dress and hats. Do as you please. The evils now afflicting the people shall be duly attended to by the Government. This is Our own word of honour. Let all understand.

By order of His Majesty,
(Signed) Pak-Chung Yang,
Acting Home and Prime Minister.

11th day, 2nd moon, 1st year of Kon-Yang.

PROCLAMATION TO THE SOLDIERS

On account of the unhappy fate of Our country, traitors have made trouble every year. Now We have a document informing us of another conspiracy. We have therefore come to the Russian Legation. The Representatives of different countries have all assembled.

Soldiers! come and protect Us. You are Our children. The troubles of the past were due to the crimes of chief traitors. You are all pardoned, and shall not be held answerable. Do your duty and be at ease. When you meet the chief traitors, viz., Cho-hui Yen, Wu-pom Sun, Yi-tu Hwong, Yi-pom Nai, Yi-chin Ho, and Kon-yong Chin, cut off their heads at once, and bring them.

You (soldiers) attend us at the Russian Legation.

(Royal Signature)

11th day, 2nd moon, 1st year of Kon-yang.

From: Bishop, I.L., <u>Korea and Her Neighbours</u>, London, 1898, Vol. II., pp.181-183.

(This proclamation was issued from the Russian Legation in Seoul, the asylum to which the Emperor had fled on February 11, 1896, in order to be free from Japanese influence. The reference to "Top-Knots" is concerned with the Royal Edict of December 30, 1895, issued under pressure from the Japanese, which called upon all Koreans to cut short their hair.)

#   #   #

February 20, 1897

MEMORIAL OF THE INDEPENDENCE CLUB

We, your Majesty's humble servants, desire to state that two important factors constitute an independent and sovereign state, namely: first, it must not lean upon another nation nor tolerate foreign interference in the national administration; secondly, it must help itself by adopting a wise policy and enforcing justice throughout the realm. The power of establishing these two great principles has been invested to your gracious Majesty by Heaven above. Whenever this power is destroyed there is no sovereignty.

The object of erecting the Independence Arch and organizing the Independence Club by your humble servants is to reverence your Majesty's august throne and to strengthen the hearts of the people in order to maintain our dynasty and the independence of our nation. Recently we, your humble servants, have observed that the condition of the nation is on the verge of destruction; great disappointment and constant discontent prevail in the heart of every citizen. The reason for this state of affairs is due to the giving away to a foreigner the authority of administering the national finance, which power must be in the hands of our own people; the controlling influence of the military department ought to be in the hands of our own officials but this also has been transferred to foreigners. Even the power of appointing and dismissing government officials has been taken from our own authorities. The dishonest and corruptive classes thus created take this opportunity to satisfy their contemptible nature by bringing foreign influence to bear upon Your Majesty and some go so far as to even oppress and threaten the Throne for their personal gain and for the interests of their foreign employers. Impossible stories and baseless reports which these classes continually bring to Your Majesty produce the most damaging effect upon Your Majesty's saintly intelligence. There is an old saying that ice is generally discovered after stepping repeatedly upon frost. Hence it is perfectly natural for us to come to the conclusion, after witnessing so many lamentable events which have taken place, that before many moons the entire power of self government will have become a matter of past record. If it is once lost, repentance can not restore it.

The only way to maintain order and achieve improvement in national life is to enforce just laws and to apply proper rules and regulations to all institutions of the government. But of late the authorities totally disregard both the old and the new laws and the rules and regulations have become worthless dead letters. Under such circumstances how can we expect other nations to consider us capable of self government? Whenever this doubt is entertained by other nations, they naturally feel inclined to interfere with our affairs; when they are once permitted to interfere, they will go still further to use coercion in order to carry out their object.

Alas! the fifteen million souls within this land of three thousand li are all Your Majesty's children and it is their duty to protect our imperial house and to defend the independent and sovereign rights of our country, but through their ignorance and self-love, the great and glorious responsibility of defending the nation's rights has been forgotten. The consequence is that the powerful neighbors have been treating us as if we are nobody, and even Your Majesty's position has become perilous. For this sad condition of affairs we blame no one but our humble selves. Having realized our crime of negligency and incompetency, we are ashamed to stand upon earth and face Heaven. We would rather be shot through our hearts or have our abdomens cut open for the sake of the country and our sovereign than to prolong our unworthy lives with the shame and humiliation of neglecting our duties and shifting our inherited responsibilities. After having resolved upon this point we humbly and unanimously pray Your Majesty to consider the welfare and interests of the fifteen million souls as Your Majesty's own; to rejoice with them when they are prosperous and happy; to weep with them when they are in distress and sorrow; to sympathize with them in all their worthy and patriotic movements. To direct Your Majesty's officials to enforce justice strictly in every department and to jealously guard against foreign infringment of our sovereign rights are what we humbly desire. If Your Majesty cooperate with Your Majesty's own subjects and elicit their loyal support, Your Majesty's august home will be the reigning house of our land unto endless years; thousands of enemies will not dare to usurp our independent power. Before the sight of Heaven we have pledged our lives to the cause of our country and we humbly take an oath before your august presence that we will not alter our decision in the matter. We pray that Your Majesty will take cognizance of our loyalty, to Your Imperial house and to the cause of our independence.

(Signed by one hundred and thirty-five members of the Independence Club.)

From: The Korean Repository, February, 1898, Vol. V, pp.75-76.

(This document is one of the earliest expressions of the independence movement in Korea and was written before the King assumed the title of Emperor. The Independence Club was organized on June 7, 1896, by a Korean, at that time an American citizen, by the name of Suh Chai Pil (Dr. Phillip Jaisohn). This organization published The Independent, the first issue of which was printed on April 7, 1896.)

# # #

September 1897

MEMORIAL URGING TITLE OF EMPEROR

It is written in the Book of Rites that he whose virtues equal those of heaven and earth is called Whang Chei. Three Whangs (pre-historic rulers of China) and five Cheis (whose successive reigns extended from 2953 to 2439 B.C.) were so called because their virtues and merits were like those of heaven. Where virtues are unsurpassable titles should be as high, and where merits are unexcelled honors should be as great. To assume the highest title because of the greatest merits, has been the practice of all holy and illustrious rulers, and is agreeable to heavenly principles and human laws. On previous occasions, we expressed fully our views on the subject; but Your Majesty was not satisfied. Our regret and sorrow at your refusal are unbearable.

Since the establishment of your dynasty, the country has been for five centuries governed by holy and wise sovereigns. The land has been pervaded and saturated with glory and peace. Our ceremonies, music, laws, literature and style of dress are modifications of those of the Han, Tang and Song dynasties, our standard being the Ming dynasty. Hence we are the direct successor of these dynasties in civilization.

In wisdom and bravery Your Majesty far excells a hundred monarchs. Your disposition is like that of heaven and earth. Your virtues extend even to spirits. You follow the principles of three emperors and inherit the ideas of five sovereigns. During your reign of three decades, good influence and merits have extended far and wide, while your methods of government are those of the classics. When we passed thro calamitous times, many dangers only strengthened the country and great anxieties displayed your powers. Thro your exertions disorders have been rectified; and the royal ancestral temples have been kept safe. The safety of the land has been made as firm as mountains, and misfortunes have been turned into blessings. In peace and prosperity the foundation of independence has been laid, and the rights of self-government are enforced. This is the time when heaven is helping us, and your dynasty is entering an era of renewed glory.

It is said in the international law that the ruler of any independent state may assume a new title and make his subjects honor the same; but that he has no right to make others recognize it. It is further stated that when the ruler of a certain state assumed the title of king or of emperor, some powers recognized the title sooner than others. This shows that we have the right to assume a title tho the right of recognition is with others. Then we need not give up our right because others may not exercise theirs. When it is said that some powers recognize sooner than others the regal or imperial title assumed by a ruler, it means that the party adopting the new title does so without first requiring the recognition of others -- the word "sooner" indicating the order of recognition after the assumption and not before it. Then, who should first seek for the recognition of others without assuming the title?

Now, in lofty virtues and in clear judgment Your Majesty is as great and as penetrating as heaven. "Whang" means greatness, "Chei" means judgment. Being, in holiness, like Hui, Rong, Yo, and Soon (four celebrated rulers of ancient China), and as the successor of Han, Tang, Song and Ming dynasties your assumption of the title of emperor is in accordance with ancient precedents and present requirements. The will of heaven and the wishes of the people should be complied with. Admiring as we do Your Majesty's modesty we don't know when ancient rulers ever refused to hear your prayers. After fasting and washing, we unanimously beg Your Majesty to grant this petition.

From: The Korean Repository, Volume IV, October 1897, Seoul, pp.387-388

(This Memorial urged that the King take the step of becoming Emperor as a symbolic act expressing the full independence of Korea from foreign suzerainty.)

\# \# \#

October 12, 1897
EDICT UPON ASSUMPTION OF TITLE OF EMPEROR

The Whang-Chei, by the grace of heaven, says:--

After Dan-Kun and Ki-Ja, the country was divided into principalities, each striving for mastery over others. But Korio absorbed the states of Ma-Han, Chin-Han, and Ben-Han. This is known is history as the Consolidation of Three Hans. When Tai jo (the founder of this dynasty) ascended the throne the territory was further extended to the north by subduing the land of Mal-Kal which produced tusks, furs and wild silk, and to the south by taking the principality of Tam-na (Quelpart) whose tributes consisted of oranges and marine products. A united realm of 4,000 li was thus established. Ceremonials, music, laws and measures were modelled after those of Tang and Woo (delebrated Chinese dynasties, 2357 B.C.). A Kingdom firm and solid was established as the heritage of our endless dynasty.

Our unworthy lot has fallen on evil days; but thro the kind care of the Supreme Being, dangers have given place to safety. The foundation of independence has been laid and the rights of self-government are exercised. Our officials and people, soldiers and merchants unanimously desired Us, in scores of petitions, to assume the title of Emperor. Our refusal was repeated but useless. Therefore, on the 17th day of the 9th moon (12th of October), after informing heaven and earth thro sacrifices, We assumed the title of Emperor in the south of the White Mountains. (Seoul). Dai Han shall be the name of Our dominion. This year shall be the first of Kwang-Mu. The altar of the god of earth shall be called Tai-sa; the altar of the god of grains, Tai-jik (formerly Sa and Jik only). The Queen Min shall be Empress and the Crown Prince, the Imperial Prince.

As the great event has been just accomplished, We, according to ancient usages, hereby proclaim a general amnesty.--

1. High ranks and generous salaries granted for the maintenance of officials are to secure their loyal service to the state. The fortunes of a state depend on the corruption or integrity of officials. When officials are corrupt bribes flourish, positions and rewards go to the unworthy and the unmerited; underlings play tricks and people are injured. From corruption rise all disorders in the body politic. From the 12th October, any official, irrespective of rank, departmental or gubernatorial, civil or military, who takes bribes or breaks the laws or oppresses the people shall be punished.

2. Officials above the age of 80 years and private citizens above 90 years of age shall be promoted one rank higher.

3. The soldiers stationed in the interior suffer many hardships. Let the War Office show substantial considerations to their families.

4. Let governors recommend talented persons, now in obscurity, to different departments for several appointments.

5. We have remitted taxes from districts suffering from either flood, or drought, or fire. If in a district, where all government dues

have been paid up, the magistrate has put the money to some unauthorized or selfish use, thus placing the people under an unjust debt, the people shall be relieved from all obligations.

6. All uncultivated lands which have no owners should be brought under cultivation by remitting taxes thereon.

7. All officials, civil or military, below the seventh rank shall be promoted a rank higher.

8. Human life is very precious. To err in pardoning a criminal is better than to err in condemning him. Hence let all judicial authorities abstain from obstinacy and bribery, endeavoring to do justice.

9. Except of those who are guilty of either rebellion, or murder, or adultery, or robbery, or swindling, or stealing, let the penalty be mitigated one degree.

10. Let local authorities extend a special protection to all the helpless and the unfortunate.

11. Let local authorities send to the proper department an estimate of the cost of repairing all dilapidated temples, sacred to mountains and streams. Such repairs should be made at once to show reverence to gods.

12. Let the local authorities keep bridges and roads in good repair for the benefit of travellers.

13. Let all provincial and magisterial authorities observe in earnest the various requirements of the edict, so that the people may enjoy the benefit thereof and that Our compassionate intentions for the masses may not be frustrated. Those who neglect their duties herein shall be punished by the Home Department.

Ah! We ascended the royal throne by the grace of heaven and have assumed the imperial title according to the wishes of the people. Our desire is to abolish old abuses and to introduce what is new, making good government and wholesome customs prevail. We proclaim this to the world: let all hear and know.

From: The Korean Repository, Volume IV, Seoul,
Korea, 1897, pp.388-390.

(By this act Korea expressed its will to become independent of foreign suzerainty. The precarious independence which Korea gained by this act was brought to an end in 1905, when Japan established a protectorate over the country.)

# # #

August 30, 1898

MARQUIS ITO'S SPEECH ON JAPANESE-KOREAN RELATIONS

Your Excellencies and Gentlemen:

I thank you sincerely for the kind words in which the Acting Minister of Foreign Affairs has just addressed me on your behalf, but at the same time I am constrained to say that I do not deserve the high compliments which he chose to confer upon me. Allow me to avail myself of the present opportunity to say a few words concerning the attitude of Japan toward this country. You doubtless know that in 1873 a group of Japanese statesmen advocated the despatch of a punitive expedition to Korea, a proposal to which I was uncompromisingly opposed from the outset, because I deemed such a war not only uncalled for, but contrary to the principles of humanity. You may imagine the magnitude of the excitement occasioned by this question, when I tell you that the split which it caused in the ranks of the Japanese statesmen led to a tremendous civil war a few years later (the Satsuma Rebellion of 1877). The point to which I wish to direct your attention is that His Imperial Japanese Majesty's Government did not hesitate to reject what it considered to be an unjust proposal even at such gigantic risk.

Japan's policy toward Korea has since been unchanged; in other words, her object has always been to assist and befriend this country. It is true that at times incidents of an unpleasant nature unfortunately interfered with the maintenance of unsuspecting cordiality between the two nations. But I may conscientiously assure you that the real object of the Japanese Government has always been to render assistance to Korea in her noble endeavors to be a civilized and independent state.

I am sincerely gratified to see that today Korea is independent and sovereign. Henceforth it will be Japan's wish to see Korea's independence further strengthened and consolidated; no other motive shall influence Japan's conduct toward this country. On this point you need not entertain the slightest doubt.

Japan's good wishes for Korean independence are all the more sincere and reliable because her vital interests are bound up with those of your country. A danger to Korean independence will be a danger to Japan's safety. So you will easily recognize that the strongest of human motives, namely self-interest, combines with neighborly feelings to make Japan a sincere well-wisher and friend of Korean independence.

Let me repeat once more that Korea may rest assured of the absence of all sinister motives on Japan's part. Friendship between two countries in the circumstances of Japan and Korea ought to be free from any trace of suspicion and doubt as to each other's motives and intentions. In conclusion, allow me to express my heartful hope that you may long remain in office and assiduously exert yourselves for the good of your sovereign and country.

> From: Ladd, G.T., In Korea with Marquis Ito, New
> York, 1908, pp.226-227.

> (Italics not in the original text.)

(Speech by Marquis Ito at dinner given by the Korean Foreign Office in Seoul on August 30, 1898. This speech was made at a time when there was intense rivalry between Japan and Russia

for the good will of Korea. Marquis Ito was responsible for
negotiations between Japan and Korea leading up to the establishment of a protectorate in 1905.)

#   #   #

February 10, 1904

JAPAN'S DECLARATION OF WAR AGAINST RUSSIA

We, by the grace of Heaven, Emperor of Japan, seated on the throne
occupied by the same dynasty from time immemorial, do hereby make proclamation to all our loyal and brave subjects as follows:

We hereby declare war against Russia and we command our army and
navy to carry on hostilities against that Empire with all their strength,
and we also command all our competent authorities to make every effort,
in pursuance of their duties and in accordance with their powers, to
attain the national aim with all the means within the limits of the law
of nations.

We have always deemed it essential to international relations and
made it our constant aim to promote the pacific progress of our Empire
in civilization, to strengthen our friendly ties with other states, and
to establish a state of things which would maintain enduring peace in
the extreme East and assure the future security of our dominion without
injury to the rights and interests of other powers. Our competent authorities have also performed their duties in obedience to our will, so
that our relations with the powers have been steadily growing in cordiality. It was thus entirely against our expectation that we have un-
happily come to open hostilities against Russia.

The integrity of Korea is a matter of constant concern to this
Empire, not only because of our traditional relations with that country,
but because the separate existence of Korea is essential to the safety
of our realm. Nevertheless Russia, in disregard of her solemn treaty
pledges to China and her repeated assurances to other powers, is still
in occupation of Manchuria and has consolidated and strengthened her hold
upon those provinces and is bent upon their final annexation. And since
the absorption of Manchuria by Russia would render it impossible to maintain the integrity of Korea and would, in addition, compel the abandonment of all hope for peace in the extreme East, we determined in those
circumstances to settle the question by negotiation and to secure permanent peace. With that object in view, our competent authorities, by our
order, made proposals to Russia, and frequent conferences were held
during the course of six months. Russia, however, never met such proposals in a spirit of conciliation, but by her wanton delays put off the
settlement of the question; and by ostensibly advocating peace on the one
hand while she was on the other extending her naval and military preparations, sought to accomplish her own selfish designs.

We can not in the least admit that Russia had from the first any serious or genuine desire for peace. She has rejected the proposals of our Government; the safety of Korea is in danger; the vital interests of our Empire are menaced. The guarantees for the future which we have failed to secure by peaceful negotiations, we can now only seek by an appeal to arms.

It is our earnest wish that by the loyalty and valor of our faithful subjects peace may soon be permanently restored and the glory of our Empire preserved.

> From: Korea: Treaties and Agreements, Carnegie Endowment for International Peace, Washington, Pamphlet No. 43, 1921, pp.52-53.

(The Anglo-Japanese Alliance had been signed two years previously on January 30, 1902, bringing Great Britain in on the side of Japan.)

#   #   #

February 23, 1904
PROTOCOL BETWEEN JAPAN AND KOREA

M. Gonsuke Hayashi, Envoy Extraordinary and Minister Plenipotentiary of His Majesty the Emperor of Japan and Major General Yi Chi-Yong, Minister of State for Foreign Affairs ad interim of His Majesty the Emperor of Korea, being respectively duly empowered for the purpose, have agreed upon the following Articles:

Article I. For the purpose of maintaining a permanent and solid friendship between Japan and Korea and firmly establishing peace in the Far East, the Imperial Government of Korea shall place full confidence in the Imperial Government of Japan, and adopt the advice of the latter in regard to improvements in administration.

Article II. The Imperial Government of Japan shall in a spirit of firm friendship ensure the safety and repose of the Imperial House of Korea.

Article III. The Imperial Government of Japan definitively guarantees the independence and territorial integrity of the Korean Empire.

Article IV. In case the welfare of the Imperial House of Korea or the territorial integrity of Korea is endangered by aggression of a third power or internal disturbances, the Imperial Government of Japan shall immediately take such necessary measures as circumstances require, and in such case the Imperial Government of Korea shall give full facilities to promote the action of the Imperial Japanese Government. The Imperial Government of Japan may for the attainment of the above mentioned object occupy when the circumstances require such places as may be necessary from strategic points of view.

Article V. The Governments of the two countries shall not in future without mutual consent conclude with a third power such an arrangement as may be contrary to the principles of the present protocol.

Article VI. Details in connection with the present Protocol shall be arranged as the circumstances may require between the representative of Japan and the Minister of State for Foreign Affairs of Korea.

                         (Signed)   HAYASHI
                                    YI CHI-YONG ((Si-Yong))

        From: Korea: Treaties and Agreements, Carnegie
              Endowment for International Peace, Division
              of International Law, Pamphlet 43, 1921,
              pp.36-37.

        (Underlining not in original text.)

(This protocol was negotiated early during the Russo-Japanese
War, which was declared on February 10, 1904. It was preliminary to the establishment of a protectorate over Korea by
Japan on November 17, 1905, which took place after the Treaty
of Portsmouth of September 5, 1905.)

                #   #   #

                                                   July 29, 1905
ROOSEVELT-KATSURA SECRET PACT ON KOREA

From Tokio,
To.............., Washington.

The following is agreed memorandum of conversation between Prime Minister of Japan and myself:

"Count Katsura and *** had a long and confidential conversation on the morning of July 27. Among other topics of conversation the following views were exchanged regarding the question of the Philippine Islands, of Korea and of the maintenance of general peace in the Far East.

"First, in speaking of some pro-Russians in America who would have the public believe that the victory of Japan would be a certain prelude to her aggression in the direction of the Philippine Islands, *** ob-served that Japan's only interest in the Philippines would be, in his opinion, to have these islands governed by a strong and friendly nation like the United States, and not have them placed either under the misrule of the natives, yet unfit for self-government, or in the hands of some unfriendly European power. Count Katsura confirmed in the strongest terms the correctness of his views on the point and positively stated that Japan does not harbor any aggressive designs whatever on the Philippines; adding that all the insinuations of the yellow-peril type are nothing more or less than malicious and clumsy slanders calculated to do mischief to Japan.

"Second, Count Katsura observed that the maintenance of general peace in the extreme East forms the fundamental principle of Japan's international policy. Such being the case, he was very anxious to exchange views with *** as to the most effective means for insuring this principle. In his own opinion, the best, and in fact the only, means for accomplishing the above object would be to form good understanding between the three governments of Japan, the United States and Great Britain, which have common interest in upholding the principle of eminence. The Count well understands the traditional policy of the United States in this respect and perceives fully the impossibilities of their entering into a formal alliance of such nature with any foreign nation, but in view of our common interests he couldn't see why some good understanding or an alliance in practice, if not in name, should not be made between those three nations in so far as respects the affairs in the Far East. With such understanding firmly formed, general peace in these regions would be easily maintained, to the great benefit of all powers concerned. *** said that it was difficult, indeed impossible, for the President of the United States of America to enter even to any understanding amounting in effect to a confidential informal agreement, without the consent of the Senate, but that he felt sure that without any agreement at all the people of the United States were so fully in accord with the policy of Japan and Great Britain in the maintenance of peace in the Far East that, whatever occasion arose, appropriate action of the Government of the United States, in conjunction with Japan and Great Britain, for such a purpose could be counted on by them quite as confidently as if the United States were under treaty obligations to take.

"Third, in regard to the Korean question Count Katsura observed that Korea being the direct cause of our war with Russia, it is a matter of absolute importance to Japan that a complete solution of the peninsula question should be made as the logical consequence of the war. If left to herself after the war, Korea will certainly draw back to her habit of improvidently entering into any agreements or treaties with other powers, thus resuscitating the same international complications as existed before the war. In view of the foregoing circumstances, Japan feels absolutely constrained to take some definite step with a view to precluding the possibility of Korea falling back into her former condition and of placing us again under the necessity of entering upon another foreign war. *** fully admitted the justness of the Count's observations and remarked to the effect that, in his personal opinion, the establishment by Japanese troops of a suzerainty over Korea to the extent of requiring that Korea enter into no foreign treaties without the consent of Japan was the logical result of the present war and would directly contribute to permanent peace in the East. His judgment was that President Roosevelt would concur in his views in this regard, although he had no authority to give assurance of this. Indeed, *** added that he felt much delicacy in advancing the views he did, for he had no mandate for the purpose from the

President, . . . He could not, however, in view of Count Katsura's
courteous desire to discuss the questions, decline to express his opinions ... . and he would forward to Mr. Root and the President a memorandum of the conversation. Count Katsura said that he would transmit
the same, confidentially, to Baron Komura."

Prime Minister quite anxious for interview. If I have spoken too
freely or inaccurately or wittingly, I know you can and will correct it.
Do not want to "butt in," but, under the circumstances, difficult to
avoid statement, and so told truth as I believe it. Count Katsura especially requested that our conversation be confined to you and the
President, so have not advised Griscom. Is there any objection? If
necessary, under your direction, Foreign Office can give him a copy.

> From: The Current History Magazine, October, 1924,
> pp.15 and 18 (with photostatic reproduc-
> tion of original document).
> See also: Dennett, T., Roosevelt and the
> Russo-Japanese War, Doubleday Page, 1925,
> pp.112-115.

(In the above memorandum, the asterisks *** refer to William How-
ard Taft, Secretary of War. Count Katsura was Premier and Foreign
Minister of Japan. On July 31, 1905, President Roosevelt wrote
Taft that: "Your conversation with Count Katsura absolutely correct in every respect. Wish you would state to Katsura that I
confirm every word you said." This executive agreement ((or pact))
preceded the Revised Anglo-Japanese Alliance of August 22, 1905,
and made in effect the United States an unsigned member of this
alliance before the Portsmouth Treaty of September 5, 1905.)

#   #   #

October 1905

LETTER OF EMPEROR OF KOREA TO PRESIDENT ROOSEVELT

Ever since 1883 ((ratification of U.S.-Korean Treaty of 1882)) the
United States and Korea have been in friendly treaty relations. Korea
has received many proofs of the good will and the sympathy of the
American Government and people. The American Representatives have always shown themselves to be in sympathy with the welfare and progress
of Korea. Many teachers have been sent from America who have done much
for the uplift of our people.

But we have not made the progress that we ought. This is due partly to the political machinations of foreign powers and partly to our mistakes. At the beginning of the Japan-Russia war the Japanese Government
asked us to enter into an alliance with them, granting them the use of
our territory, harbours, and other resources, to facilitate their military and naval operations; Japan, on her part, guaranteed to preserve the

independence of Korea and the welfare and dignity of the royal house. We complied with Japan's request, loyally lived up to our obligations, and did everything that we had stipulated. By so doing we put ourselves in such a position that if Russia had won, she could have seized Korea and annexed her to Russian territory on the ground that we were active allies of Japan.

It is now apparent that Japan proposes to abrogate their part of this treaty and declare a protectorate over our country in direct contravention of her sworn promise in the agreement of 1904. There are several reasons why this should not ḵbe done.

In the first place, Japan will stultify her self by such a direct breach of faith. It will injure her prestige as a power that proposes to work according to enlightened laws.

In the second place, the actions of Japan in Korea during the past two years give no promise that our people will be handled in an enlightened manner. No adequate means have been provided whereby redress could be secured for wrongs perpetrated upon our people. The finances of the country have been gravely mishandled by Japan. Nothing has been done towards advancing the cause of education or justice. Every move on Japan's part has been manifestly selfish.

The destruction of Korea's independence will work her a great injury, because it will intensify the contempt with which the Japanese people treat the Koreans and will make their acts all the more oppressive.

We acknowledge that many reforms are needed in Korea. We are glad to have the help of Japanese advisers, and we are prepared loyally to carry out their suggestions. We recognize the mistakes of the past. It is not for ourselves we plead, but for the Korean people.

At the beginning of the war our people gladly welcomed the Japanese, because this seemed to herald needed reforms and a general bettering of conditions, but soon it was seen that no genuine reforms were intended and the people had been deceived.

One of the gravest evils that will follow a protectorate by Japan is that the Korean people will lose all incentive to improvement. No hope will remain that they can ever regain their independence. They need the spur of national feeling to make them determine upon progress and to make them persevere in it. But the extinction of nationality will bring despair, and instead of working loyally and gladly in conjunction with Japan, the old-time hatred will be intensified and suspicion and animosity will result.

It has been said that sentiment should have no place in such affairs, but we believe, sir, that sentiment is the moving force in all human affairs, and that kindness, sympathy, and generosity are still working between nations as between individuals. We beg of you to bring to bear upon this question the same breadth of mind and the same calmness of judgment that have characterized your course hitherto, and, having weighed the matter, to render us what aid you can consistently in this our time of national danger.

(Private Seal of the Emperor
of Korea).

From: McKenzie, F.A., <u>Korea's Fight for Freedom</u>,
New York, 1920, pp. 102-103.

(This letter was conveyed secretly to President Roosevelt, who
read it and replied through diplomatic channels that it seemed
quite impracticable that any action should be based on it. See
letter of Roosevelt to Root quoted in Dennett, T., <u>Roosevelt
and the Russo-Japanese War</u>, Doubleday Page, New York, 1925,
pp.304-305.)

\#   \#   \#

October 1905

<u>STORY OF KOREA'S SECRET APPEAL TO THE U.S.</u>

(The following are the confidential remarks of Dr. Homer B. Hulbert, following his prepared address, at the session of the Korean
Liberty Conference, held in Philadelphia, Sunday, March 1, 1942:)

This is a story which has never been told. This is the time when
it might be told.

I was in Korea in 1905. There was a King marooned on a throne.
Think of it. A King marooned on a throne. There was no one he could
trust. It was in the fall of 1905 that Korea met her end.

I had a long talk with Ming Yong Whan. The outlook was bad. Korea
had to do something. I said, "Why do you not get out your treaty with
America? That treaty which says:

'If other powers deal unjustly or oppressively with either
Government, the other will exert their good offices on being informed of the case, to bring about an amicable arrangement.'"

I said, "Call America's bluff. Let's find out if she will use them
or not."

I went to Chang. He said, "This must not be a matter to go from one
foreign office to another. The King of Korea must send it to the President of the United States."

I said, "Surely, but how are we to get it there? There isn't a person we can trust."

Dr. Jaisohn had left the country. He could have taken it. Perhaps
someone from the Legation, but Mr. Allen, a friend of Korea, had been replaced by E.V. Morgan.

Then someone said, "Why not send Dr. Hulbert?"

I was just a school teacher, writing textbooks and Korean books. The matter was laid before the King. The King said, "I remember that man Hulbert. I have seen him when we have had them all in to be introduced to me. I remember his face. He is one of the three Americans who came in to guard me after the Queen was killed."

I was sent for. I said that I had no credentials from the King, and that I should have credentials. I was told, "We are afraid the Japanese will kill anyone who is sent as a servant of the King of Korea."

I said I would take the message, but that first we must write a letter that things are wrong in Korea, things that need to be amended. I would not do it clandestinely. I took that letter straight to the American Legation, to E.V. Morgan. He afterwards denied that he had ever seen me. He allowed me to send the letter in the American mail pouch. If it came in the American mail pouch, E.V. Morgan knew it. You can't get away from that.

Morgan immediately cabled to the United States State Department that I was coming with that letter. That man did not know as much about diplomacy as I knew.

They knew I was on the way. Within thirty minutes of the time I arrived in Washington, the Japanese went to the Palace and by threats of death and toture, forced three men in hhe King's cabinet to sign away their country. The King never surrendered to the Japanese. He bent, but he would not break. At the risk of his life he sent me to America.

Put it down in the annals of history that he died loyal to his people.

The letter was not accepted. It was too late, I was told.

From: Korean Liberty Conference, United Korean
      Committee in America, Philadelphia, 1942,
      pp.101-102.

(Homer B. Hulbert, a teacher and an American of long residence in Korea, was the author of The History of Korea, 2 vols., Seoul, 1905; of The Passing of Korea, New York, 1906, and of numerous articles in scholarly journals. He was closely associated with the Korean Independence Movement.)

#   #   #

November 15, 1905

MARQUIS ITO'S CONVERSATION WITH THE EMPEROR OF KOREA

The Emperor said--

"Although I have seen in the newspapers various rumours that Japan proposed to assume a protectorate over Korea, I did not believe them, as I placed faith in Japan's adherence to the promise of maintaining the independence of Korea which was made by the Emperor of Japan at the beginning of the war and embodied in a treaty between Korea and Japan. When I heard you were coming to my country I was glad, as I believed your mission was to increase the friendship between our countries, and your demands have therefore taken me entirely by surprise."

To which Marquis Ito rejoined--

"These demands are not my own; I am only acting in accordance with a mandate from my Government, and if Your Majesty will agree to the demands which I have presented it will be to the benefit of both nations and peace in the East will be assured for ever. Please, therefore, consent quickly."

The Emperor replied--

"From time immemorial it has been the custom of the rulers of Korea, when confronted with questions so mementous as this, to come to no decision until all the Ministers, high and low, who hold or have held office, have been consulted, and the opinion of the scholars and the common people have been obtained, so that I cannot now settle this matter myself."

Said Marquis Ito again--

"Protests from the people can easily be disposed of, and for the sake of the friendship between the two countries Your Majesty should come to a decision at once."

To this the Emperor replied--

"Assent to your proposal would mean the ruin of my country, and I will therefore sooner die than agree to it."

> From: McKenzie, F.A., _Korea's Fight for Freedom_, New
> York, 1920, pp.89-90.
> (Also given in _The Case of Korea_, Chung, H.,
> Revell, New York, 1921, pp.52-53.)

(Marquis Ito was the first Japanese Resident-General in Korea. He was assassinated on October 26, 1909, in Harbin, Manchuria, by a Korean by the name of Ahn Jung Keun.)

#   #   #

November 17, 1905

CONVENTION FOR JAPANESE PROTECTORATE OVER KOREA

The Governments of Japan and Korea, desiring to strengthen the principle of solidarity which unites the two Empires, have with that object in view agreed upon and concluded the following stipulations to serve until the moment arrives when it is recognized that Korea has attained national strength:

Article I. The Government of Japan, through the Department of Foreign Affairs at Tokio, will herafter have control and direction of the external relations and affairs of Korea, and the diplomatic and consular representatives of Japan will have the charge of the subjects and interests of Korea in foreign countries.

Article II. The Government of Japan undertake to see to the execution of the treaties actually existing between Korea and the other Powers, and the Government of Korea engage, not to conclude hereafter any act or engagement having an international character, except through the medium of the Government of Japan.

Article III. The Government of Japan shall be represented at the Court of His Majesty the Emperor of Korea by a Resident General, who shall reside at Seoul, primarily for the purpose of taking charge of and directing matters relating to diplomatic affairs. He shall have the right of private and personal audience of His Majesty the Emperor of Korea. The Japanese Government shall also have the right to station Residents at the several open ports and such other places in Korea as they may deem necessary. Such Residents shall, under the direction of the Resident General, exercise the powers and functions hitherto appertaining to Japanese Consuls in Korea and shall perform such duties as may be necessary in order to carry into full effect the provisions of this agreement.

Article IV. The stipulations of all treaties and agreements existing between Japan and Korea not inconsistent with the provisions of this Agreement shall continue in force.

Article V. The Government of Japan undertake to maintain the welfare and dignity of the Imperial House of Korea.

In faith whereof, the Undersigned duly authorized by their Governments have signed this Agreement and affixed their seals.

(Signed) HAYASHI CONSUKE, (Seal)
Envoy Extraordinary and Minister
Plenipotentiary.
The 17th day of the 11th month of the 38th
year of Meiji.
(Signed) PAK CHE SOON,   (Seal)
Minister for Foreign Affairs.
TThe 17th day of the 11th month of the 9th
year of Kwang-Mu.

From: <u>Korea: Treaties and Agreements</u>, Carnegie
Endowment for International Peace, Division
of International Law, Pamphlet No. 43, 1921,
pp.55-56.

(This Convention was secured from the Koreans under duress and
made public on November 23, 1905. On November 26, 1905, Mr.
Hulbert received the following secret message from the Emperor
of Korea: "I declare that the so-called treaty of protectorate
recently concluded between Korea and Japan was extorted at the
point of the sword and under duress and therefore is null and
void. I never consented to it and never will. Transmit to
American Government. Signed: The Emperor of Korea." See Mc-
Kenzie, F.A., <u>Korea's Fight for Freedom</u>, Revell, New York,
1920, pp.100-101.)

\#   \#   \#

November 22, 1905.

POLICY DECLARATION OF THE JAPANESE GOVERNMENT ON KOREA

The relations of propinquity have made it necessary for Japan to
take and exercise, for reasons closely connected with her own safety and
repose, a paramount interest and influence in the political and military
affairs of Korea. The measures hitherto taken have been purely advisory, but the experience of recent years has demonstrated the insuffi-
ciency of measures of guidance alone. The unwise and improvident action
of Korea, more especially in the domain of her international concerns,
has in the past been the most fruitful source of complications. To
permit the present unsatisfactory condition of things to continue un-
restrained and unregulated would be to invite fresh difficulties, and
Japan believes she owes it to herself and her desire for the general
pacification of the extreme East to take the steps necessary to put an
end once and for all to this dangerous situation. Accordingly, with
that object in view and in order at the same time to safeguard her own
position and to promote the well-being of the Government and people of
Korea, the Imperial Government have resolved to assume a more intimate
and direct influence and responsibility than heretofore in the external
relations of the Peninsula. The Government of His Majesty the Emperor
of Korea are in accord with the Imperial Government as to the absolute
necessity of the measure, and the two governments, in order to provide
for the peaceful and amicable establishment of the new order of things,
have concluded the accompanying compact. In bringing this agreement to
the notice of the Powers having treaties with Korea, the Imperial Government declare that in assuming charge of the foreign relations of Korea
and undertaking the duty of watching over the execution of the existing
treaties of that country, they will see that those treaties are maintained and respected, and they also engage not to prejudice in any way
the legitimate commercial and industrial interests of those Powers in
Korea.

From: <u>Papers Relating to the Foreign Relations of</u>
<u>the United States</u>, Washington, D.C., 1905,
pp.612-613.

(This well-known document announced to the world the fundamental
position of Japan relative to Korea following the Russo-Japanese
War.)

\#   \#   \#

1905

KOREAN EDITORIAL PROTESTING PROTECTORATE

When it was recently made known the Marquis Ito would come to Korea
our deluded people all said, with one voice, that he is the man who will
be responsible for the maintenance of friendship between the three countries of the Far East (Japan, China, and Korea) and believing that his
visit to Korea was for the sole purpose of devising good plans for strictly maintaining the promised integrity and independence of Korea, our people, from the sea coast to the capital, united in extending to him a
hearty welcome.

But oh! How difficult is it to anticipate affairs in this world.
Without warning, a proposal containing five clauses was laid before the
Emperor, and we then saw how mistaken we were about the object of Marquis
Ito's visit. However, the Emperor firmly refused to have anything to do
with these proposals and Marquis Ito should then, properly, have aban-
doned his attempt and returned to his own country.

But the ministers of our government, who are worse than pigs or
dogs, coveting honours and advantages for themselves, and frightened by
empty threats, were trembling in every limb, and were willing to become
traitors to their country and betray to Japan the integrity of a nation
which stood for 4,000 years, the foundation and honour of a dynasty 500
years old, and the rights and freedom of twenty million people.

We do not wish to too deeply blame Pak Che-Sun and the other ministers, of whom, as they are little better than brute animals, too much
was not to be expected, but what can be said of the Vice-Prime Minister,
the Chief of the Cabinet, whose early opposition to the proposals of
Marquis Ito was an empty form devised to enhance his reputation with the
people?

Can he not now repudiate the agreement or can he not rid the world
of his presence? How can he again stand before the Emperor? With what
face can he ever look upon anyone of his twenty million compatriots?

Is it worthwhile for any of us to live any longer? Our people
have become the slaves of others, and the spirit of a nation which has
stood for 4,000 years, since the days of Tan Kun and Ke Ja have perished

in a single night. Alas, fellow countrymen! Alas!

From: Korean Review, Vol. I, March, 1948, pp.41-42.

(This editorial appeared in the Whang So'ng Sinmun, a Seoul
paper which was immediately suppressed by the Japanese and
whose editor was thrown into prison.)

#   #   #

November 1905

SUICIDE LETTER OF MIN YONG WHAN

"To......

"I, Min Yong Whan, have been unable to do my duty as a true subject
of my country, and not having served her well, she and her people are
brought to this present hopeless condition. Foreseeing the coming death
of my country, I am now offering my humble farewell to His Majesty, my
Emperor, and to the twenty millions of my fellow countrymen, in an excess of despair and utter hopelessness. I know that my death will accomplish nothing, and that my people will all be lost in the coming
life and death struggle, but seeing that I can do nothing to prevent
this by living, I have taken my decision.

"You must know the aim and actions of the Japanese at the present
day, I therefore beseech you to use your good offices, in making known
to the world whatever injustice my people may suffer, and may you use
your magnanimous efforts in trying to uphold our independence. If you
can do this for my land, even my dying soul can rest happily. Do not
misunderstand the good intentions of my people. I trust you will not
forget our first treaty (with America) made between your republic and
my country. May there be practical proof of your sympathy from your
Government and your people; then even the dead shall know, and be thank-
ful to you.

"Yours in despair,

(Signed and Sealed), Min Yong Whan."

From: The Korea Review, 1906, Vol. 6, pp. 6-7.

(Min Yong Whan was a Prince of the Royal Blood and at one time
the Korean Minister of War. This letter of his protesting with
his life the Japanese protectorate is regarded by Koreans as one
of the most famous documents in their history.)

#   #   #

KOREAN PROTEST AGAINST JAPANESE PROTECTORATE

"Our numbers are twenty million, and we have over ten million strong men, excluding old, sick, and children. Now, the Japanese soldiers in Korea are not more than eight thousand, and Japanese merchants at various places are not more than some thousands. Though their weapons are sharp, how can one man kill a thousand? We beg you our brothers not to act in a foolish way and not to kill any innocent persons. We will fix the day and the hour for you to strike. Some of us, disguised as beggars and merchants, will go into Seoul. We will destroy the railway, we will kindle flames in every port, we will destroy Chinkokai, kill Ito and all the Japanese, Yi Wanyong and his underlings, and will not leave a single rebel against our Emperor alive. Then Japan will bring out all her troops to fight us. We have no weapons at our hands, but we will keep our own patriotism. We may not be able to fight against the sharp weapons of the Japanese, but we will ask the Foreign Consuls to help us with their troops, and maybe they will assist the right persons and destroy the wicked; otherwise let us die.

Let us strike against Japan, and then, if must be, all die together with our country and with our Emperor, for there is no other course open to us. It is better to lose our lives now than to live miserably a little time longer, for the Emperor and our brothers will all surely be killed by the abominable plans of Ito, Yi Wan-yong, and their associates. It is better to die as a patriot than to live having abandoned one's country. Mr. Yi Chun went to foreign lands to plead for our country, and his plans did not carry well, so he cut his stomach asunder with a sword and poured out his blood among the foreign nations to proclaim his patriotism to the world. Those of our twenty million people who do not unite offend against the memory of Mr. Yi Chun. We have to choose between destruction or the maintenance of our country. Whether we live or die is a small thing, the great thing is that we make up our minds at once whether we work for or against our country."

By a Korean Group in Provinces.

From: MacKenzie, F.A., Korea's Fight for Freedom, Revell, New York, 1920, pp.136-137.

(This is a representative sample of the many protests by Koreans, signed and unsigned, against the establishment of the Japanese protectorate over Korea in 1905.)

# # #

September 1906

PROCLAMATION OF GENERAL HASEGAWA

"I, General Baron Yoshimichi Hasegawa, Commander of the Army of Occupation in Korea, make the following announcement to each and every one of the people of Korea throughout all the provinces. Taught by the natural trend of affairs in the world and impelled by the national need of political regeneration, the Government of Korea, in obedience to His Imperial Majesty's wishes, is now engaged in the task of reorganizing the various institutions of State. But those who are ignorant of the march of events in the world and who fail correctly to distinguish loyalty from treason have by wild and baseless rumors instigated people's minds and caused the rowdies in various places to rise in insurrection. These insurgents commit all sorts of horrible crimes, such as murdering peaceful people, both native and foreign, robbing their property, burning official and private buildings, and destroying means of communication. Their offenses are such as are not tolerated by heaven or earth. They affect to be loyal and patriotic and call themselves volunteers. But none the less they are lawbreakers, who oppose their Sovereign's wishes concerning political regeneration and who work the worst possible harm to their country and people.

"Unless they are promptly suppressed the trouble may assume really calamitous proportions. I am charged by His Majesty, the Emperor of Korea, with the task of rescuing you from such disasters by thoroughly stamping our the insurrection. I charge all of you, law-abiding people of Korea, to prosecute your respective peaceful avocations and be troubled with no fears. As for those who have joined the insurgents from mistaken motives if they honestly repent and promptly surrender they will be pardoned of their offense. Any of you who will seize insurgents or will give information concerning their whereabouts will be handsomely rewarded. In case of those who wilfully join insurgents, or afford them refuge, or conceal weapons, they shall be severely punished. More than that, the villages to which such offenders belong shall be held collectively responsible and punished with rigor. I call upon each and every one of the people of Korea to understand clearly what I have herewith said to you and avoid all reprehensible action."

From: Oliver, R.T., Korea, Forgotten Nation, Public Affairs Press, Washington, 1944, pp.40-42. Also in McKenzie, F.A., Korea's Fight for Freedom, Revell, New York, 1920, pp.135-136.

(This document is regarded by Koreans as one of the most famous, or infamous, proclamations in the record of Japanese control over Korea. General Hasegawa became Governor-General of Korea in October 1916.)

\#   \#   \#

June 27, 1907

PETITION TO THE HAGUE BY KOREAN DELEGATION

Yi-Sang-Sul, ex-vice premier, Yj-Tjoune, former police magistrate of the Supreme Court of Korea, Yi-Oui-Tjyong, ex-Secretary of the Korean Legation to St. Petersburg, envoy of His Majesty, the Emperor of Korea, as delegate to the Peace Conference at the Hague, have the honor to inform Your Excellencies that the independence of our country was guaranteed and recognized in 1884 by all the powers of the world. In addition, our independence is recognized to the present day in your countries.

In 1905, on the 17th of December, Yi-Sang-Sul, as vice-Prime Minister witnessed the moves of Japan, who, without regard to any international law and by armed force compelled us to break the friendly, diplomatic relations which have prevailed between our countries up to that time. In view of this, allow me to inform Your Excellencies of the methods used by the Japanese, who, in order to obtain this objective, did not hesitate either to resort to threats of violence or to violate the rights and the laws of the country. For greater clarity, I shall classify our grievances into three different categories:

I. The Japanese have acted without the consent of H.M. the Emperor.
II. In order to attain their aim the Japanese have resorted to armed force against the Imperial Government.
III. The Japanese have acted without any regard for the laws and the customs of the country.

Your Excellencies' impartial judgment will decide whether the above three paragraphs are or are not a direct violation of international law.

Can we as an independent nation permit the Japanese trick to destroy the amicable and diplomatic relations which have existed up to now between ourselves and other nations and to become a constant menace for the peace in the Far East?

I regret beyond measure to have been deprived of the possibility of being present at the Hague Conference although delegated by His Majesty the Emperor to do so, by this very violation of our rights by the Japanese.

We are including in this letter a resume of all the methods used and of the acts perpetrated by the Japanese to the day of our departure and we beg you to give your kind attention to this question, which is of vital importance to our country. If you should need supplementary information or if you should wish to ascertain the full authority conferred on us by His Majesty the Emperor of Korea, please let us know; we shall have the honor of placing ourselves at the complete disposal of Your Excellencies.

Since the diplomatic relations between Korea and the other countries have not been severed by the will of Korea itself but rather as a result of the violation of our rights by Japan, we have the honor of addressing ourselves to Your Excellencies and of urging you to be kind enough to intervene so that we may take part in the Hague Convention and there defend our rights by bringing to light the behavior of the Japanese.

Please accept our thanks in advance and the assurance of our great respect.

Signed: Yi-Sang-Sul
Yj-Tjoune
Yi-Oui-Tjong

From: Courier de La Conference de La Paix, No. 14, Dimanche 30 Juin 1907, pp.2. Amsterdam - Leipzig (Translation from the French).

(Following the revelation of this petition, the Japanese brought about the abdication of Emperor Ke-Jong on July 19, 1907, and also forced upon the Koreans the Convention of July 24, 1907. Although Korea was not invited to the 2nd International Peace Conference at the Hague, three Korean delegates, duly accredited by their Government, went to the Hague to present the above petition. The Conference refused to receive the petition officially.)

#   #   #

PART II. FROM ANNEXATION BY JAPAN TO WORLD WAR II

August 22, 1910

PROCLAMATION AND TREATY OF ANNEXATION OF KOREA BY JAPAN.

The Proclamation

Notwithstanding the earnest and laborious work of reforms in the administration of Korea in which the Governments of Japan and Korea have been engaged for more than four years since the conclusion of the Agreement of 1905, the existing system of government in that country has not proved entirely equal to the duty of preserving public order and tranquility; and in addition, the spirit of suspicion and misgiving dominates the whole peninsula.

In order to maintain peace and stability in Korea, to promote the prosperity and welfare of Koreans, and at the same time to ensure the safety and repose of foreign residents, it has been made abundantly clear that fundamental changes in the actual regime of government are absolutely essential. The Governments of Japan and Korea, being convinced of the urgent necessity of introducing reforms responsive to the requirements of the situation and of furnishing sufficient guarantee for the future, have, with the approval of His Majesty the Emperor of Japan and His Majesty the Emperor of Korea, concluded, through their respective plenipotentiaries, a treaty providing for complete annexation of Korea to the Empire of Japan. By virtue of that important act, which shall take effect on its promulgation on August 29, 1910, the Imperial Government of Japan undertake the entire government and administration of Korea, and they hereby declare that the matters relating to foreigners and foreign trade in Korea shall be conducted in accordance with the following rules:

1. Treaties hitherto concluded by Korea with foreign Powers ceasing to be operative, Japan's existing treaties will, so far as practicable, be applied to Korea. Foreigners resident in Korea will, so far as conditions permit, enjoy the same rights and immunities as in Japan proper, and the protection of their legally acquired rights subject in all cases to the jurisdiction of Japan. The Imperial Government of Japan are ready to consent that the jurisdiction in respect of the cases actually pending in any foreign Consular Court in Korea at the time the Treaty of Annexation takes effect shall remain in such Court until final decision.

2. Independently of any conventional engagements formerly existing on the subject, the Imperial Government of Japan will for a period of ten years levy upon goods imported into Korea from foreign countries or exported from Korea to foreign countries and upon foreign vessels entering any of the open ports of Korea the same import or export duties and the same tonnage dues as under the existing schedules. The same import or export duties and tonnage dues as those to be levied upon the aforesaid goods and vessels will also for a period of ten years be applied in respect of goods imported into Korea from Japan or exported from Korea to Japan and Japanese vessels entering any of the open ports of Korea.

3. The Imperial Government of Japan will also permit for a period of ten years vessels under flags of the Powers having treaties with Japan to engage in the coasting trade between the open ports of Korea and between those ports and any open ports of Japan.

4. The existing open ports of Korea, with the exemption of Masampo, will be continued as open ports, and in addition Shiwiju will be newly opened so that vessels, foreign as well as Japanese, will there be admitted and goods may be imported into and exported from these ports.

The Treaty

His Majesty the Emperor of Japan and His Majesty the Emperor of Korea, having in view the special and close relations between their respective countries, desiring to promote the common weal of the two nations and to assure the permanent peace in the Extreme East, and being convinced that these objects can be best attained by the annexation of Korea to the Empire of Japan, have resolved to conclude a treaty of such annexation and have, for that purpose, appointed as their plenipotentiaries, that is to say, his Majesty the Emperor of Japan Viscount Masakata Terauchi, his Resident-General, and his Majesty the Emperor of Korea Ye Wan Yong, his Minister President of State, who upon mutual conference and deliberation have agreed to the following articles:

Article I. His Majesty the Emperor of Korea makes the complete and permanent cession to his Majesty the Emperor of Japan of all rights of sovereignty over the whole of Korea.

Article II. His Majesty the Emperor of Japan accepts the cession mentioned in the preceding article and consents to the complete annexation of Korea to the Empire of Japan.

Article III. His Majesty the Emperor of Japan will accord to their Majesties the Emperor and ex-Emperor and his Imperial Highness the Crown Prince of Korea and their consorts and heirs such titles, dignity, and honour as are appropriate to their respective ranks, and sufficient annual grants will be made for the maintenance of such titles, dignity and honour.

Article IV. His Majesty the Emperor of Japan will also accord appropriate honour and treatment to the members of the Imperial House of Korea and their heirs other than those mentioned in the preceding article, and the funds necessary for the maintenance of such honour and treatment will be granted.

Article V. His Majesty the Emperor of Japan will confer peerage and monetary grants upon those Koreans who, on account of meritorious services, are regarded as deserving such special recognition.

Article VI. In consequence of the aforesaid annexation the Government of Japan assume the entire government and administration of Korea, and undertake to afford full protection for the persons and property of

Koreans obeying the laws there in force to promote the welfare of all such Koreans.

Article VII. The Government of Japan will, so far as circumstances permit, employ in the public service of Japan in Korea those Koreans who accept the new regime loyally and in good faith and who are duly qualified for such service.

Article VIII. This treaty, having been approved by his Majesty the Emperor of Japan and his Majesty the Emperor of Korea, shall take effect from the date of its promulgation.

In faith thereof, &c.

Signed by:
Viscount Terauchi
Yen (Yee) Wan Yong

From: <u>Korea - Treaties and Agreements</u>, Carnegie Endowment for International Peace, Pamphlet No. 43, 1921, pp.64-67.

(The above Proclamation and Treaty were released on August 29, 1910.)

#   #   #

August 29, 1910

KOREAN EMPEROR'S RESCRIPT ON CESSION OF SOVEREIGNTY

Notwithstanding Our unworthiness We succeeded to a great and arduous task, and from Our accession to the Throne down to the present time We have used Our utmost efforts to follow the modern principles of administration. In view, however, of the long-standing weakness and deep rooted evils, We are convinced that it would be beyond Our power to effect reforms within a measurable length of time. Day and night We have been deeply concerned about it, and have been at a loss to find the means how to rectify the lamentable state of things. Should it be left as it goes on, allowing the situation to assume more serious phase, We fear that We will finally find it impossible to adjust it in any way. Under these circumstances We feel constrained to believe it wise to entrust Our great task to abler hands than Ours, so that efficient measures may be carried out and satisfactory results obtained therefrom. Having taken the matter into Our serious consideration and firmly believing that this is an opportune time for immediate decision, We have ceded all the rights of sovereignty to His Majesty the Emperor of Japan in whom we have placed implicit confidence and with whom we have shared joy and sorrow from long time since, in order to consolidate the peace of the Extreme East and ensure the welfare of our people.

You, all the people, are expected not to give yourselves up to commotion, appreciating the present national situation as well as the trend of the times, but to enjoy the happiness and blessings by pursuing your occupations in peace and obeying the enlightened new administration of the Empire of Japan. We have decided to take this step by no means disregarding your interest but in our eagerness to relieve you of this deplorable situation. We command you, therefore, to take due cognizance of our wishes.

From: Ireland, Alleyne, The New Korea, New York, 1926, pp.315-316.

(The above Rescript was issed under pressure from the Japanese represent in Seoul by General Terauchi. See The Russo-Japanese Treaties, Price, E.B., Baltimore, 1933, p.10.)

\#   \#   \#

August 29, 1910

JAPANESE IMPERIAL RESCRIPT ON ANNEXATION

We, attaching the highest importance to the maintenance of permanent peace in the Orient and the consolidation of lasting security to Our Empire and finding in Korea constant and fruitful sources of complication, caused Our Government to conclude in 1905 an Agreement with the Korean Government by which Korea was placed under the protection of Japan in the hope that all disturbing elements might thereby be removed and peace assured for ever.

For the four years and over which have since elapsed, Our Government have exerted themselves with unwearied attention to promote reforms in the administration of Korea, and their efforts have, in a degree, been attended with success. But, at the same time, the existing regime of government in that country has shown itself hardly effective to preserve peace and stability, and, in addition, a spirit of suspicion and misgiving dominates the whole Peninsula. In order to maintain public order and security and to advance the happiness and well-being of the people, it has become manifest that fundamental changes in the present system of government are inevitable.

We, in concert with His Majesty the Emperor of Korea, having in view this condition of affairs and being equally persuaded of the necessity of annexing the whole of Korea to the Empire of Japan in response to the actual requirements of the situation, have now arrived at an arrangement for such permanent annexation.

His Majesty the Emperor of Korea and the members of His Imperial House will, notwithstanding the annexation, be accorded due and appropriate treatment. All Koreans, being under Our direct sway, will enjoy growing prosperity and welfare, and with assured repose and security

will come a marked expansion in industry and trade. We confidently believe that the new order of things now inaugurated will serve as a fresh
guarantee of enduring peace in the Orient.

We order the establishment of the office of Governor-General of
Korea. The Governor-General will, under our direction, exercise the
command over the army and navy, and a general control over all administrative functions of Korea. We call upon all of Our officials and
authorities to fulfill their respective duties in appreciation of Our
will, and to conduct the various branches of administration in conso-
nance with the requirements of the occasion, to the end that Our subjects may long enjoy the blessings of peace and tranquillity.

(HIS IMPERIAL MAJESTY'S SIGN-MANUAL)
(Privy Seal)
The 29th day of the 8th month of the 43rd
year of Meiji (1910).

From: Ireland, Alleyne, The New Korea, New York,
1926, pp.313-314.

(This is the definitive document on the annexation, reflect-
ing, as it does, policy on the highest level.)

#   #   #

August 29, 1910
PROCLAMATION OF GOVERNOR-GENERAL TERAUCHI ON POLICY

In assuming the administration of Chosen under the command of His
Majesty the Emperor of Japan, my Most Gracious and August Sovereign, I
hereby proclaim to all the people in Chosen a general outline of the
administrative policy to be adopted in future.

It is a natural and inevitable course of things that two peoples,
whose countries are in close proximity with each other, whose interests
are identical and who are bound together with brotherly feelings, should
amalgamate and form one body. Being desirous of securing the safety and
welfare of Chosen as well as of maintaining the permanent peace of the
Extreme East, His Majesty the Emperor of Japan has, in compliance with
the wish expressed by the Sovereign of Korea, accepted the cession of all
the rights of sovereignty over the country. Hereafter the Emperor of
Korea shall be known by the title of His Imperial Highness Yi Wang (Prince
Yi), and the Crown Prince shall be called Prince Heir, so that the here-
ditary title shall endure forever, while the Ex-Emperor shall be given
the title of His Imperial Highness Tai Wang (Prince Father). Their High-
nesses shall receive the treatment of Princes of the Blood and their annual grants shall be munificent and the same in amount as heretofore. As
for the people of Chosen in General, all of them shall become subjects of
the Emperor of Japan and under the benevolent rule of His Imperial Majesty

shall receive the benefits of his enlightened and merciful reign. Especially wise and good men, who will faithfully and loyally respect and assist the new regime, shall be created peers and have conferred on them special monetary grants appropriate to their services and merits, or appointed officials of the Empire, some as members of the Privy Council, others as officials of the central or local offices in accordance with their talent and ability. Further, aged persons belonging to the Yangpan or literati classes, whose behaviour is esteemed as the model of good citizenship, shall be accorded special awards, while dutiful sons and daughters, virtuous wives and other persons whose behaviour is exemplary shall be duly rewarded and publicly honoured.

Those who were formerly in the service of local offices and who while so engaged misappropriated part of the taxes collected shall be freed from their responsibility and released from refunding the balance of the sum due. With respect to those who have contravened the laws, but the nature of whose offences is deserving of leniency, a general amnesty shall be proclaimed.

As a result of maladministration of by-gone days, not a few people in the interior seem to be in great straits, some having lost their means of livelihood and some their fortunes, while others are even on the verge of starvation. Having in view such deplorable conditions, it has been considered urgently necessary to pay special attention to the recuperation of the public strength. It has therefore been decided to exempt the people from paying the land-tax, which was due until the second year of Yungheu (1908) but remained unpaid, as well as to exonerate those who borrowed public grain until the third year of Yungheui (1909) from returning it, and also to reduce the land-tax due in autumn this year by one-fifth of the rate. Further, a sum of about seventeen million yen will be defrayed from the Treasury to be donated to 328 districts of the thirteen provinces for giving industrial work to the people, aiding in the promotion of education and providing against famine and other disasters. All these measures will be taken in connection with the inauguration of the new regime in order to show to the people at large the Imperial concern for their well-being. The people, however, should not forget that it is an established rule throughout the world, ancient and modern, as well as in the East and West for any people receiving the benefit of administration to contribute their shares according to their ability towards administrative expenses. They should appreciate the significance of those measures for their relief and take care not to neglect their duty, that of always serving the public purposes.

The fundamental object of administration is to promote the security of life and property, whereon depends the general industrial development of a nation. Hitherto in Chosen insurgents or bandits have appeared frequently at various places, killing peaceful people, plundering property and causing disturbances. In view of this, troops of the Imperial Army have been stationed at important places in all the provinces in order to be on guard against emergencies, police and gendarme officers and men distributed throughout the country to look after the maintenance of peace and order, and courts of justice established at various places to give just and impartial judgments. All these measures have been taken in order to punish the wicked and cause evil-doers to cease, but fundamentally they are aimed at keeping peace and order in the country, so that people may engage at their business and increase their well-being without any fear of danger to their lives and properties.

A survey of the physical features of Chosen shows that land in the southern part of the country is fertile and admirably suited for carrying on agriculture and the mountains in the north contain great mineral wealth, while the surrounding waters abound in marine products. There are not a few natural resources which can be developed by proper methods of exploitation so as to contribute greatly to the industrial growth of the country. But the industrial development of a country can be attained only after means of communication and transportation have been sufficiently established, for these are the primary steps required for inaugurating new enterprises. For this reason, the authorities concerned have undertaken the opening of highreads connecting all important centres of business as well as the constuction of a railway between Seoul and Wonan and of another in the southern provinces; and the railway system will be gradually extended throughout the peninsula. No doubt is entertained that even in the course of these works employment will be given to many thousands of people, helping them to alleviate the misery of poverty, not to speak of the benefit the general public is to derive after the completion of the lines.

A long-standing evil in Chosen has been the constant feud existing between certain goups of men, generally originating in the clash of personal interests. Under the circumstances when one party secured power it immediately set itself to undermining its rivals. In this way struggles have gone on between rival factions for many years, not a few persons taking part in them having lost their social standing and fortunes in consequence. It goes without saying that such factional conflicts are exceedingly harmful. People are therefore warned against organizing themselves into parties and engaging in rivalry and intrigue. But instances are not few in history showing that the sincere concern of rulers about the welfare of the masses failed to reach them, while popular wishes did not come to the knowledge of persons in power, resulting in mutual misunderstanding and distrust. In order to prevent such an undesirable state of things coming into existence, it has been decided to enlarge the scope of the Privy Council and appoint all experienced and capable persons as members of the Council, so that their advice may be sought on all important administrative affairs. Also able and wise persons shall be made provincial or district councillors and their opinions and ideas shall be duly considered in the hope that no administrative measure may be at variance with reasonable popular wishes.

Of all ills nothing is more painful than disease. In Chosen the medical art has been in a primitive stage of prcgress and on this account many people are subject to untimely death. This is really regrettable and it was with the purpose of remedying it to a certain extent that a central hospital was opened in Seoul some years ago and charity hospitals were lately established at Chonju, Chongju and Hamheung. A large number of people have since received the blessing of advanced medical science from these institutions. Nevertheless the country as a whole does not enjoy it. To enable all the people of the country to share it in future, order has been issued for the establishment of a charity hospital in every province, which will be provided with an efficient staff and plenty of good medicines.

The education of the rising generation is the most important factor for insuring the steady progress of a country along the path of civilization. Their education must aim at promoting their intellect and enhancing their moral character, so that they may become good and useful citizens. But hitherto many young men of this country have been misled by erroneous methods of education into disliking work and indulging in useless and empty talk. In future attention should be paid to the removal of this evil as well as to instilling in the minds of young men the detestation of idleness and the love of real work, thrift and diligence.

The freedom of religious belief is recognized in all civilized countries. There is indeed nothing to be said against anybody trying to gain spiritual peace by believing in whatever religious faith he or she considers to be true. But those who engage in strife on account of sectarian differences, or take part in politics or pursue political intrigues under the name of religious propaganda, do injury to good manners and customs and disturb public peace and order and as doing such shall be dealt with by law. There is no doubt, however, that a good religion, be it Buddhism, Confucianism or Christianity, has as its aim the improvement, spiritual as well as material, of mankind at large, and in this not only does it not conflict with administration but really helps it in attaining the purpose it has in view. Consequently all religions shall be treated equally and further due protection and facilities shall be accorded their legitimate propagation.

In coming to this country under the command of my Imperial Master, I have no other desire than that of increasing the welfare and happiness of the people placed under my administration. This desire on my part has induced me to point out to the people at leangth the general lines they should follow. No leniency will be shown to those who, entertaining malicious motives, try to obstruct the carrying out of any administrative measures. But all those who behave themselves loyally and abide by the law peacefully shall receive even unto their unborn generations the benefit of a judicious and benevolent rule. You, people of Chosen, should therefore take due cognizance of the new regime and be careful not to go astray.

Viscount Terauchi, Masakara
Regent-General
August 29. Meiji 43 (1910)

From: Results of Three Years' Administration of Chosen Since Annexation, Government-General of Chosen, January, 1914, pp.1-5.

(Seiki Terauchi was appointed Regent-General of Korea on May 30, 1910, and appointed Governor-General of Korea on August 29, 1910, the date of this document.)

\#　　　　\#　　　　\#

August 29, 1910

GOVERNOR-GENERAL TERAUCHI'S INSTRUCTION TO RESIDENTS

By virtue of the Treaty of Annexation promulgated today, Korea is annexed to the Empire of Japan and taking the name of Chosen becomes part of the Empire. All the people living in the new territory will come under the administration of the Imperial Government and enjoy the blessings of His Majesty's benevolent rule. The present state of things in Chosen, however, is not as yet on the same level as that in Japan. Consequently except those laws and regulations of the Empire which can be immediately adapted to Chosen, the Japanese and Korean laws and regulations actually in force in Korea, which become void as a result of annexation, will remain in force as orders of the Governor-General until they are gradually amended in accordance with the progress of time. The Japanese municipalities, being organizations composed by Japanese subjects resident in Korea while remaining as a foreign country, should by the natural order of things be incorporated in the local organs of the new regime. But in view of the existing circumstances, under which their abolition would cause no small inconvenience, their existence will be recognized for the time being and their adjustment will be effected when the local administrative system into which they are to be absorbed has been completed.

The treaties between Korea and foreign Powers shall be abrogated and those treaties between Japan and foreign Powers shall be applied to Chosen as far as circumstances permit. In consequence the subjects and citizens of the foreign Powers living in Chosen will enjoy the same rights and privileges as those in Japan and at the same time will come under the jurisdiction of the Empire. It follows that all lawsuits concerning foreigners resident in Chosen will be dealt with by our courts of justice exactly as those concerning other people in general.

With regard to the customs tariff, however, the case is somewhat different. Inasmuch as the immediate application to Chosen of the national or conventional tariff of the Empire would not only cause a sudden and momentous change in the foreign trade of the peninsula but would also seriously affect the economic conditions of the interior, the Imperial Government has decided to allow the present rates of the customs tariff to remain in operation regardless of the treaty provisions. In consequence the same customs duties will be levied as those hitherto imposed on commodities exported from and imported to Chosen as well as on those passing between Chosen and Japan.

The aim and purpose of annexation is to consolidate the bonds of the two countries, removing all causes for territorial and national discriminations necessarily existing between separate powers, so as to promote perfectly the mutual welfare and happiness in general of the two peoples. Consequently, should the Japanese people regard it as a result of the conquest of a weak country by a stronger one and speak and act under such delusion in an overbearing and undignified manner they will go contrary to the spirit in which the present step has been taken. Japanese settlers in Chosen seem to have hitherto considered that they are living in a foreign land and have often fallen into the mistake of holding themselves as superiors at the expense of the people of the coun-

energy particularly to the cultivation of moral character and thorough
propagation of the national language, and thereby inculcate the quality
and character becoming a loyal subject of the Empire. If, on the contrary, it suffers empty speculation to be preferred to practical utility,
diligence to give way to indolence, and unstable and dissolute habits
to supersede the beautiful virtues of decency and probity, then the proper
object of education will not only be lost, but the personal careers of
many will be spoilt, and indirectly much damage be done to the State.
In enforcing education, therefore, all endeavour must be made to secure
the best fruits by adapting it to the times and to the standard of
popular civilization.

Education in Chosen is roughly divided into three kinds, namely,
common, industrial and special education. The proper object of common
education rests in that children shall be taught the national language
and moral virtues, assisted to acquire a personal character suitable
to a member of our nation and such knowledge and art as are essential
for the gaining of a livelihood. In the education of girls, special
care shall be taken in nursing the virtues of chastity, fidelity and
goodness. Industrial education shall have as its aim not only the
training in knowledge and art required in the branches of industry concerned, but also the inculcation in pupils of the habit of diligence.
Special education is intended for the making of men proficient in the
higher knowledge and art required in various professions. It scarcely
need be stated that education by private schools ought to be undertaken
in accordance with the Laws and Ordinances of the State, and not be permitted to deviate from the fundamental principle underlying the Empire's
educational policy. Freedom of religion is assured to each and all.
But as the educational administration of the Empire maintains, and has
maintained from early times, the principle that the education of the
people shall stand independent of religion, no Government nor public
school, nor any school whose curriculum is fixed by the Law and Ordinance of the Empire, can be allowed to enforce religious education or
conduct any religious ceremonies. The functionaries concerned ought
always to bear in mind this statement and beware of being led into a
wrong course.

The welfare of Chosen incidental to the prosperity of the Empire
must depend upon the education of later generations. The people in Chosen, therefore, should be made to perceive this fact and induced to edu-
cate their sons and daughters according to their means and status, and
thus place the latter on the highroad to worthy and useful careers. In
this way, I hope, the people in Chosen will be able to enjoy the blessings of the highly benevolent reign of his August Majesty, lead a happy
family life, contribute to the advancement of general civilization and
discharge their duties as subjects of the Empire.

From: Results of Three Years' Administration of
Chosen Since Annexation, Government-General
of Chosen, January, 1914, pp.6-7

(Underlining not in original text.)

(This document reveals the intent of Japan to insure the

ideological identity of Korea with Japan through educational
measures in harmony with the famous Japanese Imperial Rescript
on Education of October 30, 1890.)

March 1, 1919

KOREAN DECLARATION OF INDEPENDENCE

We herewith proclaim the independence of Korea and the liberty of the
Korean people. We tell it to the world in witness of the equality of all
nations and we pass it on to our posterity as their inherent right.

We make this proclamation, having back of us 5,000 years of history, and 20,000,000 of a united loyal people. We take this step to insure to our children for all time to come, personal liberty in accord
with the awakening consciousness of this new era. This is the clear
leading of God, the moving principle of the present age, the whole
human race's just claim. It is something that cannot be stamped out,
or stifled, or gagged, or suppressed by any means.

Victims of an older age, when brute force and the spirit of plunder
ruled, we have come after these long thousands of years to experience the
agony of ten years of foreign oppression, with every loss to the right
to live, every restriction of the freedom of thought, every damage done
to the dignity of life, every opportunity lost for a share in the intelligent advance of the age in which we live.

Assuredly, if the defects of the past are to be rectified, if the
agony of the present is to be unloosed, if the future oppression is to
br avoided, if thought is to be set free, if right of action is to be
given a place, if we are to attain to any way of progress, if we are to
deliver our children from the painful, shameful heritage, if we are to
leave blessing and happiness intact for those who succeed us, the first
of all necessary things is the clear-cut independence of our people.
What cannot our twenty millions do, every man with sword in heart, in
this day when human nature and conscience are making a stand for truth
and right? What barrier can we not break, what purpose can we not
accomplish?

We have no desire to accuse Japan of breaking many solemn treaties
since 1636, nor to single out specially the teachers in the schools or
government officials who treat the heritage of our ancestors as a colony
of their own, and our people and their civilization as a nation of sav-
ages, finding delight only in beating us down and bringing us under their
heel.

We have no wish to find special fault with Japan's lack of fairness
or her contempt of our civilization and the principles on which her state
rests; we, who have greater cause to reprimand ourselves, need not spend

precious time in finding fault with others; neither need we, who require so urgently to build for the future, spend useless hours over what is past and gone. Our urgent need today is the settling up of this house of ours and not a discussion of who has broken it down, or what has caused its ruin. Our work is to clear the future of defects in accord with the earnest dictates of conscience. Let us not be filled with bitterness or resentment over past agonies or past occasions for anger.

Our part is to influence the Japanese Government, dominated as it is by the old idea of brute force which thinks to run counter to reason and universal law, so that it will change, act honestly and in accord with the principles of right and truth.

The result of annexation, brought about without any conference with the Korean people, is that the Japanese, indifferent to us, use every kind of partiality for their own, and by a false set of figures show a profit and loss account between us two peoples most untrue, digging a trench of everlasting resentment deeper and deeper the farther they go.

Ought not the way of enlightened courage to be to correct the evils of the past by ways that are sincere, and by true sympathy and friendly feeling make a new world in which the two peoples will be equally blessed?

To bind by force twenty millions of resentful Koreans will mean not only loss of peace forever for this part of the Far East, but also will increase the ever-growing suspicion of four hundred millions of Chinese – upon whom depends the danger or safety of the Far East - besides strengthening the hatred of Japan. From this all the rest of the East will suffer. Today Korean independence will mean not only daily life and happiness for us, but also it would mean Japan's departure from an evil way and exaltation to the place of true protector of the East, so that China, too, even in her dreams, would put all fear of Japan aside. This thought comes from no minor resentment, but from a large hope for the future welfare and blessing of mankind.

A new era wakes before our eyes, the old world of force is gone, and the new world of righteousness and truth is here. Out of the experience and travail of the old world arises this light on life's affairs. The insects stifled by the foe and snow of winter awake at this same time with the breezes of spring and the soft light of the sun upon them.

It is the day of the restoration of all things on the full tide of which we set forth, without delay or fear. We desire a full measure of satisfaction in the way of liberty and the pursuit of happiness, and an opportunity to develop what is in us for the glory of the people.

We awake now from the old world with its darkened conditions in full determination and one heart and one mind, with right on our side, along with the forces of nature, to a new life. May all the ancestors to the thousands and ten thousand generations aid us from within and all the force of the world aid us from without, and let the day we take hold be the day of our attainment. In this hope we go forward.

THREE ITEMS OF AGREEMENT

1. This work of ours is in behalf of truth, religion and life, undertaken at the request of our people, in order to make known their desire for liberty. Let no violence be done to anyone.

2. Let those who follow us, every man, all the time, every hour, show forth with gladness this same mind.

3. Let all things be done decently and in order, so that our behaviour to the very end may be honorable and upright.

The 4252nd Year of the Kingdom of Korea, 3rd Month.

Representatives of the People.

The signatures attached to the document are:

Son Byung Hi, Kil Sun Chu, Yi Pil Chu, Paik Long Sung, Kim Won Kyu, Kim Pyung Cho, Kim Chang Choon, Kwon Dong Chin, Kwon Byunk Duk, Na Long Whan, Na In Hup, Yang Chun Paik, Yang Han Mook, Lew Yer Dai, Yi Kop (Kap) Sung, Yi Mung Yong, Yi Seung Hoon, Yi Choong Hoon, Yi Chong Il, Lim Yei Whan, Pak Choon Seung, Pak Hi Do, Pak Tong Wan, Sin Hong Sik, Sin Suk Ku, Oh Sei Chang, Oh Wha Young, Chung Choon Su, Choi Sung Mo, Choi In (Rin), Han Yong Woon, Hong Byung Ki, Hong Ki Cho.

From: Kendall, C.W., _The Truth about Korea_, San Francisco, 1919, pp.49-52.

(This well-known Declaration of Independence was signed by thirty-three patriots, of whom fifteen were Christians, fifteen were members of the Chuntokyo ((Religion of the Heavenly Way)), and three were Buddhists. These men met secretly in Seoul on March 1, 1919, two days before the funeral ceremonies of the Korean Emperor, who had died on January 20, 1919, and signed the Declaration. Immediately afterwards they offered themselves up for arrest. At 2 p.m. on March 1, 1919, the Declaration of Independence was read publicly to the crowds on the streets of Seoul. Thus the Independence Movement was launched, only to be suppressed in the course of the next few months with great brutality.)

\#   \#   \#

March 27, 1919

PETITION BY KOREAN VISCOUNTS TO GENERAL HASEGAWA

A way of doing things is good only as it accords with the time; and a government succeeds only when it makes its people happy. If the way is not in keeping with the age, it is not a perfect way; and if a government fails to make its people happy, it is not a good government.

It is now ten years since Japan and Korea were unified, and though there has resulted from it no little profit to the people with the clearing away of abuses, it still cannot be said to have made the people happy.

Today when the call for independence is given in the street, voices without number answer in response. In ten days and less the whole nation vibrates with its echo, and even the women and children vie with each other with no fear of death in their hearts. What is the reason for such a state of things as this? Our view is that having borne with pain and stifled resentment to the point of bursting, and being unable to repress it further, at last they have found expression, and like the overflowing of the Whang-ho River the waves have broken all bounds, and once having broken away, its power will brook no return. We call this an expression of the people, but is it not rather the mind of God Himself?

There are two ways of treating the conditions today, one a kind way and one the way of repression. The liberal way would be to speak kindly, soothe, comfort so as to remove fears and misgivings. But in that case there would be no end to the demonstrations. The use of force, on the other hand, that would cut down, uproot, beat to pieces, extinguish, will but rouse it the more and never conquer the spirit. If you do not get at the cause, you will never settle the matter.

The people, now roused to action, desire that restored to them that they once possessed, in order that the shame of their slavery be removed. They have nothing but bare hands, and a tongue with which to speak the resentment they feel. You can tell by this that no wicked motive underlies their thoughts.

The good and superior man would pity and forgive such as this, and view it with tender sympathy. We hear, however, that the government is arresting people right and left till they fill the prisons. There they whip, beat, and torture them, until they die violent deaths beneath it. The government also uses weapons till the dead lie side by side, and we are unable to endure the dreadful stories we hear.

Nevertheless, the whole state only rises the more, and the greater the force used to put it down, the greater the disturbances. How comes it that you look not to the cause, but think only to cut the manifestation of it down by force? Though you cut down and kill those who rise up everywhere, you may change the face of things, but the heart of it, never. Every man has written in his soul the word Independence, and those who in the quiet of their rooms shout for it are beyond the possibility of numbering. Will you arrest and kill them all?

A man's life is not something to be dealt with as the grass that grows. In ancient times Mencius said to King Sun of Che Kingdom; "If by taking possession of the state you can make the people of Yun happy, take possession; but if taking possession will render them miserable, forbear to do it."

Though Mencius spoke, the king paid no attention, and, as a result, came to a place where he finally said that he was greatly ashamed. This is, indeed, a mirror from history worthy to be looked into. Even the sage cannot run counter to the times in which he lives. We read the mind of God in the attitude of the people. If a people are not made happy, history tells us that there is no way by which their land can be held in possession.

We, your servants, have come to these times of danger and difficulty. Old and shameless are we, for when our country was annexed we accepted the rank of nobility, held office, and lived in disgrace, till, seeing these innocent people of ours in the fire and water, are unable to endure the sight longer. Thus we, too, in privacy have shouted for the independence just like the others.

Fearing not presumption on our part, we speak forth our hearts, in the hope that Your Excellency will be in accord herewith and let His Imperial Majesty know so that the Cabinet may consider it, and set right the cause, not by mere soft words, not by force, but in accord with the opportunity that Heaven above grants and the wishes of the people speak. Thus may Japan give independence including those nations with whom she is in treaty relation. Undoubtedly, all will grant their approval, and, like the eclipsed sun and moon, Japan will once again resume the light and splendor of her way. Who will not look with praise and commendation on this act of yours?

We, your servants, behind closed doors, ill and indisposed, and knowing not the mind of the world, offer our poor woodsmen's counsel to the state. If you accede to it, countless numbers of people will be made happy; if you refuse, we two alone will suffer. We have reached the bourn of life, and so we offer ourselves as a sacrifice for our people. Though we die for it, we have no complaints to make. In our sick chamber with our age upon us, we know not how to speak parsuasively. We pray Your Excellency to kindly give this your consideration. In a word, this is what our hearts would say.

Signed: Kim Yun-Sik
Yi Yong-Chik

From: Chung, Henry, The Case of Korea, Revell, N.Y., 1921, pp.343-345.

(This petition was submitted by two men enobled by the Japanese. By thus repudiating their titles and sympathizing with the independence movement, they became national heroes. The Japanese immediately arrested the two Viscounts and sentenced them after trial to penal servitude. At this time General Hasegawa was Japanese Governor-General of Korea.)

#   #   #

April 16, 1919.

AN APPEAL TO AMERICA BY KOREAN CONGRESS IN U.S.

We, the Koreans in Congress assembled, in Philadelphia, April 14-16, 1919, representing eighteen million people of our race who are now suffering untold miseries and barbarous treatment by the Japanese military authorities in Korea, hereby appeal to the great and generous American people.

For four thousand years our country enjoyed an absolute autonomy. We have our own history, our own language, our own literature and our own civilization. We have made treaties with the leading nations of the world; all of them recognized our independence, including Japan.

In 1904, at the beginning of the Russo-Japanese War, Japan made a treaty of alliance with Korea, guaranteeing territorial integrity and political independence of Korea, to cooperate in the war against Russia, Korea was opened to Japan for military purposes and Korea assisted Japan in many ways. After the war was over, Japan discarded the treaty of alliance as a "scrap of paper" and annexed Korea as a conquered territory. Ever since she has been ruling Korea with that autocratic militarism whose prototype has been well illustrated by Germany in Belgium and Northern France.

The Korean people patiently suffered under the iron heel of Japan for the last decade or more, but now they have reached the point where they are no longer able to endure it. On March 1st of this year some three million men, mostly of the educated class composed of Christians, Heaven Worshipers, Confucians, Buddhists, students of mission schools, under the leadership of the pastors of the native Christian churches, declared their independence from Japan and formed a provisional government on the border of Manchuria. Through the news dispatches and through private telegrams we are informed that 32,000 Korean revolutionists have been thrown into dungeons by the Japanese and over 100,000 men, women and children have been either killed or wounded so far. The Koreans have no weapons with which to fight, as the Japanese had taken away from them everything since the annexation, even pistols and fowling pieces. What resistance they are offering now against the Japanese soldiers and gendarmery is with pitchforks and sickles. In spite of this disadvantage and the horrible casualty among the Koreans, these people are keeping up their resistance and this demonstration is now nation-wide, including nearly all provinces. Japan has declared martial law in Korea and is butchering by thousands these unfortunate but patriotic people every day.

The Koreans in the United States and Hawaii have sent their representatives to Philadelphia, the Cradle of Liberty, to formulate a concerted plan with a view to stop this inhuman treatment of their brethren by the "Asiatic Kaiser," and to devise ways and means to help along the great cause of freedom and justice for our native land.

We appeal to you for support and sympathy because we know you love justice; you also fought for liberty and democracy, and you stand for Christianity and humanity. Our cause is a just one before the laws of God and man. Our aim is freedom from militaristic autocracy; our object is democracy for Asia; our hope is universal Christianity. Therefore we feel that our appeal merits your consideration.

You have already championed the cause of the oppressed and held out your helping hand to the weak of the earth's races. Your nation is the Hope of Mankind, so we come to you.

Beside this, we also feel that we have the right to ask your help for the reason that the treaty between the United States and Korea contains a stipulation in article 1, paragraph 2, which states as follows:

"If other powers deal unjustly or oppressively with either government, the other will exert their good offices, on being informed of the case, to bring about an amicable arrangement, thus showing their friendly feelings."

Does not this agreement make it incumbent upon America to intercede now in Korea's behalf?

There are many other good and sufficient reasons for America to exert her good offices to bring about an amicable arrangement, but we mention only one more, which is a new principle recently formulated at the peace conference in Paris. We cannot do better than to quote President Wilson's words, who is one of the founders of this new international obligation.

"The principle of the League of Nations is that it is the friendly right of every nation a member of the League to call attention to anything that she thinks will disturb the peace of the world, no matter where that thing is occurring. There is no subject that touches the peace of the world that is exempt from inquiry or discussion."

We therefore, in the name of humanity, liberty and democracy and in the name of the American-Korean treaty and in the name of the peace of the world, ask the government of the United States to exert its good offices to save the lives of our freedom-loving brethren in Korea and to protect the American missionaries and their families who are in danger of losing their lives and property on account of their love for our people and their faith in Christ.

We further ask you, the great American public, to give us your moral and material help so that our brethren in Korea will know that your sympathy is with them and that you are truly the champions of liberty and international justice.

Philadelphia
April 14-16, 1919

Signed by:
Members of First Korean Congress
Meeting in Philadelphia, U.S.A.

From: First Korean Congress, Philadelphia, 1919, pp.29-30.

(This document is representative of many statements made in later years by patriotic Koreans in exile.)

#   #   #

April 23, 1919

PROCLAMATION OF PROVISIONAL CONSTITUTION

Official Proclamation

Korea proclaims to the nations of the world that the people of this land, with a history of 4,000 years, have now, in this age of world progress, asserted the independence and liberty of their nation.

Although the Japanese troops have overrun our country, as the Germans did Belgium, yet we will not recognize their control, and as a people, in this manner, we repudiate their government and send out these notifications.

We, the liberty-loving people of Korea, having declared our independence and having chosen our representatives for a Provisional Government, through them make this announcement.

We extend our most cordial sentiments to the friendly nations that have already had treaty relations with our land, also to the new states which have been recently formed upon principles of humanity and justice.

PROVISIONAL GOVERNMENT FOR THE NEW
KOREAN REPUBLIC

Provisional Constitution

By the will of God, the people of Korea, both within and without the country, have united in a peaceful declaration of their independence, and for over one month have carried on their demonstrations in over 300 districts, and because of their faith in the movement they have by their representatives, chosen a Provisional Government to carry on to completion this independence and so to preserve blessings for our children and grandchildren.

The Provisional Government, in its Council of State, has decided on a Provisional Constitution, which it now proclaims.

1. The Korean Republic shall follow republican principles.

2. All powers of State shall rest with the Provisional Council of State of the Provisional Government.

3. There shall be no class distinction among the citizens of the Korean Republic, but men and women, noble and common, rich and poor, shall have equality.

4. The citizens of the Korean Republic shall have religious liberty, freedom of speech, freedom of writing and publication, the right to hold public meetings and form social organizations and the full right to choose their dwellings or change their abode.

5. The citizens of the Korean Republic shall have the right to vote for all public officials or to be elected to public office.

6. Citizens will be subject to compulsory education and military service and payment of taxes.

7. Since by the will of God the Korean Republic has arisen in the world and has come forward as a tribute to the world peace and civilization, for this reason we wish to become a member of the League of Nations.

8. The Korean Republic will extend benevolent treatment to the former Imperial Family.

9. The death penalty, corporal punishment and public prostitution will be abolished.

10. Within one year of the recovery of our land the National Congress will be convened.

In the 1st Year of the Korean Republic, 4th Month.

Signed by:
THE PROVISIONAL SECRETARY OF STATE,
AND THE MINISTERS OF FOREIGN AFFAIRS,
HOME AFFAIRS,
JUSTICE,
FINANCE,
WAR,
COMMUNICATIONS.

From: Kendall, C.W., The Truth About Korea, San Francisco, 1919, pp.55-57.

(This Constitution was framed in secret by delegates from thirteen provinces meeting in Seoul on April 23, 1919.)

\#   \#   \#

April 1919

KOREAN PETITION TO VERSAILLES PEACE CONFERENCE

KOREAN DELEGATION

TO THE PEACE CONFERENCE IN SESSION AT PARIS:

THE PETITION of the KOREAN PEOPLE AND NATION for the liberation from Japan and for the reconstitution of Korea as an independent state

RESPECTFULLY SHEWETH:

The Korean People have been a nation for more than 4,200 years, with a settled life and culture and with their country forming one of the historic states of Asia. During most of these Forty-two Centuries, Korea enjoyed national independence.

Korean Independence Recognized.

2. The continued existence of Korea as a separate and sovereign state

was recognized by Japan, the United States, Great Britain and other foreign Powers in their respective treaties of peace and commerce concluded with the Korean Government.

In the Treaty with the United States, signed at Seoul on May 22, 1882, it was expressly agreed that "if other Powers deal unjustly or oppressively with either Government the other will exert their good offices, on being informed of the case, to bring about an amicable arrangement, thus showing their friendly feelings."

In the Treaty of Shimonoseki, signed on April 17, 1895, Japan insisted on China's definite recognition of the "full and complete independence and autonomy of Korea." And in the first Anglo-Japanese agreement of alliance, concluded on January 30, 1902, Japan and Great Britain affirmed and substantially guaranteed the independence of Korea. Lastly, in the Treaty of Defensive and Offensive Alliance made between the Japanese Government and the Korean Government in 1904, Japan specifically guaranteed the independence and integrity of Korea.

Korean Independence as an International Doctrine.

3. These treaties not only affirmed and confirmed the separate existence of Korea as a sovereign state, but they established, it is submitted, Korean independence on the basis of an international authority and sanction which no single Power could violate without subjecting its action to eventual revision by other Powers.

Japan's Violation of Korean Independence.

4. Such a violation of Korean independence was committed by Japan when the Japanese Government - by acts of fraud and force - compelled the conclusion of the Treaty of August 22, 1910, whereby the then Emperor of Korea purported to cede "completely and permanently to His Majesty the Emperor of Japan all rights of sovereignty over the whole of Korea," with her then population of more than Fifteen million Koreans.

The Korean Protest.

5. Against this extinction of Korean sovereignty and the incorporation of their country as a province of Japan, the Korean people and nation have strenuously protested and do still protest.

6. This protest is renewed and strengthened daily, owing to the methods applied by Japan in the administration of Korea. In ruthlessness and efficiency these methods exceed those practised by Prussia in her eastern provinces, in Schleswig-Holstein, in Alsace-Lorraine.

Not only in name but in reality, Japan is determined to turn Korea into a Japanese province. And she is trying to do this by a pitiless attempt to extirpate the great roots of patriotism - love of the soil, language of the people and the history of the nation - and also to "control" the two means which might render futile this organized attempt to destroy patriotism, i.e., education and wealth.

Japanese "Control" of Korean Education and Wealth.

7. Any and every department of modern education calculated, if pursued beyond a certain point, to encourage what Count Terauchi - the Japanese proconsul who "annexed" Korea - calls "dangerous thoughts" is either forbidden or taught in an emasculated sense in the schools of Korea under Government control. And the Korean student is absolutely prohibited from going to Europe or the United States to seek a modern education, even at his or her expense.

8. Nearly every wealthy Korean is obliged to have a Japanese over-seer at his house, controlling his properties and finances. And Koreans with deposits in the banks - which are all Japanese institutions - cannot withdraw large amounts at one time without disclosing to the banks about the purpose or purposes for which the money is to be used.

Japan and Christianity.

9. Every effort is made by the Japanese authorities - particularly through their police agents - to discourage and obstruct Christian mis-sionary work in Korea which is envisaged as opposed to vital Japanese interests in the peninsula.

Is not the gravest indictment of Japan's work in Korea to be read in the fact that Christianity is seriously regarded as a force hostile to the success of the Japanese system of government in the country?

Korea for the Japanese.

10. The Japanese authorities claim that "reforms" have been intro-duced into Korea. But it is well to remember that most of these reforms, valuable as they are, may be found in a well-regulated penal colony ("The Korean Conspiracy Case," New York), and all of them have been effected or introduced at the expense of the Korean taxpayer in the interest and for the benefit of the Japanese settler for whom the Japa-nese authorities are bent on making Korea an attractive field of colo-nization.

11. The Japanese rules and administers Korea in the spirit and by the methods of a Master-Nation or, more accurately, a Profiteer-Nation.

Except in the sense that cattle or slaves must be shown care of if they are to be of any value to their owners, the welfare of the Korean people is not an aim of government with Japan.

Japan Against the World.

12. In addition to these reasons connected directly with the fate of the Korean people, the vital interests of the world - especially the Asiatic interests of France and the Asiatic and Pacific interests of Great Britain and the United States - demand the dis-annexation of Korea and the liberation of her people from Japan.

13. In trade and commerce, Japan is gradually eliminating the

Western trader and merchant in Korea and transferring to the exclusive hands of her own people tradal interests which have had their origin in the series of treaties of peace and commerce concluded between Korea and the foreign powers.

In this elimination of Western competition, Japan continues true to that instinct for exclusion which, in the past, found expression in her rigidly guarded isolation and which, today, expresses itself in the menacing attempt to exclude Western influence in Far Asia through the application of a debased Monroe Doctrine for the Far East.

Japan's Continental Policy.

14. It is, however, in the far-reaching political aims of Japan - ralizable eventually through her continued annexation of Korea - that France, as well as Great Britain and America, must be vitally interested.

The danger of the non-Japanese world, including especially the three Latin and Anglo-Saxon powers, lies in Japan's unfettered prosecution of her Continental Policy.

This policy aims, first, at the seizure of the hegemony of Asia through the domination and control of the man-power and natural resources of China - possible by the Japanese possession of the continental point d'appui of Korea - and, next, at the mastery of the Pacific as the sole means of securing unrestricted entrance for the Japanese immigrant into Australasia and the United States.

The Policy in Operation.

15. Japan's Continental Policy as already found expression -

(a) In two successful wars which have made her the greatest military power in Asia in much the same way that Prussia's two wars made her the greatest military power in Europe;

(b) In the annexation of Korea;

(c) In the gradual substitution of Japanese for Chinese authority in South Manchuria and Eastern Inner Mongolia;

(d) In the attempt now being made to secure from the Peace Conference the succession of Japan to German holdings and privileges in the Chinese province of Shantung, including Kiaochow;

(e) In the growing subjection of China, with her incalculable man-power and resources, to Japanese domination by and through the same set of methods which made the annexation of Korea a "political necessity"; and

(f) In the Japanese possession of the "South Sea Islands north of the Equator," which bring Japan nearly two thousand miles closer to Australia and gives the Japanese Navy a base which dominates, practically, the entire land-areas of the Pacific.

The Korean Revolution.

16. The protest and opposition of the Korean people to Japanese annexation of their country and to the process of political extermination

applied to them by the Mikado's agents has now expressed itself in the Korean Revolution.

On the 1st of March, at 1 p.m., the Korean People and Nation declared their independence. This act of independence was formally done by the National Independence Union, composed of three million Koreans representing and expressing the desire and will of 18,700,000 Koreans in Korea proper, in China, Siberia, in Hawaii and in the United States.

The declaration states: "It is our solemn duty to secure the right of free and perpetual development of our own national character, adapting ourselves to the principles of the reconstruction of the world - to secure our independence, to wipe out injuries, get rid of our present sufferings, and leave our children eternal freedom instead of a bitter and shameful inheritance."

Progress of the Revolution.

17. The Korean Delegation - appointed by the New Korean Young Men's Society to which are affiliated the Korean National Independence Union and other bodies organized in the cause of Korean independence - is in receipt of several cable dispatches reporting the progress of the revolution and the national movement for independence.

A dispatch from the Korean National Independence Union received in Paris, via Shanghai, on April 7th, instant, reads in part as follows: "On March 26 we held grand demonstrations at Seoul. Our national flags were flown on the city hills. The Japanese arrested two hundred of those who participated in the demonstrations. There were casualties on both sides. Samnam (i.e., all provinces south of Seoul) are uprising every day. Korean demonstrations are taking place in Eastern Siberia and Manchuria."

The Korean Republic.

18. The same dispatch reports the organization of a Provisional Government of Korea, consisting of a President, Vice-president, Secretary of State, Minister for Home Affairs, Minister of Finance, Minister of Justice and Minister of War.

Among those included in the Provisional Government are Prince Pak Yung-hio and Messrs. Rhee Syngman, Ahm Chang Ho and Li Tong Whi. Prince Pak Yung-hio is one of the five great leaders who inaugurated what is known in Korean history as the movement of the Progressive Party in 1884. He was the chief figure among the Progressives who, in 1894, compelled the introduction of modern reforms into Korea. He was at one time Minister for Home Affairs before the annexation. Rhee Syngman is an M.A. of Harvard, U.S.A., and Ph.D. of Princeton, U.S.A. Since 1894 he has been one of the leaders of the old Korean Independence Club. As a political worker he has suffered imprisonment and he has also been tortured. Ahn Chang Ho is the founder of the Sin Min Hueh or People's Soviety and, since 1905, has been a leader of young Korean nationalists. He is the President of the Korean National Association. Li Tong Whi is a former major in the old Korean Army and a recognized leader of Korean nationalists in Siberia and Manchuria. He has been imprisoned and tortured by the Japanese authorities.

Japanese Repression.

19. Another dispatch received by the Korean delegation on April 10th inst., states that "from the 1st of March up to date, active demonstrations of the Independence movement have been very well conducted all over Korea. Representatives prefer passive revolution, including lecturing and distribution of manifestoes. Girls more active. Strikes have occurred in enemy (Japanese) factories, stores, etc. Our churches, schools and stores closed everywhere. Thirty-two thousand men and women are in prison. About 100,000 have been injured, including old people, girls and children. Interior traffic communications severed. Terrible outrages committed by enemy (Japanese). Missionaries are sending truth to world."

In a further dispatch which reached the Korean delegation on April 11th inst., Japanese atrocities are reported: "Japan has begun massacring in Korea. On March 28 over 1,000 unarmed people were killed during a three-hour demonstration held in Seoul. The shooting, beating and hooking (bayoneting) of people are in merciless progress throughout Korea. Churches, schools and homes of leaders have been destroyed. Women are being stripped naked and beaten before crowds, especially female members of leaders' families. The imprisoned are being tortured. Doctors are forbidden to attend the wounded. We ask urgently aid from Foreign Red Cross. We have decided to fight for freedom until last Korean falls. We solicit help in the name of God."

Of the main news dispatches on the subject appearing in the American and European press, it must suffice here to quote the latest from the Tokio correspondent of the London "Times." It appeared in the issue of the London paper on April 17th inst., under the caption "Korea's Rights": "While it is recognized that there can be only one outcome of the disturbances in Korea, the Government's decision to reinforce the military establishment in the peninsula evokes universal press comment, the feature of which is the recognition that it will be inevitable, when opportunity occurs, to replace the Military Governor by a Civilian Governor. The 'Nichi-Nichi' attributes the disturbances chiefly to a mistaken conception of the principle of self-determination, also to the inimical influence of missionaries. The 'Jiji' says it is evident that many reforms are necessary in Korea. Another journal dwells on the fact that the Koreans are not an inferior people...."

Abrogation of the Treaty of Annexation.

20. The Korean people submit that the Treaty of Annexation of August 22, 1910, should be declared Null and Void or otherwise abrogated by the Peace Conference for the reasons set forth in this petition and further elaborated in the memorandum hereto attached and more especially for the reasons following:

I. The said Treaty of annexation was concluded in curcumstances of Fraud and Force which vitiated its validity as a legal and international document, even assuming that the then Emperor of Korea had the right to hand over to "His Majesty the Emperor of Japan" Fifteen Million Koreans and a country that had existed as a separate and sovereign state for more than 4,200 years.

II. The Korean people and nation have consistently denied the right of the then "puppet" Emperor of Korea to deal with them in terms of the said Treaty of Annexation. Being men and not cattle, they hold that their consent is and has been an essential condition to the validity of the said treaty. This consent has never been given.

III. That said Treaty of Annexation was and is a direct violation by Japan of the International guarantees entered into by the Japanese Government with Korea and other Powers regarding Korean independence and integrity.

IV. In the several Treaties concluded between Korea and Japan and other Powers, and by Japan with China, with Russia and with Great Britain, regarding Korea, the existence of the latter as a separate and sovereign state is - as to all these treaties - explicitly recognized and its political independence and territorial integrity is - as to some of them - also explicitly guaranteed in terms establishing the same on the basis of a public law of nations which no single Power - especially Japan - could violate without subjecting its action to eventual revision by the Powers assembled in an international congress like the present Peace Conference.

V. The Peace Conference meets in order to secure a settlement of the affairs of the member-nations according to the principles expressed in President Wilson's Fourteen Points. The principles underlying this statement of views is defined by the President in his message to Congress on January 8, 1918, as "the principle of justice to all peoples and nationalities and their right to live on equal terms of liberty and safety with one another, whether they be strong or weak."

As one of the allied and associated states in the war, Japan has expressly accepted the Fourteen Points with their underlying principle of justice. Inasmuch as this principle of justice is clearly violated by the Mikado's continued exercise of "all rights of sovereignty over the whole of Korea" without the consent and against the wishes of the Korean People and Nation, it becomes the right and duty of the Peace Conference to declare the nullification or otherwise decree the abrogation of the aforesaid Treaty of Annexation.

VI. In virtue of rights founded in International Law and of the New Justice which is to redress the wrongs of nations, the Korean People have a just claim for the Reconstruction of Korea as an Independent State unless, indeed they are to be excluded from the scope of the principles which have already found expression in the reconstitution of Poland after almost one and a half centuries of partitions and annexations and in the disannexation of Alsace-Lorraine after nearly half a century of Prussian rule.

It is less than ten years since Japan effected the annexation of Korea. And the fact that the outbreak of the war did not find Japan an ally of the Central Powers - a political combination that had always been envisaged by the German-trained advisers of the Mikado - is no reason why the Korean People should be suffered by the Peace Conference to continue to live under a system of military government which is a denial of every principle for which men have lately died on the soil of France.

This petition is presented in the name and on behalf of the Provisional Republican Government of Korea and of the eighteen million seven hundred thousand Koreans living in Korea proper, in China, Siberia, Hawaii, the United States and elsewhere as well as of the five thousand and more Koreans who fought for the Allied cause on the Eastern Front before the treaty of Brest-Litovsk - in the aggregate forming and constituting the Korean People and Nation - by the undersigned John Kiusic Soho Kimm, the duly accredited member of the Korean Delegation appointed by the New Korean Young Men's Society, etc., etc.

J. Kiusic S. Kimm
Delegate of New Korean Young Men's
Society,
Delegate of the Korean National
Association,
Delegate of the Provisional Government of the Korean Republic,
etc., etc., etc.

From: Kendall, C.W., <u>The Truth About Korea</u>, San Francisco, 1919, pp.60-70.

(No action was taken on this petition at the Versailles Peace Conference.)

#   #   #

August 19, 1919

JAPANESE IMPERIAL RESCRIPT ON REORGANIZATION

We have ever made it Our aim to promote the security and welfare of Our territory of Korea, and to extend to the native population of that territory as Our beloved subjects a fair and impartial treatment in all respects, to the end that they may without distinction of persons lead their lives in peace and contentment. We are persuaded that the state of development at which the general situation has now arrived calls for certain reforms in the administrative organization of the Government-General of Korea, and We issue Our Imperial command that such reforms be put into operation. The measures thus taken are solely designed to facilitate the working of administration and to secure good and enlightened government in pursuance of Our settled policy, and in fulfilment of the altered requirements of the country. Specially in view of the termination of the war in Europe and of the rapid changes in the conditions of the world do We consider it highly desirable that every effort should be made for the advancement of the national resources and the well-being of the people. We call upon all public functionaries concerned to exercise their best endeavors in obedience to Our wishes in order that a benign rule may be assured to Korea, and that the people, diligent and happy in attending to their respective vocations, may enjoy the blessing of peace and contribute to the growing prosperity of the country.

From: Ireland, Alleyne, The New Korea, New York,
1926, pp.317-318.

(Underlining not in original text.)

(This Rescript announcing reforms in Korea was intended to calm the Korean people who at that time were greatly stirred by the independence movement which began on March 1, 1919.)

#   #   #

September 1919

STATEMENT BY JAPANESE PREMIER HARA ON KOREA

Nearly ten years have elapsed since Korea was incorporated into the Empire of Japan, and in view of significant changes which meanwhile have presented themselves in the conditions of the country, a plan of various reforms in the Korean administrative system for some time has been engaging my attention. Unfortunately, in March last disturbances broke out in several parts of the peninsula which for obvious reasons have retarded the introduction of the contemplated reforms. It will not be necessary at this moment to file a full account of those disturbances.

It is much to be regretted that, as is generally the case under the circumstances, they gave birth to wild and baseless representations, some of which even went so far as to make new stories out of old incidents antedating the annexation. Being determined to be perfectly just and fair in the conduct of affairs connected with the recent uprisings, the Government will admit no excuse for any culprit, whether he be a Government official or a private citizen. Take the Suigen occurrence, for instance. There the Government has caused the responsible officers who had already been subjected to administrative censure to be brought for trial before a courtmartial.

In proceeding to the reorganization of the system of the Governor-General of Korea, I regret to announce the resignation of Marshal Hasegawa, Governor-General, and of Yamagata, Director-General of Administration, both of whom have rendered eminent service to the State at the important posts which they have occupied for several years. To fill the vacancies caused by their retirement, Baron Saito and Mr. Midzuno have now been appointed respectively as Governor-General and Director-General of Administration. Baron Saito, who had long distinguished himself as a Minister of State, requires no introduction for his high personality and powers of statesmanship.

Nor is there any need to refer to the high esteem in which Mr. Midzuno is held at home and abroad as a public servant who has not only filled with credit several important executive posts during a period of more than twenty years, but also held a Ministerial portfolio in the late Cabinet. I have no doubt that these two gentlemen will prove equal to the trust placed in them for carrying out the contemplated reforms in Korea in conformity with the expressed wishes of the Government. Korea is united geographically with the main islands of Japan and the two peoples are closely related to each other in race, in manners and customs, and in sentiments.

No distinction of inequality should be allowed to exist between them as loyal subjects of the same sovereign, whether politically, socially, or otherwise. These considerations are understood invariably to have been kept in view in the imperial rescript issued at the time of the annexation, as well as in that which has just been issued. It should be noted that the existing administrative system of Korea is not meant to be of a permanent and unalterable nature, but that it embodies provisional arrangements calculated to meet the passing needs of the transitory period until the final goal is reached.

In pursuance of this policy the Government are now decided to carry out various reforms in Korea, and it is their fixed determination to forward the progress of the country in order that all differences between Korea and Japan proper in matters of education, industry, and of the civil service may finally be altogether obliterated. The Government are, moreover, confidently looking forward to the eventual adoption in Korea of a system of provincial and municipal administration similar to that in operation in Japan proper, so far as circumstances would permit. For a speedy attainment of the objects one naturally cannot rely solely on the force of organ and machinery: a great deal must necessarily depend upon the efforts of Koreans themselves toward their own upliftment.

I am well aware that the system of gendarmery prevailing in Korea is being made a subject of criticism at home and abroad, but I would call attention to the fact that the institution originated in attempts to meet the exigencies of the situation under the regime of residents-general and was never intended to be a permanent arrangement. It is now proposed to have gendarmery replaced by a force of police to be placed under the control of local governors in a manner similar to that which obtains in Japan proper, except in districts where conditions make immediate elimination inadvisable.

It is not possible at this moment to make any further announcement on the details of the contemplated reforms, which it remains for the newly appointed authorities to work out. To sum up, however, it may be stated that Korea and Japan proper, forming equally integral parts of the same empire, no distinction should in principle be made between them, and that it is the ultimate purpose of the Japanese government in

due course to treat Korea as in all respects on the same footing with
Japan proper. In this wise may be attained the only true object of annexation, and on these lines may be expected the permanent advance and
and enlightenment of the Koreans. I trust that the above brief observations may assist the public at home and abroad to arrive at a full
comprehension of the true intentions and policy of the Japanese government.

From: Cynn, H.H.H.W., <u>The Rebirth of Korea</u>, New
York, 1920, pp.166-169.

(Premier Hara, the first commoner to become Premier of Japan,
held office between September 29, 1918, and November 12,
1921. The above statement reflects the new spirit of liberal-
ism which was evident in many quarters in Japan during the
decade of the 20's. It is known that Premier Hara drew up
this statement of policy toward Korea after discussion with
the Korean leader Lyou Un Hyeung of the Shanghai headquarters
of the Korean Provisional Government in exile.)

#   #   #

September 10, 1919

JAPANESE GOVERNOR-GENERAL SAITO'S PROCLAMATION TO THE PEOPLE

On my assumption of duty as Governor-General, the organization of the
Government-General was revised. Accordingly, I desire to address a few
words to the people at large.

That the administrative policy of Chosen should be based on the
great principle of placing the Japanese and Korean peoples on an equal
footing and should aim at promoting their interests and happiness, as
well as at securing the permanent peace of the Far East, was determined
upon at the very beginning. Those successively charged with the administration of this Peninsula duly appreciated its meaning and strove to
improve and develop its people and resources. The people, too, diligently engaged in their business. It is now recognized at home and
abroad that the present development of Chosen came as the result of
their joint efforts. It goes without saying, however, that all administrative institutions must be planned and executed in conformity with
the standard of popular living and the progress of the times, so that
appropriate measures may be carried out and popular desires prevented
from taking a wrong course. The times have progressed so much and civilization too that it is difficult to draw a comparison between this and
former days. Since the great European War was brought to an end, moreover, the condition of the world and human psychology have undergone a
marked change. In deference to this hard fact, His Majesty's Government,
through a revision in the Organic Regulations, enlarged the sphere of
appointment for the Governor-General, reformed the police system, and
made such provision for simplification and prompt transaction of state

business and the diffusion of enlightened administration as to bring them in perfect accord with the forward movement of this age. On assuming my present duty by Imperial order I determined in my own mind to pursue faithfully the State policy and vindicate the spirit of annexation. I am determined to superintend officials under my control and encourage them to put forth greater efforts to act in a fairer and juster way, and promote the facilities of the people and the unhindered attainment of the people's desires by dispensing with all formality. Full consideration will be given to the appointment and treatment of Koreans so as to secure the right men for the right places, and what in Korean institutions and old customs is worthy of adoption will be adopted as a means of government. I also hope to introduce reform in the different branches of administrative activity, and to enforce local self-government at the proper opportunity, and thereby ensure stability for the people and enhance their general well-being. It is most desirable that the government and governed throw open their hearts and minds to each other and combine their efforts to advance civilization in Chosen, solidify its foundation of enlightened government, and thus answer His Majesty's benevolent solicitude. If anybody is found guilty of unwarrantably refractory language or action, of misleading the popular mind, and of impeding the maintenance of public peace, he will be met with relentless justice. May it be that the people at large will place reliance on all this.

September 10, 1919   BARON MAKOTO SAITO,
                                Governor-General of Chosen.

        From: Ireland, Alleyne, The New Korea, New York,
                1926, pp.322-324.

    (This proclamation was in effect an appeal by a more liberal
     administrator for better relations between Korea and Japan.)

                    #   #   #

                                                    October 1, 1925

GOVERNOR GENERAL SAITO'S STATEMENT ON
FIFTEENTH ANNIVERSARY OF ANNEXATION

        Today we celebrate the fifteenth anniversary of the new regime in Chosen and our minds are naturally filled with memories of the past. Fifteen years ago the present regime was established immediately following the annexation. The annexation itself was a great epoch-making event in modern history and was brought about with the high aim of insuring for the millions in this peninsula the enjoyment of peace and enhancement of thier welfare, while perpetuating the peace in the Orient and safeguarding the security of the Empire. Since Japan and Chosen are adjacent to each other across a narrow strip of water and possess vital interests closely interwoven, together with homogenity of race and culture, it is but natural as well as logical for them to be united into one body politic for their mutual benefit. Chosen was for long pre-occupied with internal strife, besides labouring under constant pressure from neighbouring powers, and so eventually became exhausted, and even today she finds herself lagging behind other countries in civilization. To lift up Chosen from this deplorable state of natural existence it was of first importance to develop her economic resources and help her overwrought masses so that they might keep pace with the progress of the world, and there was no better means to do this than to make one family of Japan and Chosen and establish here in this land a complete and liberal government. Annexation, therefore, was really an inevi-table yet natural consequence. Since the new regime was instituted we have exerted ourselves to the utmost in the interests of Chosen by undertaking various enterprises commensurate with the cultural require-ments of the times, with the result that these new subjects of the Empire have begun to appreciate how good the change has been for them. I was appointed to Chosen in August 1919 when reorganization of the government machinery was effected, and, in obedience to the Imperial wishes expressed at the time, laid down a platform, the main points of which consisted in maintenance of law and order, deference to popular will, security of living, promotion of culture, etc. I have since de-voted my whole energy toward realization of this policy and have been fortunate enough to see the peninsula begin another chapter of improvement in all important lines of human activity - education, sanitation, indus-try, traffic, and finance. As a matter of fact, if we compare these days with those previous to annexation what a change do we not see? Admin-istration of Chosen, nevertheless, is a long continuing task, and the progress so far experienced is nothing more than a beginning. Comple-tion of the great work requires more time and labour, and we are bound by duty to redouble our efforts for attainment of our great goal. I sincerely hope that government and people will continue to cooperate in overcoming every difficulty in the way and will finally place this coun-try on a par with the most civilized countries in the world, so that its eighteen million inhabitants may for ever enjoy the full bliss of an enlightened rule. This is the hope I desire all in the country may share with me on this felicitous commemoration day.

> From: Annual Report of Administration of Chosen,
> 1927-28, Compiled by Government-General of
> Chosen, Keijo, December 1929, pp.156-157.

(This statement is significant as evidence of the more liberal policy of Japan at home and abroad that was evident in certain Japanese quarters during the 20's. The date of this document was two years before General Yamanashi was appointed Governor-General of Korea in December 1927 by the new Premier of Japan, G. Tanaka, known for his militaristic leanings.)

#   #   #

June 30, 1932

GOVERNOR-GENERAL UGAKI'S INSTRUCTION TO GOVERNORS

I am deeply gratified to have the opportunity of seeing you in person at this Gubernatorial Conference at which I have the pleasure of listening to you as well as of expressing my own ideas.

It goes without saying that the grand aim of the amalgamation of Japan proper and Chosen is to secure the permanent peace of the Far East, to ensure stable harmony in the relations between the two peoples, and to effect the happiness and well being of all. More than twenty years have elapsed since the amalgamation, and thanks to the constant efforts of successive administrators, various phases of the administration have attained perfection. Industry has been markedly enhanced, while all, diligently striving at their daily tasks, pay reverence to the Imperial Family whose bountiful blessings they gratefully enjoy. But on the eighth of January last, outside the Sakurada Mon a treacherous Korean made a sudden attempt on the Imperial Cortege, an act that disturbed me most profoundly and my feelings of deepest regret were shared by the twenty million people of this peninsula. As the one responsible for the administration of Chosen I feel the gravity of my duty, and eagerly desire to fulfil the August Will by making clear to the people the fundamental character of our Empire, by purifying the minds of the masses, by accelerating the harmonious cooperation of all the inhabitants, by showing our sincerity in our reverence of the Emperor, and by encouraging the spirit of patriotism.

Peace and quietness now prevail in the four corners of the peninsula and it is most gratifying that the dispatch of the Imperial Army to the neighbouring country ((Manchuria - 1931)) seems to have deepened the sense of trust on the part of the Korean masses, but the mental uneasiness of peoples outside this country coupled with the successive occurrences of deplorable incidents in Manchuria naturally cause unsettling ideas to rise in the thoughts of the people of this country and it is difficult to feel entirely assured that some may not dare to imitate radical actions.

Taking advantage of the economic depression and inactive rural conditions now prevailing, some people have attempted to interfere with the smooth working of administrative regulations, and to disturb peace by inciting heedlessly the feelings of the masses. In view of the above I desire to solicit your closest attention at all times to the trend of popular feelings, to afford opportunities for enlightenment and guidance toward the proper directions, to maintain peace in the strictest sense of the term and to correct wrong doing. I beg you to fulfil carefully these instructions and thus to eliminate satisfactorily all unsettling feelings.

In examining the prevailing condition of the world, it appears that the depression is becoming increasingly serious, and that no ray of hope for recovery is yet in sight. The thoughts of the people are getting into a state of still greater complexity showing that the nations of the world have fallen into such a desperate situation as has never been experienced before. The reason that the world has been brought into such unsolvable difficulties on every side, is chiefly that the nations have declined into

an excessively materialistic form of civilization. The affairs of the
Governments and of social activities are organized on a basis of materialistic economy. The people too are absorbed in a life of production,
distribution and consumption of wealth and they ignore the spiritual
life of which little evidence is now apparent. It is of paramount importance that as a way by which to alleviate these grave difficulties,
we should emphasize and encourage spiritual living among the people
assisting them to liberate themselves from the fetters of economic
dominance. More particularly in Chosen, considering the existing condition of culture, economics and society in general, we should reform
education, and encourage art and religion, through the aid of which
spiritual ideas may be awakened, and moral culture emphasized. To attain this object, increasing attention should be paid to educational
institutions in the endeavour to turn out steady and promising material,
besides trying to purify thoughts and cultivate virtue through which
the spiritual life of the people may be made sound. It is with this
desire that we have effected recently the creation of a Civic Course in
secondary schools, the revision of the Normal School regulations, the
arrangement of vocational Continuation Schools, and the enforcement of
the long term practical training course in the rural schools.

Besides the work in enlightening the students in the schools, we
have been enlisting the assistance of religionists, educationists and
other men of intelligence, in a closer cooperation between officials and
private citizens in the advancement of this movement. For the attainment
of this goal an increase in the expenditure was necessary and a special
appropriation in the supplementary budget was made and the reorganization
of offices in the Government-General was effected. Such being the case,
you are asked to encourage those responsible in enforcing sternly the
rules of the schools, who by self-teaching and by self-respect in attending to the training of pupils who may keep their thoughts on the institutions of social education, in endeavouring to aid the uplift of the
spiritual world, thereby coming to closer harmony with the administrative
measures of the Government-General to cope with the present grave situation. The question of the security of living of the large agrarian population is a vital issue from the industrial and social point of view,
especially at the present time of serious depression, and this solution
is a most urgent one. Needless to say the consistent realization of
relief of this kind is not an easy task but the soundest way by which
agriculturalists may attain a secure living is through their own thrift
and their own hard work. It appears to me that to make Korean farmers
self-supporting should be a comparatively simple task for there is plenty
of arable land utilizable and plenty of manpower available while methods
of intensive cultivation should be applicable. Thus these farmers, by
increasing their earnings from an extension of their labours, should
make themselves financially, independent. The difficulty in the rural
community today is two-fold. The widely spread use of too simple farming
methods and the rapid increase of money tightness, may be designated as
the underlying cause, with the fluctuation of the prices of agricultural
products resulting from the financial depression, as the immediate cause.
Thus, in guiding the rural community in the future, we should effect
changes in farm management into synthetic and amalgamated farming basing
the principles on thrift and diligence, instilling in the farmers a spirit
of self-dependence, by making them self-supporting thereby placing the

agricultural communities on a sound financial foundation. The farming problem is no longer a mere industrial and economic one, but involves those of peace, education and social welfare as well as other questions of local administration, all of which require careful study and the hearty cooperation of all concerned.

The Government-General expects to introduce a partial change in its organization with a view to lessen the burden on agriculture, to increase farm earnings and to alleviate their financial difficulties. Thus measures will be effected for a system more unified than the one now existing for raising the financial status, and we hope to attain success in the relief of this condition.

All forms of local administrative and educational organs should establish a consistent amalgamation plan by keeping still more perfect relationship with each other, while endeavouring to elevate the spiritual life of the rural community by encouraging thrifty and intelligent living. It is hoped that the local organs may take measures to assist a large number of farmers to establish a foundation of life in conformity with the policy of the Government-General and the Provincial Government.

On the outbreak of the Manchurian incident in September last year, the Imperial Army was despatched there for the purpose of securing our acquired rights and of protecting our compatriots. This was followed by the Shanghai incident where our army was sent likewise for the protection of our citizens. By the desperate fighting and the great efforts of our gallant and loyal soldiers the Imperial Army's prestige has been greatly enhanced. As a result a New Nation has been created and truce concluded in the Shanghai district, showing signs that the dark clouds in the Orient are gradually being swept away, for which we wish to offer our hearty congratulations.

Especially do we hope that the newly born State of Manchukuo, having "Wangdao" (Rule of Justice) as the fundamental spirit in the founding of that Nation, may make a healthy development. This, we believe, is the means for securing the peace of the Far East.

Physically, Chosen is closely joined to Manchuria and they have had very close relationship from of old. Especially as Chosen is situated between Japan proper and Manchuria, in any attempt to form cultural or economic measures in favour of this New Nation, a close relation should be maintained under a unified system and so that no discord may be caused, but instead that mutual accord and mutual prosperity may be realized. In effecting measures to secure the living of our compatriots there and to aid their cultural and economic development, we must also keep in close relationship with the measures of that Nation by which means the most suitable policy may be established and put in operation to serve the practical needs of both peoples.

We most deeply regret that many of our compatriots residing in that country suffered loss. In this connection a relief fund for these sufferers has been most graciously granted by His Majesty the Emperor by whose August Will in bestowing such gracious benevolence we were most deeply affected. The Government-General, under the gracious Will of His Majesty, endeavouring to the best of its ability to distribute this efficiently effected prompt and proper measures for the relief and protection of our compatriots from Chosen who had taken refuge in the South Manchuria Railway zone and almost all of these have now returned to their original places. In short, our beloved country now faces a most critical time in politics, economics, thoughts and other affairs. To cope with this situation, it demands the cooperation of every one in the nation. An emergency cabinet has already been formed and the work of relief has begun under its direction. It is most important that all, regardless whether big or small, official of responsible position or private individual should undertake to save this grave situation.

The foundation of the nation's destiny lies in the man. In times of national difficulties capable men are called. In supervising your subordinates, you should choose the right man for the right place and not effect too frequent changes, making them feel their own responsibilities in their duties, enforcing strict official discipline, opening new channels of hope, uplifting ethical idea of political thoughts, and promoting the well being of the people.

The above is an outline of my cherished opinions. Further details will be given to you by the Vice-Governor-General and other Directors of Bureaus. I hope you will fully understand the policy of the Government-General and contribute in the administration of the Provinces.

From: Annual Report on Administration of Chosen, 1933-34, compiled by Government-General of Chosen, Keijo, December 1934, pp.200-203.

(Underlining not in original text.)

(This document is significant because it reflects the ideological orientation of Japanese political leaders toward Korea after the Manchurian Incident of September 18, 1931, which led to the setting up by Japan of the new state of "Manchukuo." General Ugaki served as Governor-General of Korea from July 1931 to August 1936. Further documents for the period between 1931 and 1941 are not included in this collection because the indigenous independence movement was effectively suppressed in Korea by the Japanese and existed only underground and in exile. Korea was more firmly attached to Japan as Japan started her invasion of China on July 7, 1937.)

#   #   #

PART III. FROM WORLD WAR II TO THE KOREAN CRISIS ON 1950

December 1, 1943

CAIRO DECLARATION (U.S.A., U.K., CHINA)

The several military missions have agreed upon future military operations against Japan. The Three Great Allies expressed their resolve to bring unrelenting pressure against their brutal enemies by sea, land, and air. This pressure is already rising.

The Three Great Allies are fighting this war to restrain and punish the aggression of Japan. They covet no gain for themselves and have no thought of territorial expansion. It is their purpose that Japan shall be stripped of all the islands in the Pacific which she has seized or occupied since the beginning of the first World War in 1914, and that all the territories Japan has stolen from the Chinese, such as Manchuria, Formosa, and the Pescadores, shall be restored to the Republic of China. Japan will also be expelled from all other territories which she has taken by violence and greed. The aforesaid three great powers, mindful of the enslavement of the people of Korea, are determined that in due course Korea shall become free and independent.

With these objects in view, the three Allies, in harmony with those of the United Nations at war with Japan, will continue to persevere in the serious and prolonged operations necessary to procure the undonditional surrender of Japan.

Signed: Franklin D. Roosevelt
Winston Churchill
Chiang Kai-Shek

From: Dept. of State Bulletin, Vol. IX, p.393.

(Underlining not in original text.)

(The Cairo Conference was held on November 22-26, 1943. The Soviet Union was not represented as it did not declare war on Japan until August 8, 1945. The Cairo Declaration was issued by the White House on December 1, 1943. The Potsdam Declaration of July 26, 1945, reaffirmed the Cairo pledge that Korea should "in due course be free and independent.")

\#   \#   \#

December 27, 1945

EXTRACT FROM MOSCOW DECLARATION ON KOREA (U.S.A., U.K., U.S.S.R.)

III. Korea

1. With a view to the reestablishment of Korea as an independent state, the creation of conditions for developing the country on democratic principles and the earliest possible liquidation of the disastrous results of the protracted Japanese domination in Korea, there shall be set up a provisional Korean democratic government which shall take all the necessary steps for developing the industry, transport and agriculture of Korea and the national culture of the Korean people.

2. In order to assist the formation of a provisional Korean government and with a view to the preliminary elaboration of the appropriate measures, there shall be established a Joint Commission consisting of representatives of the United States Command in southern Korea and the Soviet command in northern Korea. In preparing their proposals the Commission shall consult with the Korean democratic parties and social organizations. The recommendations worked out by the Commission shall be presented for the consideration of the Governments of the Union of Soviet Socialist Republics, China, the United Kingdom and the United States prior to final decision by the two Governments represented on the Joint Commission.

3. It shall be the task of the Joint Commission, with the participation of the provisional Korean democratic government and of the Korean democratic organizations to work out measures also for helping and assisting (trusteeship) the political, economic and social progress of the Korean people, the development of democratic self-government and the establishment of the national independence of Korea.

The proposals of the Joint Commission shall be submitted, following consultation with the provisional Korean Government for the joint consideration of the Governments of the United States, Union of Soviet Socialist Republics, United Kingdom and China for the working out of an agreement concerning a four-power trusteeship of Korea for a period of up to five years.

4. For the consideration of urgent problems affecting both southern and northern Korea and for the elaboration of measures establishing permanent coordination in administrative-economic matters between the United States command in southern Korea and the Soviet command in northern Korea, a conference of the representatives of the United States and Soviet Commands in Korea shall be convened within a period of two weeks.

Signed: V. Molotov
Ernest Bevin
James F. Byrnes

From: Korea's Independence, Bulletin of the Department of State, (No. 2933), October 1947, pp.18-19.

(This Declaration was made on December 27, 1948, more than
four months after V-J Day, August 15, 1945. The Soviet
Union had declared war on Japan on August 8, 1945, affirm-
ing in its declaration its agreement with the Potsdam Declaration regarding Korea of July 26, 1945. The division of
Korea by the 38° parallel was a military decision confirmed
later in General MacArthur's General Order No. 1 of September 2, 1945, for the surrender of Japan.)

\#   \#   \#

March 11 and 20, 1946

STATEMENTS OF THE U.S. AND U.S.S.R. DELEGATIONS ON
THE JOINT AMERICAN-SOVIET COMMISSION

(Statement by Lt.-General John R. Hodge, Commanding General, U.S. Army
Forces in Korea:)

On the eve of the convening of the Joint Commission, it is consid-
ered appropriate to state the aims of the U.S. delegation in the Joint
Soviet-American Commission and the steps taken thus far by the American
Command to prepare for the achievement of these aims.

First and foremost, it has been the object of the American Forces
to establish and perpetuate the freedoms of speech, assembly, religion
and press in Korea. These freedoms are not mere words to be used to
gain political favor. They represent principles on which any genuine
democracy must be based and are as old as democracy itself. Furthermore,
they are absolute and not relative or subject to exceptions. They apply to
all democratic persons, all democratic schools of thought, all democratic parties, no matter how small their following or whether or not
their programs may correspond to the ideas of the existing authorities.
Thus in South Korea it has been the American policy to permit all democratic groups, whether moderates or extremists, capitalist or communist
to establish their own parties, hold their own meetings, broadcast their
own speeches, propagate their own ideas and philosophies and publish
their own newspapers without censorship, restriction or special privilege. These freedoms are basic in the American idea of democracy.
They are also what we believe the vast majority of the Korean people
want, and it is what the American delegation of the Joint Commission
wants to help the Koreans to attain throughout their entire country.

The purpose of the Joint Commission as stated in the Moscow Communique is to assist the formation of a provisional Korean government and
to undertake the preliminary elaboration of appropriate measures to that
end. It is also the task of the Joint Commission, with the participation
of the provisional Korean democratic government and of the Korean democratic organizations, to work out measures for assisting the political,
economic, and social progress of the Korean people, the development of
democratic self-government and the establishment of the national inde-

76.

pendence of Korea. The Communique specifies that in preparing their proposals the Commission shall consult with the Korean democratic political
parties and social organizations.

It is of course impossible to say at this time the precise manner in
which the details will be worked out, since this is a matter to be determined by the Joint Commission and approved by the four great powers. However, it is the view of the American delegation that one of the primary
requisites for accomplishing the Commission's tasks is the early unification of Korea both economically and politically. Until the economic en-
tity of the country has been restored and the effects of the 38° parallel
eliminated in the internal functions of Korea and until all democratic
elements of the country have freedom to hold meetings, to confer among
themselves, to propagate their ideas by speeches, by radio and by the
press, and to organize parties, recruit members, and carry on political
activities not only in North and South Korea separately, but between the
two areas, it is not considered possible to form a genuinely representative democratic government. In the carrying out of its functions as
part of the Commission it is the intention of the American delegation to
travel throughout the country and to confer freely with representatives
of democratic political and social organizations. It is the American
view that Korean political leaders of all democratic parties both in the
north and in the south should enjoy the same opportunities.

In its efforts to assist in forming a provisional government for
Korea, it is not the purpose of the American delegation to bring about
a government of any particular group or wing. It is their purpose to see
that a government that corresponds to the views of the majority is established. The programs thus far published by the political parties in
Southern Korea differ considerably from those of the leading parties in
America, but these programs have not been opposed nor will they be opposed by the American authorities so long as they represent the views
held by most of the truly democratic Koreans. At the same time it is the
earnest intention of the American delegation to prevent the domination of
Korea by small minorities, no matter how vocal and well organized or how
energetic they may be in their political activities.

This statement is to present the attitude of the American members of
the Joint Commission in solving the problems of Korea. The Soviet members of the Commission represent another great nation that fought for
liberation of Korea from the Japanese, was a signatory to the Moscow
Agreement and is greatly interested in making Korea an independent democratic nation. Therefore, it is safe to assume that the two delegations
will work together harmoniously and in a truly cooperative effort to accomplish the aims expressed in that agreement.

—   —   —

(Statements of Lt. General John R. Hodge and Col. General Terenty Shtikov,
Head of the Soviet Delegation, at the opening session of the United States-
Soviet Joint Commission, March 20, 1946:)

GENERAL HODGE: General Shtikov, members of the Joint Commission and
visitors at the opening session, it is with great pleasure and expectation

that I welcome the Soviet delegation to Seoul and open the initial meeting of the Joint Russian-American Commission in Korea to carry out the provisions of the Moscow Agreement.

Today is an important day in Korean history. It is a day to which all Koreans have looked forward with great hope for the future of their nation and should be a day Koreans will celebrate in the future as the start of a new era in Korean history. The eyes of the entire world, as well as of the Korean people, will be watching our deliberations here. The results of the work of this Commission will prove the ability of two great nations of the world to cooperate fully in capitalizing upon their victory over oppression and despotism and to restore a less fortunate, long-oppressed nation to an independent sovereign status among the family of free nations. Our successful results in the councils of this Commission will have a lasting effect upon the peace and happiness of the world as well as the future of Korea.

As a respresentative of the United States, I express my hope and confidence that our joint efforts here will be able to solve amicably and justly all Korean problems presented, whether they be political, economic or administrative.

General Shtikov, I repeat my sincere welcome to you and your distinguished co-workers. I and my fellow representatives of the United States look forward with confidence to our coming relationships in our efforts to help Korea.

GENERAL SHTIKOV: General Hodge, gentlemen, our Joint Commission representing the American and Soviet Commands is called upon to carry out the historic decisions of the Moscow Conference of the Foreign Ministers of the Soviet Union, the United States of America and the United Kingdom pertaining to Korea. These decisions express the good will and the wishes of the Great Allied Powers to assist by all means in the rehabilitation of an independent Korea, and in the creation of conditions for the development of this country on a democratic basis.

The great armies of the United States of America and the Soviet Union, having crushed the Japanese Imperialists, have forever eliminated Japanese domination in Korea and liberated the Korean people.

Korea has entered a new stage in her development - a stage of national rebirth and reestablishment of state independency.

Gentlemen, the people of Korea with their ancient culture vividly expressed national self-consciousness, year after year suffering hardships and the humiliation of colonial slavery. This people deserves the best future possible. With their blood and innumerable sufferings, the Korean people earned the right for independence and a free way of life.

The Soviet people warmly supported this right of the Korean people. The Soviet Union has always championed and will always champion their self-determination and free existence of any nation, without exception.

As all of us are convinced, the people of Korea are bent upon and have already shown their determination to create, with the help of the Allied Powers, a free democratic Korean government, friendly to all the freedom-loving nations.

The great aims of creating a democratic independent Korean state have brought to life wide political activity of the whole of the people of Korea.

The Korean people have formed their democratic parties, public organizations, people's committees as organs of democratic self-government.

However, in the way of gradual democratization of the whole of the internal life of the Korean people, there stand serious difficulties, brought about by the furious resistance of reactionary and anti-democratic groups and certain elements whose object is to undermine the work of creating and firmly establishing a democratic system in Korea.

The task of the United States-Soviet Commission is to help the Korean people to create a provisional Korean democratic government capable of fulfilling the tasks arising from the democratization and reconstruction of the country.

The future provisional Korean democratic government must be created on a basis of wide unification of all the democratic parties and organizations, supporting the decisions of the Moscow Conference of the Ministers of Foreign Affairs.

Only such a government will be able to abolish entirely the remnants of the former Japanese domination in the political and economic life of Korea, to launch a decisive battle with reactionary anti-democratic elements inside the country, to carry out radical measures in the rehabilitation of economic life, to give political liberties to the Koreans and to fight for peace in the Far East.

The Soviet Union has a keen interest in Korea being a true democratic and independent country, friendly to the Soviet Union, so that in the future it will not become a base for an attack on the Soviet Union.

The task of the Joint United States-Soviet Commission deriving from the decision of the conference of the three ministers concerning Korea consists also in working out, with the participation of the provisional Korean democratic government and assistance of Korean democratic organizations, the measures of aid and assistance with respect to trusteeship in political, economic and social progress of the Korean people and the development of democratic self-government and in establishing the sovereign independence of Korea. Such temporary trusteeship corresponds with the fundamental interests of the Korean people, inasmuch as it assures the condition of a most rapid national reconstruction and a revival of independence on a democratic basis.

General Hodge, concluding my speech, I wish on behalf of the Soviet delegation, to extend my sincere greetings to you and your distinguished delegates, and to express my deep gratification that we shall work together with the representatives of the American Command in the interests and for the good of the Korean people.

I am fully assured that our joint work will proceed in a spirit of mutual understanding and friendship and that we shall successfully and honorably fulfill the will of our governments, expressed in the decisions of the Moscow Conference of the Foreign Ministers concerning Korea.

From: The Voice of Korea, Vol. III, No. 57, April 6, 1946.

(On May 8, 1946, the Joint Commission was suspended due to a deadlock resulting from differences of opinion on what Korean political groups would be "consulted" in working out a program for the unification of the country. The Joint Commission was reconvened on May 20, 1947, but became dead-locked again.)

    #   #   #

November 1, 1946

APPEAL TO THE U.N. BY KOREAN REPRESENTATIVE DEMOCRATIC COUNCIL

To the United Nations General Assembly:

Your urgent attention is respectfully invited to the dangerous situation in Korea which calls for immediate action.

The arbitrary division of our country with the military forces of the United States in the South and of the Union of Soviet Socialist Republics in the North is paralyzing the economy and the people of Korea.

This intolerable condition constitutes a direct threat not only to the peace of the Orient but to the peace of the whole world. It contains every element of international disaster to a world still in the throes of misery resulting from World War II. It holds the same threat to the future of the United Nations that Japan's invasion of Manchuria presented to the League of Nations. Surely the United Nations has no wish to repeat the tragic mistakes of the League of Nations.

As a sovereign nation, with forty-two centuries of uninterrupted national existence, Korea is dedicated to liberty and self-government with no interference or dictation from any foreign power.

The Korean people are proud of their long and unbroken record as a peace-loving nation that has never waged aggressive war. But we, the people of Korea, are ready to fight and, if need be, to die for the preservation of our liberty. We take real pride in the fact that we proved to the treacherous Japanese and to the whole world that, despite forty

years of Japanese tyranny and oppression, the soul of Korea remained un-
conquered and unconquerable.

May I remind this great Assembly, consisting in the main of small
nations, that only because Korea was a small nation did she fall victim
to a big nation - Japan. Can this Assembly of small nations afford, for
a single moment, to overlook the historic and tragic fate that it was
the betrayal of a small and friendly nation which wrecked the peace of
Asia and paved the way for World War II?

Please tell us, why are we, the Korean people, still denied our
freedom? Why are we forced to suffer the humiliation of seeing our
nation torn in half and ruled by two powerful nations - nations with
opposing ideologies?

Japan, which proved herself so treacherous an enemy, has already
been allowed her own civil government, but not Korea.

Japan has already been permitted a free election, but not Korea.

Only Germany, the despoiler of small nations, is subjected to the
treatment which peaceful Korea is still forced to endure.

Denied the right and privilege of a government of our own, the Korean people take this means to appeal to your great Assembly. Peace in
our time - peace at any time - will be impossible while Korea, a nation
of thirty millions of your fellow human beings, is divided and enslaved.

The leaders of the Korean people respectfully but solemnly warn
this Assembly of the increasing difficulty of maintaining order in the
midst of a disheartened population which reposed faith in the promise of
the great Powers that the defeat of the common enemy, Japan, would bring
the restoration of Korean national independence.

With the approach of winter, the situation daily grows more perilous.
Needed supplies from northern Korea, particularly coal, are not permitted
entry to southern Korea. Needed foodstuffs from the South are denied
movement into the North. You, who aim to insure world peace, surely
realize that cold and starvation are always and everywhere the foes of
law and order.

The Korean people view with increasing dismay growing inflation,
utterly inadequate housing, the care of more than 100,000 refugees from
the North, and the denial of the right to trade with other nations.

Nor do we understand the continued imposition of military rule on a
peaceful, friendly nation as compatible with the principles of democracy
or with the oft-stated ideals of the great Powers.

The Korean Representative Democratic Council of South Korea, in the
name of justice and humanity - and for the preservation of the United
Nations and world peace - specifically requests that:

1. The Cairo Declaration and the Potsdam Declaration, assuring the

Korean people their freedom and independence, be immediately
enforced;

2. All American and Russian military forces be withdrawn from
Korea; and

3. The interim Korean Government be immediately admitted to membership in the United Nations.

We request that the American military government in southern Korea
be terminated and a Korean civilian government be inaugurated in that
area. In the event of delay in the retirement of the Soviet authorities
from northern Korea, we urge the retention of the American military
forces, under the able leadership of Lieutenant General John R. Hodge,
until such time as the Russian forces withdraw.

As a member of the United Nations, having the privilege of diplomatic relations with other powers, the interim Korean Government would
be in a position to negotiate directly with the Government of Soviet
Russia regarding the elimination of the artificial 38th parallel division of our country, and the withdrawal of Russian military forces. The
interim KoreanGovernment could take immediate steps to create a permanent Korean Government through the medium of a truly national democratic
election....

Two tragic world wars within the lifetime of a single generation
have taught the salutary lesson that no nation, no matter how strong,
can achieve security and peace by denying a small nation the right to
security and peace.

The people of Korea are convinced that the strength of the United
Nations does not rest on might but on justice - justice for all nations,
large and small. And it is because of this firm conviction that we
gladly place Korea's cause in your keeping. We ask for nothing which
violates the principles of the United Nations. We ask only that you do
notexclude us from the protection of the United Nations for which countless millions had to die before its beneficent principles could be
brought to life.

From: New Cycle in Asia, Isaacs, H.R., New York,
1947, pp.91-94.

(This appeal was submitted by a delegate of the Korean Representative Democratic Council. As no official member delegation in the UN was willing to sponsor this appeal, it was
not presented formally to the UN General Assembly. The
text given above is that issued by the Korean delegation in
New York City. The Korean Representative Democratic Council
was organized on February 14, 1946, as an all-Korean advisory
body to the U.S. Commanding General of South Korea. Its
president was Dr. Syngman Rhee and its members represented
the views of the Korean Provisional Government in exile rather
than the Korean People's Republic, which had been organized
after V-J Day in Korea but had received little support from
the U.S. Military Government.)

#   #   #

September 17, 1947

SECRETARY MARSHALL'S SPEECH ON KOREA IN THE U.N.

(Extract from Address by Secretary Marshall before UN General Assembly.)

I turn now to the question of the independence of Korea. At Cairo in December 1943, the United States, the United Kingdom, and China joined in declaring that in due course Korea should become free and independent. This multilateral pledge was reaffirmed in the Potsdam Declaration of July 1945 and subscribed to by the Union of Soviet Socialist Republics when it entered the war against Japan. In Moscow in December of 1945, the Foreign Ministers of the U.S.S.R., the United Kingdom, and the United States concluded an agreement designed to bring about the independence of Korea. This agreement was later adhered to by the Government of China. It provided for the establishement of a Joint U.S.-U.S.S.R. Commission to meet in Korea and, through consultations with Korean democratic parties and social organizations, to decide on methods for establishing a provisional Korean government. The Joint Commission was then to consult with that provisional government on methods of giving aid and assistance to Korea, any agreement reached being submitted for approval to the four powers adhering to the Moscow Agreement.

For about two years the United States Government has been trying to reach agreement with the Soviet Government, through the Joint Commission and otherwise, on methods of implementing the Moscow Agreement and thus bringing about the independence of Korea. The United States representatives have insisted that any settlement of the Korean problem must in no way infringe the fundamental democratic right of freedom of opinion. That is still the position of my Government. Today the independence of Korea is no further advanced than it was two years ago. Korea remains divided at the 38th parallel with Soviet forces in the industrial north and United States forces in the agricultural south. There is little or no exchange of goods or services between the two zones. Korea's economy is thus crippled.

The Korean people, not former enemies but a people liberated from 40 years of Japanese oppression, are still not free. This situation must not be allowed to continue indefinitely. In an effort to make progress the United States Government recently made certain proposals designed to achieve the purposes of the Moscow Agreement and requested the powers adhering to that Agreement to join in discussion of these proposals. China and the United Kingdom agreed to this procedure. Soviet Delegations to the Joint Commission have not even been able to agree on a joint report on the status of their deliberations. It appears evident that further attempts to solve the Korean problem by means of bilateral negotiations will only serve to delay the establishment of an independent, united Korea.

It is therefore the intention of the United States Government to present the problem of Korean independence to this session of the General Assembly. Although we shall be prepared to submit suggestions as to how the early attainment of Korean independence might be effected, we believe that this is a matter which now requires the impartial judgement of the other members. We do not wish to have the inability of two powers to reach agreement delay any further the urgent and rightful claims of the Korean people to independence.

From: Korea, 1945 to 1948, U.S. Department of State, Publication No. 3305, October 1948, pp.47-48.

(This speech followed an extended exchange of correspondence between the U.S. State Department and the Foreign Ministry of the U.S.S.R., the texts of which are given in U.S. Department of State Publication No. 2933, op.cit.)

#   #   #

November 13, 1947

A.A. GROMYKO'S SPEECH ON KOREA IN THE U.N.

(Extract from Address by A.A. Gromyko before U.N. General Assembly.)

Considering the importance of the question of Korea, the Soviet delegation deems it necessary to state its position on this subject also at the plenary meeting of the General Assembly. This is necessary if only for the reason that the resolution adopted by the Political Committee and submitted for approval to the Assembly does not provide a solution to this problem. Moreover, this resolution, which, as we know, has been imposed by the United States, only complicates the whole problem, since it is based, not on the interests of the Korean people but on the plans of the United States, which has thwarted, and continues to thwart, a proper settlement of the future of Korea.

When setting forth the position of the Soviet Government on the Korean question in the Political Committee, the U.S.S.R. delegation dwelt in detail on all the principal aspects of this important issue, with the idea of helping other delegations to understand what it is really about. We proceeded from the fact that the attitude of the Soviet Union to the Korean question is as a rule presented in a false light, and often directly misrepresented. This has been done by the Government of the United States and its official representatives both here, in the U.S.A., and in southern Korea.

Of course, the detailed discussion of this question in the Political Committee relieves the Soviet delegation of the necessity of going into the details of the problem at the plenary meeting of the Assembly. I shall therefore only dwell on the more important questions arising out of the discussion of the Political Committee's resolution, touching chiefly on the Soviet and American proposals concerning Korea.

First of all, it is necessary to state that the Soviet Government has done everything in its power to secure a settlement of the Korean question in strict conformity with the obligations which the U.S.S.R., the U.S.A., and Great Britain took upon themselves under the Moscow Agreement of December 27, 1945, with which later China associated herself. According to these obligations, the Allied Powers were to ensure the re-establishment of Korea as an independent state, the setting up of a Provisional Korean Democratic Government, and the creation of conditions for developing the country on democratic principles.

Besides this, the United States and the Soviet Union, which maintains troops on the territory of Korea, took upon themselves special obligations under this agreement. They pledged themselves, through the U.S.S.R.-U.S. Joint Commission set up under the terms of the Agreement, to prepare appropriate recommendations, according to which, after they had been considered by the four Powers, the Governments of the U.S.A. and the U.S.S.R. were to take final decisions in furtherance of the aforesaid aim, the creation of an independent democratic Korean state.

The agreement also envisaged the methods by which the Governments of the two Powers were to fulfil the tasks they had assumed. It was stipulated that, at working out its recommendations, the U.S.S.R.-U.S. Joint Commission was to consult with the democratic political parties and social organizations of Korea. This is quite understandable, since it is impossible to ignore the opinion of the Korean people when elaborating decisions determining their future.

Unfortunately, the work of the U.S.S.R.-U.S. Commission reached a deadlock almost as soon as it had begun, since the United States refused to carry out the obligations it had assumed, primarily with regard to the question of consultation I have already mentioned. In spite of the undertaking of the two states to consult with the democratic parties and social organizations, the U.S. representatives in the Commission insisted on holding such consultations with anti-democratic parties and organizations, which are moreover conducting a fight against the Moscow Agreement, and categorically objected to democratic parties and organizations of southern Korea being invited to the consultations, such as the Korean Federation of Trade Unions, the All-Korea Women's Alliance, the All-Korea Youth Alliance, the All-Korea Peasants' Union, which embraces upwards of three million Korean peasants, etc.

Already in the initial period of the work of the U.S.S.R.-U.S. Joint Commission it had become clear that the Government of the U.S.A. had in fact agreed to the obligations of the Moscow Agreement only as a maneuvre, for the behaviour of the American representatives in the Commission was directly contrary to what the agreement had stipulated.

The Soviet Government repeatedly, through its representatives in the Commission, as well as in letters from Foreign Minister V.M.Molotov to U.S. Secretary of State Marshall insisted on the necessity for the strict observance of the Moscow Agreement. After an interruption which lasted from May 1946 to April 1947, the Commission resumed its activities, but without any tangible result, owing to the fact that the attitude of the U.S.A. toward the question of consultation, an attitude contradictory to the Moscow Agreement to set up an independent democratic state, remained unaltered.

The United States thus grossly violated its obligations and thwarted the carrying out of the Moscow Agreement. I consider it necessary to declare this once again, since at the Assembly the U.S. delegation, in following the example of the American representatives in the U.S.S.R.--U.S. Commission in Korea, misrepresents the true state of affairs and tries to blame the U.S.S.R. for the failure until now to settle the Korean question, although, as we know, the American delegation has not been able to cite a single fact in support of its assertions, or in justification of its attitude generally. Nor is this surprising, for the facts themselves disclose the real state of affairs in Korea, expose the double game which the United States has hitherto played in the Korean question, and confirms the correctness of the position of the U.S.S.R., which has stubbornly insisted on the necessity for the strict discharge by the Allied states of the obligations they have assumed with regard to Korea.

One cannot refrain from pointing out that the U.S. State Department and the American representatives in the U.S.S.R.--U.S. Commission have systematically given the press information regarding the situation in Korea and the work of Commission which does not correspond to the facts. Falsification of facts has become their favourite method, and this cannot but give rise to still greater doubt as to whether the ruling circles of the U.S.A. intend, in conjunction with the other Allied states, to settle the question of Korea's future in genuine conformity with the interests of the Korean people, by seeking to establish an independent and democratic Korea. There was a sort of competition in this respect between the State Department and the American Military Command in southern Korea. Behind all this tendentious propaganda it was impossible not to discern a desire to bury the entire plan for the settlement of the Korean question laid down by the Moscow Agreement, and to replace it by a separate plan of the United States, which is evidently pursuing its own aims in Korea, if we judge not from the statements of U.S. official spokesmen, but by the facts.

Having done everything it could to have the United States and the Soviet Union act in strict conformity with the obligations they have assumed with regard to Korea, and becoming convinced that the Government of the U.S.A., for reasons of its own, did not desire to carry out its obligations, and was delaying and thwarting the work of the U.S.S.R.--U.S. Joint Commission, the Government of the U.S.S.R., on September 26 of this year, submitted through its representatives in this Commission new proposals on the subject of Korea. The substance of these proposals was that all foreign troops on the territory of Korea should be withdrawn from that country in the beginning of 1948. This implied that the Korean people should themselves decide their domestic affairs; hold elections to representative institutions, set up a National Government of Korea, create their own armed forces and, without any outside pressure or interference, arrange their internal political and economic life on democratic principles. It will be easily seen that the new Soviet proposals correspond with the fundamental national interests of the Korean people, which cannot but coincide with our common interest in maintaining international peace and security.

These Soviet proposals provide a radical solution of the Korean problem; they would at once remove all the difficulties and complications which stood in the way of the discharge by the Allied Powers of the obligations previously undertaken, at the same time providing the Korean people with full opportunity to decide their own internal affairs of state. These new proposals offer a simple solution of the Korean problem. Add to what has been said that the Soviet proposals coincide with the national sentiment of the Korean people and reckon with their natural sense of national dignity, and the significance of these proposals will be still clearer.

How were these Soviet proposals met in Korea? They met with the full approval of the Korean people. Not only do democratic leaders and democratic political parties and social organizations hail these proposals; they are hailed even by many leaders of Right parties and organizations. Quite a number of reports have been published recently to this effect, notably in the American press. It was affirmed, for instance, in an article by Rosenthal in the New York Times on the 5th of this month.

Among the Koreans themselves, only arrant enemies of the Korean people are opposed to the withdrawal of the foreign troops from Korea, only the hopeless reactionaries on whom the American Military Command in southern Korea relies in its activities. These people know that they will not dare to meet their own people face to face if the American troops leave southern Korea. They are prepared to sell and betray the interests of their people to the advantage of their foreign masters.

As regards the leading circles of the United States, the Soviet proposals, as may be seen from the attitude of the American delegation at the General Assembly, have completely upset the cards of these circles and, of course, of the American delegation at the Assembly.

Until now the assertion that the United States was allegedly interested in the earliest withdrawal of the foreign troops from Korea held a prominent place in American propaganda on the subject of Korea's future. But when the Soviet proposal to withdraw all foreign troops from Korea was introduced, instead of supporting this proposal, the U.S.A. vigorously objected to it. It thereby demonstrated the hypocrisy of the assertions that it desired the troops to be withdrawn from Korea as soon as possible.

When the Soviet proposals were examined in the Political Committee, the U.S. delegation actually evaded a discussion of these proposals and confined itself to certain minor and rather uncoordinated remarks which evidenced that the American delegation fears even to discuss these proposals, realizing apparently that it cannot bring forward any convincing arguments against them.

Meanwhile, the U.S. delegation hammered away in the Political Committee on one point, trying to hasten the vote on its proposals, which, as is well known, radically differ from the Soviet proposals. In the U.S. proposals everything is placed topsy-turvy. According to them, the withdrawal of foreign troops from Korean territory should not precede the election of representative bodies and the formation of a democratic government of Korea, but, on the contrary, is to constitute the last of a series of measures proposed by this American plan. Moreover, no definite date at all is fixed for the withdrawal of the foreign troops from Korea. The proposals contain a non-committal formula simply to the effect that the troops should be withdrawn "as soon as possible" after the elections and the formation of a Korean government. Is it not obvious what the authors of these proposals are out for? According to the American plan, as we see, the election of representative institutions, including the People's Assembly of Korea, and the formation of a Korean National Govern- ment are, to be held with foreign troops present in the country. This, of course, cannot be regarded as otherwise than an attempt to arrange the elections in a situation of foreign interference in the internal affairs of Korea with the object of securing the election to representative insti- tutions and the inclusion in the government of people upon whom the Ameri- can military authorities have long been relying, that is, of thoroughgoing reactionaries, who are concerned not so much for the fate of their own people as for the advantage of their foreign patrons and themselves.

This American plan would not permit the Korean people freely to ex- press their will; but it would play into the hands of the anti-democratic groups and political leaders in Korea, since it would help them to remain in power. The calculations of the U.S.A. are, as we see, rather simple, but the trouble is that they do not conform either to the interests of the Korean people or to our common interest of promoting international coopera- tion, since their implementation would imply the creation, not of a Korean democratic state, but of an anti-democratic state, and one moreover depen- dent upon the United States and virtually its colony. This conclusion follows inevitably from the character of the American proposals, which were taken as a basis for the resolution adopted by the First Committee as well as from the attitude of the U.S. Government to the Soviet proposals.

It was apparently in order to conceal the real meaning of the Ameri- can proposals that the U.S. delegation made the recommendation, which has also been approved by the First Committee, to set up a so-called United Nations Temporary Committee, which, as the sponsors of the recommendation conceive it, is virtually to exercise control over Korea both in the per- iod of elections and in the period of formation of a Korean National Gov- ernment. But the setting up of such a Commission, would not alter any- thing. Moreover, the decision to set up this Commission makes this entire American plan still more crude and still more unacceptable to all who gen- uinely desire the creation of a democratic Korea, and who do not play with words which serve as a mask for reactionary projects designed to enslave the Korean people to the American monopolies.

The formation of such a Commission would be impermissible, since it contradicts the right of the Korean people to self-determination. This commission would only become a screen for unilateral actions on the part of the United States of America in southern Korea aimed at converting Korea into an American colony.

What I have said is corroborated by the practices of the American military authorities in southern Korea. In the course of the debate in the Political Committee, the Soviet delegation cited a number of facts showing that the American authorities in southern Korea are pursuing an anti-democratic policy. In southern Korea the U.S.A. has been banking on small reactionary groups isolated from the Korean people, and giving every encouragement to the activities of these groups which are directed against democratic parties and organizations. They likewise encourage by their connivance the terrorist activities of semi-fascist organizations, which have embarked on an open struggle against the democratic forces of the country, even going so far as the physical extermination of prominent leaders of Korean democratic parties and social organizations. This policy of the American military authorities in southern Korea has caused the legitimate indignation of the entire Korean people. This is expressed, for example, in a letter of the People's United National Democratic Front of northern Korea written two months ago in the name of its numerous affiliated political parties and social organizations and addressed to the Governments of the U.S.A., and the U.S.S.R. In this letter it is stated: "What is happening in South Korea today surpasses the gloomiest days of the riot of reaction." The letter exposes the anti-popular policy of the American Military Command. The U.S. delegation continues to remain silent about this letter.

Almost daily reports appear in the world press, including the American press, showing that the reactionary and terrorist semi-fascist groups in southern Korea are, with the support of the American authorities, becoming more and more brazen, and that the discontent of the whole people--workers, peasants and intellectuals--is growing from day to day. No wonder, for in southern Korea, as distinct from northern Korea, no democratic reforms have been carried out. The land, which has been the cherished dream of the Korean peasants for centuries, is still not distributed among those to whom it rightly belongs. The peasant in southern Korea still remains landless, unlike the peasant of northern Korea. Can the Korean peasant really be expected under these circumstances to support the existing order in southern Korea? Of course not. There is therefore no need to be surprised at the statement made in PM on November 3, 1947, by a correspondent, Mark Gayn, who had been in Korea: "The Russians have created a lot of friends for themselves. We have none." We agree with him.

I might quote many facts to confirm that the condition of the Korean worker in southern Korea is no better than that of the peasant, but that is widely known throughout the world. The condition of the worker is evidenced by the numerous strikes and demonstrations of protest against the policy of the American authorities in southern Korea and of their Korean reactionary puppets.

In view of all this, need we be surprised that many people who have visited southern Korea, on their return sharply criticize the American Command. Even many Americans are outraged by the situation to be observed in southern Korea and say that, far from improving, the position is growing worse, and that the American authorities display complete indifference to the fate of the Korean people. This same correspondent, Mark Gayn, reports a conversation he had regarding the plight of the peasants with an American official, who, he says, told him that the Koreans were "used to this system."

Bearing in mind all these facts, it becomes clear why the United States delegation vigorously objected to the Korean question being discussed in the General Assembly in the presence of elected representatives of the Korean people. It evidently feared to hear the voice of the Korean people, it evidently feared to hear the truth about the situation in southern Korea, which the delegation of the U.S.S.R. insisted on being heard, for its view is that we cannot examine the substance of the Korean question without hearing the opinion of representatives of the Korean people.

As you know, the United States succeeded in preventing the voice of the Korean people from being heard in the General Assembly, and the resolution approved by the Political Committee was adopted in the absence of Korean representatives. This is a result of ignoring the interests of the Korean people. Such decisions are incompatible with the national dignity of the Korean people.

The meaning of the American proposals will become even more clear if we consider not only the practices of the U.S. military authorities in southern Korea, but also the statements made by certain American official persons about Korea and its significance for the United States of America.

The Soviet delegation has already referred in the course of the debate in the Political Committee to General Hodge's statement that the Americans have "dug-in in Korea" and will remain there until they fulfil their mission. It also referred to the statement of former Assistant Secretary of State General Hilldring, expressing the fear that the withdrawal of the American troops from Korea "might bring about serious reaction in the East."

Due credit must be given to the frankness of these people. Such statements throw light on the plans of the United States, in particular with regard to southern Korea, which, economically, the American authorities in Korea are beginning more and more to adapt to the economy of the United States. Politically, it is beginning to turn southern Korea into a centre of reaction in East Asia. Territorially, Korea is evidently regarded as a sort of base of the United States. No wonder the more reactionary American press is already stressing the strategical importance of Korea, and making transparent and unambiguous hints as to how and against whom this base might and even should be used. The eyes of these press organs are directed from Korea to the north and northwest.

And it is under such conditions that we are asked to accept the American plan for the settlement of the Korean question, a plan which is not designed to settle it at all, but would only put difficulties in the way of its settlement. Obviously, it is those who impose such plans that are primarily responsible for this situation.

As to the Soviet Union, it will continue in the future to expose all the efforts of those who, under the label of the United Nations, are striving to use Korea for the furtherance of interests which have nothing in common with the maintenance of peace and international security. It will work for a decision on the future of Korea which corresponds with the fundamental national interests of the Korean people and at the same time accords with our common interest in consolidating the peace and security of nations. The Soviet delegation has already declared in the Political Committee that it is impossible to examine the Korean question in substance at the General Assembly and adopt decisions in the absence of representatives of the Korean people. Since the majority of the Committee did decide to examine this question in substance and adopt decisions, the

U.S.S.R. delegation declared that it did not consider it possible to take part in the voting on the American proposal for the reasons stated above.

For the same reasons, the Soviet delegation likewise does not consider it possible to take part in the voting on the Committee's resolution at the plenary meeting of the General Assembly.

From: The Soviet Union and the Korean Question, (Documents), Ministry of Foreign Affairs of the U.S.S.R., Moscow, 1948, pp.55-56.

(This document summarizes the position which led the Soviet Union from the date on to oppose the actions of the United Nations relative to Korea.)

#   #   #

November 14, 1947

U.N. RESOLUTION ESTABLISHING TEMPORARY COMMISSION ON KOREA
(UNTCOK)

A

Inasmuch as the Korean question which is before the General Assembly is primarily a matter for the Korean people itself and concerns its freedom and independence, and

Recognizing that this question cannot be correctly and fairly resolved without the participation of representatives of the indigenous population,

The General Assembly

1. Resolves that elected representatives of the Korean people be invited to take part in the consideration of the question;

2. Further resolves that in order to facilitate and expedite such participation and to observe that the Korean representatives are in fact duly elected by the Korean people and not mere appointees by military authorities in Korea, there be forthwith established a United Nations Temporary Commission on Korea, to be present in Korea, with right to travel, observe and consult throughout Korea.

B

The General Assembly,

Recognizing the urgent and rightful claims to independence of the people of Korea;

Believing that the national independence of Korea should be reestablished and all occupying forces then withdrawn at the earliest practicable date;

Recalling its previous conclusion that the freedom and independence of the Korean people cannot be correctly or fairly resolved without the participation of representatives of the Korean people, and its decision to establish a United Nations Temporary Commission on Korea (hereinafter called the "Commission") for the purpose of facilitating and expediting such participation by elected representatives of the Korean people,

1. Decides that the Commission shall consist of representatives of Australia, Canada, China, El Salvador, France, India, Philippines, Syria, Ukrainian Soviet Socialist Republic;

2. Recommends that the elections be held not later than 31 March 1948 on the basis of adult suffrage and by secret ballot to choose representatives with whom the Commission may consult regarding the prompt attainment of the freedom and independence of the Korean people and which representatives, constituting a National Assembly, may establish a National Government of Korea. The number of representatives from each voting area or zone should be proportionate to the population, and the elections should be under the observation of the Commission;

3. Further recommends that as soon as possible after the elections, the National Assembly should convene and form a National Government and notify the Commission of its formation;

4. Further recommends that immediately upon the establishment of a National Government, the Government should, in consultation with the Commission: (a) constitute its own national security forces and dissolve all military or semi-military formations not included therein; (b) take over the functions of government from the military commands and civilian authorities of north and south Korea; and (c) arrange with the occupying Powers for the complete withdrawal from Korea of their armed forces as early as practicable and if possible within ninety days;

5. Resolves that the Commission shall facilitate and expedite the fulfilment of the foregoing programme for the attainment of the national independence of Korea and withdrawal of occupying forces, taking into account its observations and consultations in Korea. The Commission shall report, with its conclusions, to the General Assembly and may consult with the Interim Committee (if one be established) with respect to the application of this resolution in the light of developments;

6. Calls upon the Member States concerned to afford every assistance and facility to the Commission in the fulfilment of its responsibilities;

7. Calls upon all Members of the United Nations to refrain from interfering in the affairs of the Korean people during the interim period preparatory to the establishment of Korean independence, except in pursuance of the decisions of the General Assembly; and thereafter, to refrain completely from any and all acts derogatory to the independence and sovereignty of Korea.

From: Korea, 1945 to 1948, U.S. Department of State, Publication No. 3305, October 1948, pp.66-67.

(This resolution was adopted by the General Assembly by a vote
of 43 to 0 with 6 abstentions.)

\#   \#   \#

January 6, 1948

STATEMENT BY DR. SYNGMAN RHEE

The Koreans got caught, by no fault of their own, between the two
wheels of conflicting ideologies, democracy and communism. The Soviets
are pushing ahead whenever and wherever possible, persistently and
ruthlessly.

The Americans, devoid of self-interest and desirous of peace, seem
short-sighted and vacillating.

The Koreans have been, since the early days of their independence
movement, upholding the American principle of democracy.

In 1919, inspired by President Wilson's declaration of self-determination principles, they inaugurated a passive revolution against Japan.
They declared Korea an independent republic, with a constitution modelled
after that of the United States, and established a provisional government,
the first government-in-exile known to history.

But the Koreans were bitterly disappointed when the U.S. appeased
the totalitarian empire of Japan in suppressing the democratic spirit of
the Korean people.

This appeasement policy continued until the Pearl Harbor disaster.
The Koreans, who had repeatedly warned the Americans of such a disaster,
were once again sadly disappointed.

They repeatedly requested the State Department officials for material
assistance to their army in China so that they could help defeat Japan and
prevent the danger of the Communist invasion of Korea, but not a single
rifle from "the arsenals of democracy", nor a dollar from "the lend-lease
aid" so freely given to every other struggling nation, went to the Koreans.

The New Deal statesmen joined with Russia in the arbitrary division
of Korea into two occupation zones.

The very thing against which the Koreans had repeatedly warned the
State Department officials (those officials are not there now) orally
and in writing, both for the sake of Korean independence and U.S. security,
has been allowed to take place.

The Communists rushed into northern Korea from Siberia and Manchuria,
together with the Soviet Army, and threatened the south by anti-American
agitations, strikes, riots and terrorism.

If the Koreans, at the time of surrender, had been allowed to hold a general election and set up their own government in the south, there would have been no Communist problem, at least in the United States zone.

But unfortunately they were not.

The reason the Koreans in south Korea   failed to vote and set up a government of their own, while all the occupied countries and enemy nations have had elections, was due to the fact that under the New Deal policy General Hodge, the occupation commander, had to appease Russia and hold a neutral attitude toward the Nationalists and Communists.

I told General Hodge that I could not support him any longer, and went to Washington.

He also went to Washington later and promised that as soon as the interim Legislature had adopted the election law we would have the election.

General Hildring, then an Assistant Secretary of State, told me that the south Korea interim election should be held at the earliest possible date and that the government set up by it will represent both north and south.

When I was in Tokyo in March, 1947, General MacArthur told me the election was the best step to take toward the ultimate solution, and further remarked that General Hodge would cooperate with me in this.

I returned to Seoul with high hopes.

My great optimism was based upon President Truman's new world policy.

But to my surprise I was to learn that the Truman doctrine had been meagerly promulgated and the evidence of its effect regarding the Communists was almost nil.

We were allowed no election.

Meanwhile, another sad disappointment came to the Korean people.

It was announced through the press that General MacArthur had been by-passed by the State Department, and had nothing more to do with Korea.

The Koreans held General MacArthur in high esteem, not only as a great soldier, but a great statesman.

What they most appreciate in him is the fact he has never hesitated to testify openly that the Koreans are ready for independence.

They regard General MacArthur as their true friend, and a friend of their cause.

Now the Koreans earnestly hope that the UN Commission will carry out the policy of President Truman and General Marshall in spirit and letter, and help the Koreans to hold an election free and unhampered for a national congress truly representative of the people, without any interference either by the USA or USSR in favor of Communists or coalitionists.

We know that the result will be in the interest of Korean independence and American security.

From: New York Journal-American, Jan 6, 1948.

(This statement was written by Dr. Rhee in his capacity as President of the Korean Nationalist Association and telegraphed from Seoul to the New York Journal-American. Dr. Rhee was elected President of the Republic of Korea ((South)) on July 20, 1948.)

#   #   #

February 26, 1948

RESOLUTION ON KOREA OF THE U.N. INTERIM COMMITTEE

Whereas the Chairman of the United Nations Temporary Commission on Korea, accompanied by the Assistant-Secretary-General, consulted the Interim Committee on the following questions:

"Is it open to or incumbent upon the Commission, under the terms of the General Assembly resolutions of 14 November 1947, and in the light of developments in the situation with respect to Korea since that date, to implement the programme as outlined in resolution II in that part of Korea which is occupied by the armed forces of the United States of America?

"2. If not,

"(a) Sould the Commission observe the election of Korean representatives to take part in the consideration of the Korean question, as outlined in resolution I of 14 November 1947, provided that it has determined that elections can be held in a free atmosphere? and

"(b) Should the Commission consider such other measures as may be possible and advisable with a view to the attainment of its objectives?"

The Interim Committee,

Bearing in mind the views expressed by the Chairman of the United Nations Temporary Commission on Korea;

Deeming it necessary that the programme set forth in the General Assembly resolutions of 14 November 1947 be carried out and as a necessary step therein that the United Nations Temporary Commission on Korea proceed with the observance of elections in all Korea, and if that is impossible, in as much of Korea as is accessible to it; and

Considering it important that the elections be held to choose representatives of the Korean people with whom the United Nations Temporary
Commission on Korea may consult regarding the prompt attainment of freedom and independence of the Korean people, which representatives, constituting a National Assembly, may establish a National Government of
Korea;

Resolves

That in its view it is incumbent upon the United Nations Temporary
Commission on Korea, under the terms of the General Assembly resolution
of 14 November 1947, and in the light of developments in the situation
with respect to Korea since that date, to implement the programme as
outlined in Resolution II, in such parts of Korea as are accessible to
the Commission.

From: Department of State Bulletin, March 7, 1948,
pp.297-298; and U.N. Document A/AC 18/31.

(In accordance with the above resolution the UN supervised
election in South Korea took place on May 10, 1948. The UN
Commission in Korea had not been able to get in touch with
the authorities in North Korea for the holding of nation-
wide elections. The Soviet delegation in the UN argued that
the above resolution of the UN Interim Committee was "illegal"
because the Interim Committee ("Little Assembly") was itself
an "illegal" body.)

\#   \#   \#

April 22-23, 1948

STATEMENT BY KIM KOO AND KIM KIU-SIC ON UNITY

Our trip to north Korea was in a great measure a fulfillment of the
desire for unity by the great number of our people as well as a refuta-
tion of the doubts of the outside world in regards to the unity of the
Korean people. Moreover, the Unity Conference of north and south Korean
political parties and social organizations has once again proved by action that the Korean people can surmount their differences in political
concepts and parties for the sake of the restoration of their fatherland
and for the welfare of the people.

It was the unanimous decision of the Unity Conference that the construction of a free, democratic Korea demands the absolute opposition to
the separate elections and to the setting up of a separate government in
south Korea. In complete agreement, the leaders of north Korea have clearly indicated that they would not undertake to establish a separate government in north Korea. This agreement constitutes a new forward step in the

history of our independence movement, and brightens the future hopes of our people.

The Unity Conference, through the formal declaration of the north and south political parties and social organization, has pointed the road to the construction of a united, democratic nation. It is a further testimonial that Korea, freed of foreign interference, can begin a prosperous, national life in peace.

The basis of national unity envisaged by the Unity Conference and expressed in its formal declaration are:

1. Withdrawal of the two occupation armies from Korea.

2. The organization of a provisional government by a national political conference immediately after the withdrawal of troops.

3. The adoption of a national constitution and the formation of a united national government by representatives to be elected through a national election.

We wish to make it clear that, regardless of any difficulties arising in the future, we shall adhere to the above program of the Unity Conference, and refuse to betray our people. Human hunger can not be satisfied by the first mouthful; the unity program in itself can not be the final fulfilment. The ultimate achievement of our purpose will depend on the joint struggle of our people with the weapons of our past experiences.

It is regretful that the Unity Conference was not able to secure the necessary international cooperation and resolve the international questions related to our future. However, the question as to which foreign nation is in fact rendering aid to our independence will be easily determined by the actual deeds of the foreign nation itself. As to other unsettled problems confronting us, we believe that their solutions lie only in the continued cooperation of the leaders of north and south Korea.

The Unity Conference has proved not only in words but in action that the Korean people can by their own undertaking solve any problems confronting them. For example, the question of electricity being sent to south from north as well as the question of developing water power near Yun-ahn and Pai-chun can be solved by the Korean people themselves.

As to our request to permit Cho Man-sik to accompany us to southern Korea, the north Korean leaders considered it inadvisable at present, but agreed to facilitate it in the near future.

Finally we wish to express our gratitude to those compatriots who have been concerned with our welfare, to those north and south representatives and press who provided us with comfort and understanding, and to the commanders of the two occupation armies.

                              Signed:
                                  KIM KOO
                                  KIM KIU-SIC.

From: Korean Independence, Los Angeles, June 10, 1948, p.1.

(This statement was issued by Kim Koo and Kim Kiu-sic, two outstanding political leaders of South Korea, upon their return to Seoul from the National Unity Conference held in Pyongyang, North Korea, on April 22-23, 1948.)

# # #

April 30, 1948

KOREAN UNITY CONFERENCE DECLARATION AGAINST SOUTHERN ELECTIONS

The Conference issued the followingjoint communique:

"As the result of detailed and comprehensive discussion, an understanding has been reached on the following questions:

"1. Under present conditions the immediate and simultaneous withdrawal of foreign troops from the territory of our country in conformity with the proposal made by the Soviet Union is the only correct and just solution of the Korean problem. All those who desire the unity of democratic Korea should support this reasonable proposal.

"Since the expulsion of the Japanese, our people have matured sufficiently to be perfectly capable of settling affairs of state without outside interference. Our country possesses sufficient trained personnel for this purpose. The United States must accept the fair proposal made by the Soviet Union and withdraw its army from South Korea, thus providing a practical solution to the problem of Korean independence.

"2. The leaders of parties and public organizations of North and South Korea declare that after the withdrawal of foreign troops they will never permit an outbreak of civil war or any disturbances which militate against the Koreans' desire for unity. The people's indomitable desire to achieve the unity of the nation, and the understanding reached between the biggest parties of North and South, constitute a reliable guarantee of full order in the country.

"3. After the withdrawal of foreign troops, the parties and organizations listed below will immediately, at an all-Korean political conference, form a democratic government representing all sections of the Korean people, which will assume power in the country and responsibility for its economic, political, and cultural life.

"It will be the most urgent task of this government to hold a really free general election, with direct, equal and secret vote, of a single legislative body for Korea, which will then set up a single democratic government and adopt a new Constitution.

"4. Inasmuch as the separatist elections in South Korea are opposed by political parties and public organizations of North and South with a membership of more than ten million, which constitutes an absolute majority of citizens entitled to vote, these elections, even if they are held, can never reflect the will of our people. They can be nothing but sham elections, and it is not accidental that they are being prepared in an atmosphere of gross coercion and terror.

"In view of the foregoing, the leaders of the political parties and public organizations who have signed the present communique will not recognize the results of these elections or support any separatist government which may be set up after the elections."

The communique is signed by the leaders of 15 political parties and public organizations of North Korea, and 26 parties and organizations of South Korea.

From: Soviet News, London, May 5, 1948.

(This declaration was issued by a special conference on unity held in Pyongyang by northern and southern political leaders, following the National Unity Conference of April 22-23, 1948. The UN-supervised election took place in South Korea on May 10, 1948)

# # #

May 1948

REPORT OF PROGRESS BY PREMIER KIM IL SUNG OF THE

KOREAN DEMOCRATIC PEOPLE'S REPUBLIC (NORTH)

Delegates!

Before making a report on the situation in Northern Korea I should like to say a few words regarding the political significance of this conference.

This conference is of significance not only from the standpoint of Korea, but also internationally.

The significance of this conference lies in the fact that representatives of all political parties and social organizations both in Southern and Northern Korea have met together here for the first time since the liberation of our fatherland from Japanese imperialism.

And this conference is significant, on the other hand, because it has been convened particularly at this juncture when our fatherland is confronted with the danger of a split, when the attempt by American imperialists to colonize Southern Korea is becoming more and more candid, and when the crisis confronting our fatherland today is very serious - the worst of this kind ever experienced by our fatherland since her liberation.

Such being the case, this joint conference should discuss, straight-forwardly and rightly, the political situation both in Southern and Northern Korea and work out fundamental measures to cope with the national crisis with which our fatherland is confronted.

Delegates!

At present the political situation of our fatherland is very com-plicated and tense. The reason for this is, on the one hand, that American imperialists backed by the former pro-Japanese collaborators and national traitors, are maneuvering to split us thirty million Korean people and colonize our land. With the object of realizing this dark am-bition, they, under the subterfuge of the United Nations Korean Commission, are attempting to enforce separate elections in Southern Korea for the establishment of a so-called "unified national government."

Our fatherland is confronted with crisis. Before us thirty million Korean people the danger of enslavement has arrived again.

And the reason the political situation of our fatherland is very complicated and tense is, on the other hand, that the colonial policy of American imperialists today toward our fatherland has brought a life and death struggle to the Korean people. For the entire Korean people, who have risen in protest to the policy of American imperialists to colonize and enslave our fatherland, are opposing the election comedy in Southern Korea. And this resistance movement is greatly helping unite all demo-cratic forces throughout Korea, crying for the establishment of a united, democratic, independent Korea.

We thirty million Koreans are a nation of a single identity which has enjoyed unity throughout its history of fifty centuries. Notwith-standing this, however, our fatherland is artificially divided across the 38th Parallel. This is a peculiarity of the political situation of our fatherland.

The division between South and North has compelled the Korean people to fight for the glory, liberty and democratic independence of our father-land.

The people in Northern Korea, under genuine and friendly support of the Soviet Union, have achieved great results in connection with the his-torical work of democratic reconstruction of our fatherland.

But the people in Southern Korea are groaning under the severe rule of these reactionary elements who are piloted by the U.S. army as they did under the rule of Japanese imperialists. As a matter of fact, they are now in straitened conditions, politically and economically. This fact has been known through publications in Southern Korea and even through American publications.

In order to analyse this complicated political situation in our fatherland it is necessary to view the issue historically.

We groaned under the colonial regime of Japanese imperialists for thirty-six years. These thirty-six years marked a miserable period of unjust oppression upon and enslavement of our nation. Japanese imperialists built in Korea not for the prosperity of our fatherland or for the future development of our nation, but as preparations to launch their beastly aggressive war in the eastern Asia.

We Korean people were offered as a slave labor power for the colonial robber of Japanese imperialism.

The Japanese colonial robbers looked down upon us Korean people as an inferior nation, thus excluding Koreans from the work of directing industrial undertakings or state institutions.

Only a small minority of pro-Japanese collaborators and national traitors who had been isolated from the people turned into loyal hounds of Japanese imperialism, and served for Japanese imperialists.

With an aim of blunting the awakening of the Korean people, the Japanese imperialists endeavored to erase our national cultures with a long history of fifty centuries by forcing us to speak Japanese, adopt Japanese customs, and worship Japanese literature and the so-called Japanese religion - Shintoism.

In August 1945 the Red Army drove away the Japanese army from the soil of our country. And the Red Army entered into our country as they liberated freely the Korean people. Thus, the Korean people was enabled to put an end to a bitter era of humiliation and enslavement of the Korean people. At the same time, the bright path of regeneration of the Korean people had been opened.

Even our descendants forever will remember glorious service rendered by the Red Army which heroically fought at the sacrifice of lives.

The U.S. army landed on Southern Korea after the termination of the war without using a single bullet. Under the war-time arrangement between the U.S. and Soviet governments, the area north of the 38th parallel was temporarily assigned for occupation by the Red Army and that south of the 38th parallel by the U.S. army. As such, the 38th parallel became a temporary line between the Soviet and U.S. Armies.

But this 38th Parallel line, as every one of you well know, has actually become a frontier rather than a temporary line, thereby artificially dividing our fatherland between South and North, despite the fact that our fatherland is a single piece of land. The fact that the Red Army occupied the area north of the Parallel line and the U.S. army that south of it, caused both Southern and Northern Korea to pursue opposite directions.

As everyone of you well know, both the Soviet Union and the United States toward the end of 1945 signed the Moscow Decisions regarding Korea.

I am refraining from making any detailed remarks on this issue. What I want to point out here is only the fact that the Red army in occupation of Northern Korea has been constantly pursuing the path leading to the realization of the Moscow Decisions whereas the U.S. army in occupation of Southern Korea has been pursuing the path leading to disrupting these Decisions. With regard to the actual situation in Southern Korea I believe all the delegates from Southern Korea will make detailed reports based on innumerable facts they have to date witnessed with their own eyes. But allow me to point out only one fact.

Shortly after the liberation of our fatherland from the colonial rule of Japanese imperialism the people's committees began to be created in every part of Southern Korea and Northern Korea. In fact that these committees came into being was mainly due to people's creative initiatives, and in many cases spontaneously. This phenomenon was nothing more or less than a manifestation of justifiable desire on the part of the Korean people to organize autonomous organs with their own hands for their liberated fatherland so as to stabilize the people's livelihood and preserve peace and order as speedily as possible. And it is a well known fact that an all-Korea conference of the people's committees thus organized was scheduled to be convened in Seoul.

But a trend such as this entirely was far from suitable to the taste of American imperialists. To those American imperialists who attempted to realize their gruesome scheme to enslave our fatherland, it was their desire to see political power fall not into the hands of the people, but into the hands of those national traitors and reactionary elements who would faithfully put into force their plot by selling down the river their fatherland and people.

Therefore, American imperialists dissolved the people's committees in Southern Korea by resorting to ruthless methods which are beyond description.

And thus, the American Military Government seized the entire political power in its hands and left no stone unturned to disrupt the Moscow Decisions instead of putting them into force.

Southern Korea, instead of being enabled to reconstruct our fatherland democratically and establish a people's regime by a great spontaneous movement of a liberated nation, has turned out to be what a member of the so-called United Nations Korean Commission describes as a "police state."

The situation in Northern Korea is different fundamentally from that in Southern Korea, the cause for it being that the Red army in occupation of Northern Korea enforced from beginning to end the Moscow Decisions on Korea and granted freedom of a wide scope to the people of Northern Korea.

Thus, the people in Northern Korea were enabled to organize institutions of a regime with their own hands.

The people's committees in Northern Korea, instead of being dissolved like in Southern Korea, enjoyed freedom of action, and were able to preserve order in the country and stabilize security of the people's livelihood.

And these autonomous organs directed the magnificent work of reconstructing the state by restoring industries, transportation, communications and commerce which was launched by the people in Northern Korea.

Through this magnificent state reconstruction work the people's committees already achieved great results in 1945 and 1946, thus enjoying high prestige among the wide masses of the people.

New leaders, who emerged from the people, have been trained through the process of actual works carried out by organs of the people's regime, various political parties and social organizations in Northern Korea.

Many of those who directly participated in activities at the time the people's committees were brought into being are today known as prominent leaders of the people's regime. That the form of the people's regime is most suitable to developments of our fatherland is clearly attested to by the fact that the prestige of the people's committees is growing day by day, for it has been examined through actual works carried out amidst most complicated circumstances under which the administrative institutions of Japanese imperialism had to be replaced by new ones.

As the political, economic and cultural life of Northern Korea grew day by day, the people in Northern Korea, with the object of legally preserving this form of regime, carried out elections for the people's committees in provinces, cities and counties toward the end of 1946, and for the people's committees in hamlets (MYON) and villages toward the beginning of 1947.

These elections for the people's committee of all ranks were carried out under a democratic principles of a wide scope and in accordance with the universal, equal, direct, and secret votes.

This means for the first time in Korean history democratic elections were held, for through the medium of this event the people were able to express their views most widely and freely. In the work of preparing for, and enforcing these elections, representatives of people of every strata and walks of life, and those representing all political parties and social organizations took part with greatest enthusiasm. For example, at the time of elections for the people's committees in provinces, cities and counties, 80,470 persons participated in elections committees.

Of this 9 percent were women, this being the first time for Korean women to participate in the state work. Those who were not capable of participating in the first elections in accordance with election rules numbered only 4,380; they were the proven former pro-Japanese collaborators and insanes, or those who had been deprived of their election rights as a result of public trials.

This number represented only one thousandths of the total voters. The elections were enforced amidst an overflowing political enthusiasm demonstrated by the entire voters. In the elections for the people's committees of all ranks were participated in by 99.6 percent of the total voters.

This bears witness to the fact that the prestige of the people's committees has been uplifted among the masses of the entire people.

As the result of elections for the people's committees in provinces, cities, counties, hamlet (MYON), and villages, 70,217 members were elected. This figure frankly shows how widely the masses of the people in Northern Korea are taking part in organs of the regime.

The people's committees are composed of those representing peasants, workers, clerks, intelligentsias, businessmen, industrialists, religionists, and all walks of life and strata.

The people's committees are composed of those representing all democratic political parties and social organizations in Northern Korea; of those elected as members of the people's committees, 13.1 percent represents women.

In February 1947 a convention of the people's committees was held. On the occasion, the Northern Korea Supreme People's Assembly, highest organ of the Northern Korea people's regime, was brought into being. Like the people's committees this assembly is also composed of those representing people of all walks of life and strata, as well as of those representing all political parties and social organizations in Northern Korea. As such, elections for the people's committees were completed from bottom to top, and these elections for the people's committees legally consolidated the new form of the people's regime.

Since then, one year has already elapsed.

During the past one year the people's committees have become organizations stronger than ever. And leaders of the people's regime have gained great experiences through democratic construction, demonstrated their excellent capabilities as they put into execution various measures, and at the same time demonstrated their wonderful abilities how to solve the most complicated problems in connection with the political, economic, and cultural life of our fatherland.

This is a stern fact smashing to pieces vicious propaganda being carried on by those American imperialists who look down upon the Korean people, saying in derision that the Korean people are still far from capable of constructing their own state with their hands.

In all directions the people's committees have achieved great results, the most important of all being various great democratic reforms which have been enforced in Northern Korea.

Particularly what I want to point out here is that these great democratic reforms were enthusiastically supported by the masses of the people since they were enforced for the interest of the people.

Democratic reforms uplifted the patriotic enthusiasm of the masses

of the people in Northern Korea, for the people once more firmly recognized the fact that the people's committees, which they had created
with their own hands, most faithfully are enforcing aspirations and ex-
pectations of the people. Through actual works of the people's committees the people have been convinced of this fact....

(Section on economic and educational reforms omitted.)

Toward the beginning of this year (1948) the Northern Korea Supreme
People's Assembly organized a Constitution Enactment Committee, decision
having been reached to put to discussion by the people a provisional
Korean constitution drafted by this committee. In fact, discussion is
being carried on regarding the draft of the provisional Constitution, the
most important phenomenon being that an absolute majority of the people
not only in Northern Korea but in Southern Korea as well are enthusiastically supporting the draft of the Provisional Korean Constitution.

Of course, this is by no means an accident.

For this Constitution has contributed to strengthen all the democratic reforms already enforced in Northern Korea, and at the same time the
path the entire Korean people shall follow has been clearly shown by it.

To date, the Constitution Enactment Committee has received 55,000
letters of gratitude along with documents containing decision in favor
of the draft of the Constitution as well as recommendations regarding
the draft of the Constitution. This bears witness to the fact that the
entire Korean people are greatly interested in adopting a genuine democratic Constitution.

The fact that the entire Korean people are supporting the draft of
the Provisional Korean Constitution must be considered as their supporting all those great democratic reforms that have been put into force
throughout Northern Korea. In other words, this means that the entire
Korean people are wholeheartedly supporting the works of the Northern
Korea People's Committee.

Delegates!

In order to rightly evaluate the actual situation in Northern Korea
I cannot help but relate how the people in Northern Korea are being
united in their struggle to construct a democratic, autonomous, independent state.

The unity of the people in Northern Korea has a firm foundation.
That is to say, the entire people in Northern Korea have been united on
the foundation of supporting the people's committees which are an agency
of political power of their own, as well as on the foundation of supporting all those democratic reforms which have been enforced in Northern
Korea for the interests of the masses of the people. The crystalliza-
tion of unity of the people in Northern Korea is the Northern Korea Democratic National Front, which embraces all political parties and social
organizations, as well as a wide scope of the masses of the people representing all strata and walks in life throughout Northern Korea.

At present there are 3 big political parties, 16 social organizations and 17 trade unions under the leadership of the Northern Korea Democratic National Front.

All the political parties and social organizations in Northern Korea are holding identical views and opinions regarding the political issues. For they are supporting the people's committees and democratic reforms, and are active in the struggle to construct a united, democratic, autonomous, independent state. The Northern Korea Democratic National Front is embracing 6 million persons as its organized forces; its strength and unity having already been demonstrated.

This was clearly shown by the fact that the wide masses of the people enthusiastically supported the candidates recommended by the Northern Korea Democratic National Front at the time elections were held for the people's committees.

All this magnificent strength shows that it is possible to mobilize the entire people in Northern Korea to participate in the struggle to construct a democratic, independent state of Korea.

Delegates!

The actual situation in Northern Korea can be briefly evaluated as follows.

Firstly, the political power in Northern Korea has fallen into the people's hands, for the people have become a complete master in every field of political, economic and cultural life. Taking advantage of the free conditions created by the Red army, the people in Northern Korea have created an agency of political power of their own in the form of the people's committees, strengthened and developed it.

Secondly, in Northern Korea democratic reforms suitable to the interests of the wide masses of the people have been enforced, with the result that the leadership of the masses of the people in every field of political, economic and cultural life has been guaranteed. On the other hand, the foundation of reactionaries has been fundamentally uprooted. In other words, the enforcement of democratic reforms has prevented the reactionary elements in Northern Korea from holding any foundation of their own whatever.

Thirdly, the enforcement of democratic reforms in Northern Korea has created very favorable conditions for future restoration and developments of the people's economy. At the same time, by achieving great results in restoring and developing the people's economy the democratic reforms have constantly elevated the material and cultural standard of the masses of the people.

Fourthly, all these great achievements in Northern Korea have been seized by us through our struggle. Moreover, these achievements have become a firm material foundation on which the entire people in Northern Korea are united like steel around the people's committees, an agency of political power of their own.

Contrary to this, the situation in Southern Korea, a half of the territory of our fatherland, is entirely different. In Southern Korea the U.S. occupation army has grabbed the entire political power in its hands, thereby preventing the Korean people from controlling and administering their country with their own hands. Democratic reforms still remain to be enforced in Southern Korea, with the result that centuries-old aspirations of the Korean people have not yet been realized. Lately reactionary publications in Southern Korea widely talk about the enforcement of "land reform". This so-called "land reform" is intended not only to deceive the Korean peasants in Southern Korea but also this scheme is, in actuality, nothing but an insult to those Korean peasants in Southern Korea who are being oppressed.

The material situation of the masses of the people in Southern Korea is deteriorating more and more, which fact is admitted even by the reactionary elements in Southern Korea. And the reactionary elements in Southern Korea, under the aegis of the American military government, are cudgelling their brains in working out all sorts of traitorous and anti-popular measures to suppress the democratic forces in Southern Korea.

Consequently, Southern Korea of today has been transformed into a state of anarchy where terrorism is rampant in the broad daylight.

And yet Americans, notwithstanding they have made such a mess out of Southern Korea, are still far from satiated as they are indulged in wild dreams for a world domination; they are actually scheming to permanently enslave Southern Korea.

At present our fatherland is confronted with a grave national crisis where our fatherland is likely to fall victim to the aggressive policy of American imperialism. Therefore, we people in Northern Korea are seriously worried about the destiny of our compatriots, our parents, our brothers and sisters in Southern Korea south of the 38th parallel. At the same time, we are sending our warmest encouragement and support to those compatriots in Southern Korea who are now carrying on a patriotic struggle for the glory, dignity and freedom of our fatherland against the enslavement policy of American imperialists. And we are united with our fighting compatriots in Southern Korea in our common struggle to construct an independent state.

Delegates!

From the first day of their landing on the soil of our fatherland the American imperialists have been uninterruptedly enforcing their crafty aggressive policy.

The conference of the foreign ministers of the Soviet Union, the United States and the United Kingdom, held in Moscow in December 1945, adopted decisions on Korea.

These historical decisions adopted by the Moscow conference foresaw reconstructing Korea as an autonomous independent state on the foundation of democracy. But these decisions could not be realized. Every one of you are well aware of the main reasons for it. The Soviet-U.S. joint conference was held on two different occasions to come to an agreement for the enforcement of the decisions, only to prove it vain.

We Korean people are well aware of the causes for the failure of the task of the Soviet-U.S. joint conference; they know who is to blame. The task of the Soviet-U.S. conference having thus resulted in failure, the Soviet government in September 26, 1947, proposed simultaneous withdrawal of both the Soviet and U.S. occupation forces from Korea toward the beginning of 1948, so that the Korean people themselves could settle their own problems. In other words, had this proposal been put into execution, the Korean people could have autonomously elected a supreme legislative organ, established a united democratic government, formed a national army, and reconstructed the political and economic life of our fatherland on the foundation of democracy without intervention or pressure from any foreign country.

This proposal by the Soviet government was enthusiastically supported by the entire Korean people who were determined to solve the Korean unification issue with their hands by causing the Soviet and U.S. occupation forces to withdraw from the soil of Korea. But a handful of the pro-Japanese collaborators, national traitors and reactionaries in Southern Korea were opposed to this proposal. Why? Because these traitorous elements feared they could no longer continue their treacherous acts against the interest of the people in the event the U.S. occupation forces withdrew from Southern Korea.

Rhee Syngman and his traitorous gang came out in opposition to the withdrawal of the U.S. occupation forces from Southern Korea. This act disclosed in the broad daylight the true feature of those treasonous reactionary elements.

And this crime by these treacherous elements once more demonstrated before the Korean people that Rhee Syngman and his gang were loyal hounds of American imperialism selling our fatherland and the interest of our nation to the American imperialists.

The proposal by the Soviet government also caused a pandemonium even among the American imperialists. In point of fact, the U.S. government rejected it, for the withdrawal of its troops from Southern Korea entirely runs counter to aggressive schemes of the American imperialists. The Korean issue was part of the whole issues outstanding between the Soviet and U.S. governments which could be settled only through good offices of the two governments. In other words, the Korean issue was entirely out of the scope of the United Nations. Notwithstanding this, the U.S. government illegally brought it up at U.N. general assembly and attempted to cause the Korean issue to be solved favorable to it. The U.S. government, taking advantage of those automatic hand-raising machines created within the United Nations which are, politically and economically enslaved to the American monopoly capitalists, caused the U.N. general assembly to reject the Soviet proposal, and adopt instead tricky decisions based upon military and political schemes of the American imperialists.

As every one of you well know, the so-called United Nations Korean

Commission, in accordance with the decision of the U.N. general assembly, was formed, its function being to supervise the enforcement of elections and the establishment of a Korean government as well as of a Korean national army.

The Korean people refused to recognize this decision of the U.N. general assembly. Toward the end of last year (1947) when this decision was adopted by the U.N. general assembly, they carried out solemn demonstrations and held mass rallies in every nook and corner of Southern and Northern Korea in protest against this decision.

The Korean people believed that the U.N. general assembly would, as a matter of course, invite their representatives to discussions on the Korean issue and that discussion could be held only under participation by the Korean representatives.

At the U.N. general assembly the Soviet delegation proposed inviting the representatives of the Korean people, and this proposal was supported by the representatives of many democratic countries.

But the U.N. general assembly refused to invite the Korean representatives. This was purely due to high-handed demand by the U.S. delegation who feared that the Korean representatives would expose before the eyes of the world the colonial policy now being enforced by the American imperialsits in Southern Korea.

This measure taken by the U.N. general assembly was a ruthless and insulting act trampling under foot even the elementary rights of the Korean people.

We Korean people could not permit the U.N. general assembly to determine our destiny without participation by our representatives. Therefore, the Korean people resented the act of the U.N. general assembly in discussing the Korean issue in such a way - so much so that they were compelled to carry out a nationwide strong protest movement against the U.N. decision.

The trouble lies not only in the fact that the U.N. general assembly discussed the Korean issue in an unreasonable method, but also in the fact that it, in accordance with the high-handed demand from the American imperialists, adopted decisions detrimental to the interests of the Korean people. Why is it that the Korean issue has been settled in this way?

Why is it that the U.N. general assembly rejected the most legitimate proposal to let the Korean people establish their own government with their hands, but that it adopted the proposal to organize the so-called U.N. Korean Commission which is antagonistic towards the Korean people?

That is because the U.N. general assembly is being gradually transformed into a tool of the expansion policy of American imperialism and because those countries economically enslaved to the United States are dancing to the tune of the American imperialists. More than that, this is because the withdrawal of the U.S. troops from the soil of Korea runs counter to the scheme of the colonial plunderers of American imperialism. The American imperialists are maneuvering to establish a separate government in southern Korea by partitioning our fatherland. Herein lies the objective of aggressive schemes of the American imperialists.

In order to split our fatherland the American imperialists are causing the so-called U.N. Korean Commission to play a Herculean role.

The U.N. Korean Commission is nothing but a tool whereby individual actions of the U.S. government in Southern Korea and the U.S. policy to split our fatherland can be legalized and whereby with the aim of establishing a separate government in Southern Korea an election comedy is to be performed.

We Korean people are well aware of political significance of the U.N. Korean Commission as well as of its schemes. Therefore, the entire Korean people are openly antagonistic towards the U.N. Korean Commission, for they consider it as nothing but a scheme to intervene in Korean internal affairs. And the Korean people are demanding the speedy withdrawal of the U.N. Korean Commission from our fatherland.

We demand that the Korean people be granted the right and possibility of independently establishing a united democratic people's government without interference from the outside.

The U.N. Korean Commission, after having sized the fact that the entire Korean people are dead set against the establishment of a separate government in Southern Korea, asked the U.N. general assembly for instructions for its future activity, so that it might avoid the responsibility for splitting Korea.

In accordance with the recommendations by the U.N. Korean Commission that elections be permitted to be held even in Southern Korea alone and in accordance with insistent demand by the American imperialists, the U.N. little assembly adopted a decision to hold separate elections in Southern Korea so as to establish a separate government.

This decision was adopted by 31 countries against 2 countries which opposed it and 11 others which waived the right to vote. The United States had expected that its proposal would be absolutely supported because of the absence of the delegates of the Soviet Union and all other Eastern European democratic countries, and it had actually left no stone unturned for this purpose.

But the U.N. little assembly failed to come to a unanimous decision.

At the time the decision on the Korean issue was being discussed at the U.N. little assembly, the Swedish and Norwegian delegates were opposed to enforcing separate elections in Southern Korea.

The Swedish delegate held the view that he was opposed to enforcing elections only in Southern Korea, not only because of lack of official data regarding the actual situation in Southern Korea, but because of the fact that the United Nations was not brought into being as an instrument to discuss the post-war mediation issues.

On the other, the Norwegian delegate declared that by adopting the U.S. decision the U.N. little assembly was abusing the right accorded it by the U.N. general assembly.

Besides this, it must be pointed out that even a member of the so-called U.N. Korean Commission admitted the fact that those supporting the establishment of a separate government in Southern Korea were only the faithful servant of the American imperialists, Syngman Rhee, and the Korean Democratic Party composed of the pro-Japanese collaborators, big landlords and industrialists under the leadership of Kim Sung Soo.

The said delegate also confessed that not only the leftists and the middle-of-the-roaders, but also even many of the rightists leaders were opposed to enforcing separate elections under the subterfuge of establishing a "national government", for they realized that separate elections in Southern Korea would split Korea permanently.

Even within the so-called U.N. Korean Commission 4 out of 8 members voted in favor of enforcing separate elections in Southern Korea, but 2 others voted against it while 2 others waived the right to vote.

But the U.S. delegate, who acted as the master of the U.N. little assembly, trampled underfoot this legitimate opposition by the delegates of many countries. At the U.N. little assembly the American imperialists candidly unmasked themselves and brought pressure to bear upon the U.N. little assembly to adopt their decision guaranteeing their administration in Southern Korea.

At present, the American military government, under the subterfuge of the so-called U.N. Korean Commission, is preparing for separate elections in southern Korea.

What attitude are the entire Korean people both in Southern and Northern Korea taking regarding separate elections in Southern Korea?

In order to answer this question, we must clarify what the entire Korean people want, how they are fighting against the colonial policy of the American imperialists, and what must be done.

We Korean people are well aware of the fact that the purpose of separate elections to be enforced in Southern Korea on May 10, 1948, is to split Korea permanently, so that the American imperialists may convert Southern Korea into a U.S. colony as well as into their political and military base.

We are a nation with a history of 50 centuries. How can we tolerate the realization of such a reactionary and anti-popular scheme of the American imperialists aiming at splitting our people?

Therefore, the entire Korean people throughout Korea are strongly demanding that outside intervention in internal affairs of our fatherland be terminated and that the U.N. Korean Commission withdraw from the soil of our fatherland.

In protest against the U.N. Korean Commission in numerous factories workers and clerks throughout Southern Korea are carrying on strikes, which started on January 8, 1948 - the first day the U.N. Korean Commission set foot on the soil of our fatherland.

As every one of you well know, January 8, 1948, all factory workers and clerks in Seoul struck.

Toward the beginning of February a magnificent strike was carried out by communication and factory workers throughout Southern Korea.

According to reports of the Korean News Agency in Seoul, this general strike completely paralyzed Southern Korea.

The strikers demanded Lieutenant General John R. Hodge, commander of the U.S. occupation forces in Southern Korea (now retired--Ed.). that the U.N. Korean Commission and the U.S. occupation troops be withdrawn from the soil of Korea.

Even American newsmen stationed in Seoul reported the masses of the people demonstrating in protest against the U.N. Korean Commission came into bloody clashes with police.

These strikes are still going on. This fact the delegates from Southern Korea know more than anyone else.

It is not only the workers in Southern Korea but also the peasants in Southern Korea who in cooperation with the entire workers and people are carrying on a heroic struggle for the unification of our fatherland and the establishment of a united democratic government.

Delegates from Southern Korea!

The entire people in Northern Korea are wholeheartedly supporting your sacrificial and heroic struggle against the split of our fatherland. The entire people in Northern Korea are absolutely behind you with national enthusiasm and brotherly encouragement.

The people in Northern Korea are in conditions entirely different from those in which the people in Southern Korea find themselves. The people in Northern Korea have become the masters of their land. In the hands of the people in Northern Korea there are land, political power and industry.

As already mentioned above, the people in NorthernKorea have carried out great historical democratic reforms.

But Korea still remains to be unified, and because our fatherland has not as yet been unified under a united democratic government, the democratic reforms are not capable of attaining greater achievements. Everyone of us well knows this.

The people in Southern Korea are determined to share life or death, or comfort and hardship with our parents, brothers and sisters in Southern

Korea, regardless of what conditions and environment we may find ourselves, until the unification of our fatherland against its split is
assured.

We know that splitting our fatherland will once more impose the
painful yoke of colonial enslavement upon the 30 million Korean people.

Therefore, the people in Northern Korea will deal with any kind of
separate government with antagonism and undauntedly advocate unifying
Southern and Northern Korea, and continue to fight for the attainment
of this objective.

The people in Northern Korea consider it the most urgent task to
present a nation-wide united front with their compatriots in Southern
Korea - the descendants of the same blood - in their common struggle to
frustrate the aggressive scheme of the American imperialists to split
Korea.

The people in Northern Korea have - through demonstrations, rallies,
protests, decisions, and manifestoes - demonstrated their definite political attitude against criminal activities being perpetrated by the so-
called U.N. Commission on Korea as well as against foreign intervention
in the Korean question.

The masses of the people in Northern Korea are appealing to the people in Southern Korea that they rise like one man and participate in
our common struggle for freedom and independence of our fatherland by
extricating ourselves from the complicated political situation created
in our country.

The masses of the people in Northern Korea are encouraging the people
in Southern Korea to carry out all the more positively and decisively
their struggle to boycott separate elections which will ruin our country.

It is the biggest political task for the entire Korean people to
boycott and frustrate the Southern Korea separate elections which are
against the interest of the people and which will ruin our country.

You, representatives from Southern Korea, can firmly believe that
your compatriots in Northern Korea will share life and death or happiness
and hardship with our compatriots in Southern Korea and fight, to the
bitter end, against the separate elections in Southern Korea as well as
against the establishment of a separate government in Southern Korea.

Those who are, at this moment of today, supporting the enforcement
of separate elections in Southern Korea are nothing but national traitors whose treason is worse than that committed by Song Byung Choon and
Lee Wan Yong, the two worst traitors the Korean People ever had for
fifty centuries of their national life. We have already mentioned the
traitor Rhee Syngman.

Everyone of the entire Korean people well knows that Rhee Syngman
is the most despicable traitor of the Korean people. And everyone of
the entire Korean people well knows that Rhee Syngman is a hound of the

American imperialists as it is a common knowledge that he has been raised by the American imperialists for the past forty years.

He is willing to do whatever his American masters dictate. But we don't talk about only Rhee Syngman himself. For we consider as a traitor anyone who supports separate elections in Southern Korea, no matter who he may be.

We must expose such traitors of the Korean people, we must isolate and ostracize them from the people, and we must cause the entire people to spit on them, hate them, and deal with them with antagonism. At the same time, we must clearly interpret to the masses of the people the significance of aggressive scheme behind the Southern Korea separate elections.

Every true Korean patriot must realize that these separate elections will inevitably lead Southern Korea to the abyss of ruin, thereby transforming Southern Korea into a U.S. colony.

Therefore, any who truly loves his fatherland must boycott these separate elections, no matter who he may be.

In this nation-wide struggle, regardless of party, religion, and political views, the entire Korean patriots throughout the country must be united.

Unity alone is the prerequisite to our victory. Therefore, this conference must work out measures how to all the more strongly strengthen our unity and to what direction we should lead this united strength for the attainment of the supreme cause of the Korean people in connection with our great historic work of unifying our fatherland and establishing a united democratic government.

The political situation in Northern Korea as well as the most basic and characteristic feature of the political life of our fatherland can be briefly summarized something as follows:

As everyone of you can realize, this conference has been convened under such a complicated environment of our fatherland as well as under conditions embracing various difficult problems. Therefore, at this conference we must frankly and without reservation, discuss the political situation created in our fatherland, and work out the only and common measure to fight against the split of our fatherland, maneuvers of the U.N. Commission on Korea, and the Southern Korea separate elections.

We must disrupt aggressive schemes of the American imperialists.

We must carry out a struggle to unite our fatherland as an autonomous, independent state and establish our united government on the wide democratic basis.

At this grave moment our fatherland is confronted with a crisis; we must be united, we must repulse the danger of splitting our fatherland,

and smash the scheme of the American imperialists to colonize Southern Korea. If we fail to work out this great measure for the salvation of our fatherland, we must bear in mind that we are going to commit a sin against the entire Korean people as well as against our coming descendants - the sin which can't be wiped out for centuries to come.

The most fundamental political conclusion which starts from the prevailing political situation created in our fatherland is as follows:

Long live a united democratic Korea!

The U.N. Commission on Korea must leave the soil of our fatherland!

May those truly Korean patriots who are carrying on a sacrificial struggle against the colonial aggressors of American imperialism have victory and glory!

Long live the great democratic reforms enforced in Northern Korea!

From: Korean Independence, Los Angeles, Vo. VII, No. 6, 7, 8, 9, 10, February 1949.

(This report was made before the special conference on unity held in May 1948 in Pyongyang by northern and southern political leaders. It gives the fullest and most authoritative expression of any document in this collection of the ideological position on Korean affairs held by the Democratic People's Republic ((North)).)

\#   \#   \#

July 12, 1948

CONSTITUTION OF THE DEMOCRATIC REPUBLIC OF KOREA (South)

PREAMBLE

We, the people of Korea, with a glorious tradition and history from time immemorial, following the indomitable spirit of independence, as manifested in the establishment of TAI HAN Republic in the course of the SAM-IL independence movement,

Now at this time engaged in reconstructing a democratic, independent country, are determined:

To consolidate national unity by justice, humanity, brotherly love and the elimination of all kinds of social evils,

To offer equal opportunities to every person,

To provide for the fullest development of the equality of each individual in all fields of political, economic, social and cultural life,

To permit every person to discharge his duties and responsibilities,

To promote the welfare of the people, to maintain permanent international peace, and thereby to assure Security, Liberty and Happiness of ourselves and our posterity,

Do hereby ordain and establish this Constitution on the 12th day of July in the year One Thousand Nine Hundred and Forty-Eight in the National Assembly composed of our freely and duly elected representatives.

CHAPTER I. GENERAL PROVISIONS

Article 1
Korea shall be a democratic republic.

Article 2
The sovereignty of the Korean Republic shall reside in the people as a whole. All state authority shall emanate from the people.

Article 3
The requirements for Korean citizenship shall be determined by law.

Article 4
The territory of Korea shall consist of the Korean Peninsula, and its accessory islands.

Article 5
The Democratic Republic of Korea shall guarantee liberty and equality and the initiative of each individual in the fields of political, social and economic life. It shall be responsible for their protection and adjustment for the promotion of the public welfare.

Article 6
The Democratic Republic of Korea shall denounce all aggressive wars. The mission of the national military forces shall be to perform the sacred duty of protecting the national territory.

Article 7
The duly ratified and published treaties and the generally recognized rules of international law shall be valid as a binding constituent part of the law of Korea. The status of aliens shall be guaranteed within the scope of international law and international treaties.

CHAPTER II. RIGHTS AND DUTIES OF CITIZENS

CHAPTER III. NATIONAL ASSEMBLY

CHAPTER IV. GOVERNMENT

CHAPTER V. COURTS

CHAPTER VI. ECONOMY

CHAPTER VII. FINANCE

116.

CHAPTER VIII. LOCAL AUTONOMOUS ORGANIZATIONS

CHAPTER IX. AMENDMENT TO THE CONSTITUTION

CHAPTER X. SUPPLEMENTARY RULES

From: The Voice of Korea, Washington, D.C., Vol. V,
No. 112, August 14, 1948, pp.1-5.

(This constitution was signed by Syngman Rhee on July 17, 1948.)

#　　　　#　　　　#

August 12, 1948

U.S. DECLARATION ON RECOGNITION OF REPUBLIC OF KOREA (South)

In the Joint Declaration issued at Cairo on December 1, 1943, the
three subscribing Powers - the United States, China and Great Britain -
expressed their determination "that in due course Korea shall become
free and independent." This determination was reaffirmed in the Potsdam Declaration of July 26, 1945, with which the Soviet Union associated itself upon its declaration of war against Japan on August 8 of
that year. On December 27, 1945, in Moscow the Foreign Ministers of
the Soviet Union, the United States and Great Britain concluded an
agreement, later adhered to by the Government of China, designed to
reestablish Korea as an independent state.

Although the annexation of Korea by Japan was effectively terminated with the occupation of that country by the armed forces of the
Soviet Union and the United States in August and September, 1945, the
freedom and independence of Korea so solemnly pledged by the Four
Powers have proved slow of realization. After nearly two years of
painstaking but unavailing effort to those pledges through negotiations
with the other Occupying Power, the United States Government, on September 17, 1947, laid the problem of Korean independence before the
General Assembly of the United Nations. The will of an overwhelming
majority of that body was expressed in two Resolutions adopted by it
on November 14, 1947, the purpose of which was to make it possible for
the Korean people to attain their long-sought freedom and independence
through the holding of free and democratic elections and the establishment, on the basis thereof, of a National Government.

In pursuance of those Resolutions, elections were held in Korea on
May 10 of this year, under the observation of the United Nations Temporary Commission on Korea, for the purpose of electing representatives
to a National Assembly which might in turn form a National Government.
The National Assembly so elected convened on May 31 and has proceeded
to form a Government - a Government in which it is hoped that the people
of north Korea, who were prevented from participating in the May 10 elections by the refusal of the Soviet Union to permit the implementation of

the General Assembly Resolutions in its zone of occupation, will be free
in due course to assume their rightful role. Notification of the formation of the new Government was communicated to the United Nations Temporary Commission on Korea on August 6, 1948.

It is the view of the United States Government that the Korean Government so established is entitled to be regarded as the Government of
Korea envisaged by the General Assembly Resolutions of November 14,
1947. Pending consideration by the General Assembly at its forthcoming
Third Session of the report of the United Nations Temporary Commission
on Korea, the United States, pursuant to its responsibility as Occupying
Power, is sending a Special Representative to Seoul who will be authorized to carry on negotiations with that Government, in consultation with
the United Nations Temporary Commission on Korea, concerning the implementation of the further provisions set forth in paragraph 4 of the second
of the General Assembly Resolutions of November 14, 1947. As such Special
Representative the President has named the Honorable John J. Muccio of
Rhode Island, who will have the personal rank of Ambassador.

> From: Korea, 1945-1948, U.S. Department of State,
> Publication No. 3305, October 1948, pp.100-
> 101.

(Full recognition by the U.S. was granted January 1, 1949,
after the U.N. resolution of December 12, 1948.)

#   #   #

August 15, 1948

GENERAL MACARTHUR'S SPEECH AT THE INAUGURATION OF
THE REPUBLIC OF KOREA (South)

Mr. President, General Hodge and citizens of Korea:

I am profoundly moved to stand on the soil of Korea in this historic
hour to see liberty reborn, the cause of right and justice prevail. For
forty years I have observed with admiration the efforts of your patriots
to cast off the oppressive bonds of foreign power. Their unyielding
firmness in refusing to compromise with destiny the freedom of the Korean
people has exemplified before the world the immutable truism that the
spirit once infused in the human heart never dies.

Yet in this hour, as the forces of righteousness advance, the triumph
is dulled by one of the great tragedies of contemporary history - an artificial barrier has divided your land.

This barrier must and will be torn down. Nothing shall prevent the
ultimate unity of your people as free men of a free nation. Koreans come
from too proud a stock to sacrifice their sacred cause by yielding to any
alien philosophies of disruption.

118.

As on this soil of the Asiatic mainland you face to the West where fear and threat and tragedy now fill men's minds, as people are locked in mortal combat and ideological pressures are exerted in search of weaknesses in freedom's shield you must realize that events in the making here and beyond that western horizon may well determine the issue of a world at peace or a world at war.

For three years my country's guns have been silent as we have sought in concert with all other peoples to fashion from the moral resources of the modern world a norm of human relationship which effectively would preserve the peace. Our efforts have been retarded by an evil spirit of greed and avarice and lust for power but your national rebirth today is living proof that the concept of human freedom is far too deeply rooted in human society to ever perish.

As you embark upon your destiny as a free and independent Republic, the measure of the wisdom of your chosen leaders will do much to provide the measure of your strength as a nation.

If they secure the well-being of the individual and establish his position upon a plane of personal dignity with the opportunity of progress limited only by the nature and degree of his industry, you will evolve here a strong nation of happy and industrious citizens which will prove an impregnable bulwark against the assaults of all dissident elements.

For the defense of the democratic way of life rests more than all else in the human spirit. He alone is fit to enjoy the blessings of personal libertywho is ready at all times resolutely to defend it.

The people of my country have long entertained a close friendship for the people of yours.

As early as the year of 1882 in a treaty of amity and commerce between our peoples, it was proclaimed that there should be "perpetual peace and friendship" between the United States and Korea. The American people have never deviated from this pledge and you may rely upon the invincible continuance of the friendship.

President Rhee, you and the distinguished group which has been chosen to assist you in the leadership of this infant Republic will face issues of the most complex nature known to political experience. The manner in which these issues are resolved will determine in large measure not only the unity and well-being of your own people but also the future stability of the continent of Asia.

I have faith in you and your countrymen and pray that Almighty God may sustain you in your hallowed task.

From: Contemporary Japan, Tokyo (periodical in English), July-December 1948, pp.409-410.

(On this occasion celebrating the third anniversary of V-J Day and the inauguration of the new Republic of Korea ((South)), other important speakers included President Syngman Rhee and

Lt. General John R. Hodge. General MacArthur's opinion on the future of the dividing line of the 38° parallel are expressed in the second and third paragraphs of the above speech.)

#   #   #

September 3, 1948

CONSTITUTION OF THE DEMOCRATIC PEOPLE'S REPUBLIC OF KOREA (North)

Chapter I. FUNDAMENTAL PRINCIPLES

Article 1. Our country is the Korean People's Democratic Republic.

Article 2. The sovereignty of the Korean People's Democratic Republic is in the people. The people shall exercise their Sovereignty through the people's committees, the new form of the state Sovereignty, which was brought into existence in accordance with the free will of the people simultaneously with the August 15 Liberation of 1945.

Article 3. All the organs representing the Sovereignty shall be elected by from the ri (or village) people's committee up to the supreme people's committees. Elections for the organs of the Korean People's Democratic Republic shall be held on the basis of the principles of general, equal and direct elections.

Article 4. Representatives and committee members of all the organs of the Sovereignty shallhold themselves responsible for their works and activities before their voters. In the event any representative or committee member of the organs of the Sovereignty loses confidence from the voters, the voters can recallhim even before his tenure of office has expired.

Article 5. Natural resources buried underground, forests, rivers, portations, communications, broadcasting stations, banks, hydro-electricity, water works, mineral fountains, natural energies, the properties formerly owned by the Japanese, and all the properties of Korean national traitors shall belong to the entire people, i.e., to the State. Foreign trade shall be conducted by the State and also under the supervision of the State.

Article 6. The former landownership by the Japanese State and by the Japanese subjects, that by Korean landlords, and the tenancy system shall permanently be abolished. Land can be had only by one who tills it. No one can own land beyond what is stipulated by the Law. The scope of land one can own shall separately be stipulated by the Law. Landownership by the individuals as well as by the State and the cooperative organizations shall be granted. The area of land to be owned by the State as well as by the cooperative organizations shall be limitless. The State shall grant special protection to the interests of the toiling peasants, and assist them by various methods as permitted by its economic policy.

120.

Article 7. For those areas within Korea where land reform has not yet been enforced, the land reform shall be enforced on the date to be fixed by the Supreme People's Assembly. Land reform for these areas shall be enforced on the basis of the ordinances regarding the land reform carried out in Northern Korea.

Article 8. Individual ownership of land, trucks, farming tools, other means of production, middle and small commercial organs, raw materials, manufactured goods, houses, all other auxiliary household equipments, household utensils, incomes, and savings shall be protected by the Law. The inheritance right of individual ownership shall be guaranteed by the Law. Initiative of individual management shall be encouraged.

Article 9. The State shall encourage developments of the people's cooperative organizations. The ownership by the cooperative organizations shall be protected by the Law.

Article 10. With the object of reasonably utilizing all economic resources as well as all the potential economic resources in the country for the interests of the people, the State shall draw up a single people's economic plan, and at the same time shall direct economic and cultural recovery and developments in the country on the basis of this people's economic plan. In enforcing this people's economic plan the State shall permit the branch of individual economy to participate in this plan on the basis of the ownership by the States and the co-operative organizations.

Chapter 2. FUNDAMENTAL RIGHTS AND DUTY OF THE CITIZEN

Chapter 3. SUPREME SOVEREIGN ORGANS

Chapter 4. THE STATE CENTRAL EXECUTIVE ORGANS

Chapter 5. DISTRICT SOVEREIGN ORGANS

Chapter 6. THE COURT OF JUSTICE AND THE PUBLIC PROCURATOR'S OFFICE

Chapter 7. NATIONAL BUDGET

Chapter 8. NATIONAL DEFENSE

Chapter 9. THE STATE SEAL, THE NATIONAL FLAG, AND THE CAPITAL

Chapter 10. PROCEDURES TO AMEND THE CONSTITUTION

From: Korean Independence, Los Angeles, Vol. VII, Nos. 19, 20, 21, May 1949.

(This Constitution was first made public for general discussion by the Provisional Constitution Draft Committee ((North)) on February 7, 1948. The text was approved on May 1, 1948, by the Joint North and South Conference. On July 10, 1948, the North Korean People's Council approved the document. On September 3,

1948, it was finally ratified by the Supreme People's
Democratic Assembly at Pyongyang in North Korea. The
Democratic People's Republic of Korea ((North)) was pro-
claimed on September 10, 1949.)

\#   \#   \#

September 20, 1948

SOVIET ANNOUNCEMENT ON WITHDRAWAL OF TROOPS

On the 10th September the Supreme People's Assembly of Korea adopted
the text of a message to the Governments of the Soviet Union and of the
United States of America with a request for the simultaneous withdrawal
of American and Soviet troops from Korea. It also stated that the fact
that a Supreme People's Assembly of Korea had been set up and that this
Assembly had formed a single Korean Government of representatives of
various political trends of North and South Korea, representing the will
of the overwhelming majority of the population of northern and southern
Korea, was a guarantee that during and after the withdrawal of foreign
troops from Korea complete order and public peace would prevail throughout Korea.

It is known that in the autumn of 1945 Soviet troops, after smashing
the Japanese Kwantung Army, liberated Korea from the Japanese invaders
and, on the basis of an agreement among the Allies, remained in Korea
north of the 38th parallel, while American troops remained on Korean
territory south of the 38th parallel. While remaining in northern Korea
the Soviet forces afforded the Korean population the full opportunity of
setting up democratic administrative bodies and invariably rendered
friendly assistance in the national regeneration of Korea. At the same
time the number of Soviet troops in northern Korea was gradually reduced.

In September 1947 the Soviet Government proposed to the Government
of the United States of American that the Soviet and American troops
should be simultaneously withdrawn from Korea. After that it has time
and again confirmed its readiness immediately to withdraw the Soviet
troops from northern Korea, if the Government of the United States of
America simultaneously withdrew the American troops from southern Korea,
to which, however, the Government of the United States of American has
so far not given its consent.

The question put by the Supreme People's Assembly of Korea about the
simultaneous withdrawal of Soviet and American troops from Korea was
submitted by the Soviet Government to the Presidium of the Supreme Soviet
of the U.S.S.R. which examined the aforementioned message of the Supreme
People's Assembly of Korea and found it timely to evacuate the Soviet
troops from northern Korea, expressing the hope that the U.S.A. Government would also agree to evacuate the American troops from southern Korea, in accordance with the wish expressed by the Supreme People's
Assembly of Korea.

In fulfilment of the decision of the Presidium of the Supreme Soviet of the U.S.S.R., the Council of Ministers of the U.S.S.R. has decided:

1. To evacuate to Soviet Union Territory the Soviet troops remaining on the territory of northern Korea.

2. To instruct the Ministry of the Armed Forces of the U.S.S.R. to begin the evacuation of Soviet troops from northern Korea not later than in the second half of October this year and to complete it by January 1, 1949.

Ministry of Foreign Affairs of the
U.S.S.R.

From: <u>The Soviet Union and the Korean Question</u>
(Documents), Moscow, 1948, pp.78-79.

(On December 30, 1948, the U.S.S.R. announced that all Soviet troops had been withdrawn from North Korea.)

#   #   #

September 20, 1948

U.S. STATEMENT ON WITHDRAWAL OF TROOPS

It has been the consistent view of this government that the best interests of the Korean people would be served by the withdrawal of all occupying forces from Korea at the earliest practicable date. This same view was embodied in the U.N. General Assembly Resolution of November 14, 1947 in which provision was made for such withdrawal as soon as practicable after the establishment of the Korean Government which it was the intention of that Resolution to bring into being. Had the Soviet Union co-operated in carrying out the provisions of the Resolution of November 14, 1947, the question of troop withdrawal from Korea would doubtless have been already resolved.

The United States Government regards the question of the withdrawal of occupying forces as but one facet of the entire question of the unity and independence of Korea. The General Assembly of the UN has taken cognizance of this larger question as evidenced by the Resolution referred to above, and may be expected to give further consideration to the matter at its forthcoming meeting.

U.S. Department of State

From: <u>Korea, 1945-1948</u>, U.S. Department of State
Publication No. 3305, October 1948, p.116.

(On July 8, 1949, the United States announced the completion as of June 29, 1949, of the withdrawal of its troops from South

Korea. A U.S. Military Advisory group remained in Korea
to advise the military forces of the Republic of Korea
((South)), and a Military Assistance Aid program for
Korea was inaugurated by the U.S. Government in 1949.
On January 26, 1950, a Mutual Defense Assistance Agree-
ment was signed by the U.S. and the Republic of Korea
((South)).)

#   #   #

October 8-12, 1948

CORRESPONDENCE BETWEEN NORTH KOREA AND U.S.S.R. ON RECOGNITION

The Establishment of Diplomatic Relations Between the Soviet Union and the
Korean People's Democratic Republic

To Mr. Joseph Vissarionovitch Stalin, Chairman of the Council of Ministers
of the U.S.S.R.:

On behalf of the government of the Korean People's Democratic Republic, I have the honor to address you, most esteemed Mr. Chairman, in the
present letter, and to convey to you the following desire of my government:

During the three years that have elapsed since the liberation of
Korea from long years of colonial oppression by Japanese imperialism,
profound changes, which have tremendous significance for the history of
our country, have occurred in the lives of the Korean people. Nation-
wide elections have been held throughout Korea to the sole, nation-wide,
legislative organ--the Supreme People's Assembly of Korea. As a result
of the elections a government of the People's Democratic Republic was
formed, which consists of representatives from all social strata of the
population from the north of Korea to the south, and which has elicited
the warm approval and unanimous support of the entire Korean people. The
government of the Korean People's Democratic Republic has undertaken to
fulfill its obligations and has begun to work for the welfare of the
Korean people.

Expressing the unanimous aspiration of the entire Korean people, I,
in behalf of the government, address myself to you and, in your person, to
the government of the U.S.S.R., with the request to establish diplomatic
relations with the Korean People's Democratic Republic and to exchange ambassadors. Along with the establishment of diplomatic relations, I likewise beseech the government of the U.S.S.R. to establish close economic
relations between the two states for the common welfare of our peoples.

I am profoundly convinced that the establishment of diplomatic relations between the Korean People's Democratic Republic and the U.S.S.R.
will help to strengthen friendly relations between our peoples and will
serve the cause of peace and security in the Far East.

124.

Very respectfully yours,

KIM IL-SENG
Chairman of the Cabinet of
Pyongyang, Korea, October 8, 1948   Ministers of the Korean
People's Democratic Republic

—   —   —

To Mr. Kim Il-seng, Chairman of the Cabinet of Ministers of the Korean
   People's Democratic Republic, Pyongyang:

I acknowledge receipt of your letter of October 8, in which you inform
me that the government of the Korean People's Democratic Republic has
undertaken to fulfill its obligations, and in which you propose the establishment of diplomatic relations with the U.S.S.R., the exchange of
ambassadors, and also the establishment of corresponding economic relations between the two states.

The Soviet government, which invariably defends the right of the
Korean people to create its own united, independent state, welcomes the
formation of the Korean government and wishes it success in its work for
the national rebirth and democratic development of Korea. The Soviet
government expresses its readiness to establish diplomatic relations between the U.S.S.R. and the Korean People's Democratic Republic, and to
exchange ambassadors, and along with this to establish corresponding
economic relations.

J.Stalin
October 12, 1948   Chairman of the Council of
Ministers of the U.S.S.R.

From: Soviet Press Translations: Far Eastern
       Institute, University of Washington, Seattle,
       December 1, 1948

(Full Recognition of the Korean People's Democratic Republic
((north)) by the Soviet Union preceded the full recognition of
the Democratic Republic of Korea ((south)) by the United States
by two and a half months, although the United States had extended de facto recognition to the Democratic Republic of
Korea((south)) earlier on August 12, 1948.)

#   #   #

December 12, 1948
U.S. - AUSTRALIA - CHINA RESOLUTION ON KOREA IN UN

THE GENERAL ASSEMBLY

Having regard to its resolution No. 112 of November 14, 1947, concerning the problem of the independence of Korea;

Having considered the report of the United Nations Temporary Commission on Korea (hereinafter referred to as the "Temporary Commission"), and the report of the Interim Committee regarding its consultation with the Temporary Commission;

Mindful of the fact that due to difficulties referred to in the report of the Temporary Commission, the objectives set forth in the resolution of November 14, 1947 have not been fully accomplished; and in particular that unification in Korea has not yet been achieved;

(1) Approves the conclusions of the reports of the Temporary Commission;

(2) Declares that there has been established a lawful government (the Government of the Republic of Korea), having effective control and jurisdiction over that part of Korea where the Temporary Commission was able to observe and consult in which the great majority of the people of all Korea reside; that this Government is based on elections which were a valid expression of the free will of the electorate of that part of Korea and which were observed by the Temporary Commission; and that this is the only such Government in Korea;

(3) Recommends that the occupying powers withdraw their occupation forces from Korea as early as practicable;

(4) Resolves that, as a means to the full accomplishment of the objectives set forth in the resolution of November 14, 1947, a commission on Korea consisting of _____ be established to continue the work of the Temporary Commission and carry out the provisions of the present resolution, having in mind the status of the Government of the Republic of Korea as herein defined, and in particular to;

   a. Lend its good offices to bring about the unification of Korea
      and the integration of all Korean security forces in accordance
      with the principles laid down by the General Assembly in the
      Resolution of November 14, 1947;

   b. Seek to facilitate the removal of barriers to economic, social,
      and other friendly intercourse caused by the division of Korea;

   c. Be available for observation and consultation in the further
      development of representative government based on the freely
      expressed will of the people;

   d. Observe the actual withdrawal of the occupying forces and veri-
      fy the fact of withdrawal when such has occurred; and for this
      purpose, if it so desires, request the assistance of military
      experts of the two occupying powers;

(5) Decides that the Commission:

   a. Shall, within thirty days of the adoption of this resolution,
      proceed to Korea, where it shall maintain its seat;

b. Shall be regarded as having superseded the Temporary Commission established by the resolution of November 14, 1947;
c. Is authorized to travel, consult and observe throughout Korea;
d. Shall determine its own procedures;
e. May consult with the Interim Committee with respect to the discharge of its duties in the light of developments and within the terms of this resolution;
f. Shall render a report to the next Regular Session of the General Assembly and to any prior Special Session which might be called to consider the subject matter of this resolution, and shall render such interim reports as it may deem appropriate to the Secretary-General for distribution to members;

(6) Requests that the Secretary-General provide the Commission with adequate staff and facilities, including technical advisers as required; and authorized the Secretary-General to pay the expenses and per diem of a representative and an alternate from each of the states members of the commission;

(7) Calls upon member states concerned, the Government of the Republic of Korea, and all Koreans to afford every assistance and facility to the Commission in the fulfillment of its responsibilities;

(8) Calls upon member states to refrain from any acts derogatory to the results achieved and to be achieved by the UN in bringing about the complete independence and unity of Korea;

(9) Recommends that member states and other nations, in establishing their relations with the Government of Korea, take into consideration the facts set out in paragraph (2) of this resolution.

From: Department of State Bulletin, December 19, 1948, p.760.

(Underlining not in original text.)

(This resolution was adopted by the Political and Security Committee of the General Assembly on December 8, 1948, by a vote of 41 to 6, and accepted by the Assembly on December 12, 1948. Previously the Political and Security Committee had rejected a resolution proposed by Czechoslovakia recommending that representatives of North Korea be invited to participate in the discussion of the Korea question.)

March 17, 1949

U.S.S.R.-KOREAN AGREEMENT ON ECONOMIC AND CULTURAL COOPERATION

The Presidium of the Supreme Soviet of the Union of Soviet Socialist Republics and the Presidium of the Supreme National Assembly of the Korean People's Democratic Republic, striving for the further promotion and strengthening of economic and cultural relations between the U.S.S.R. and the Korean People's Democratic Republic, convinced that the consolidation and promotion of these ties meets the vital interests of the peoples of both countries and will in the best way facilitate their economic and cultural development, have decided to conclude to these ends the present agreement and to appoint as their plenipotentiary representatives:-

The Presidium of the Supreme Soviet of the Union of Soviet Socialist Republics -- Andrei Yanuarovich Vyshinsky, Minister of Foreign Affairs of the U.S.S.R.;

The Presidium of the Supreme National Assembly of the Korean People's Democratic Republic -- Kim Ir Sen, Chairman of the Council of Ministers of the Korean People's Democratic Republic,

Who upon exchange of their credentials, found to be in proper order, have agreed upon the following:-

ARTICLE I. The contracting parties will in every way promote and consolidate trade relations between them on the basis of cooperation, equality and mutual benefit. The Governments of both contracting parties will from time to time conclude agreements determining the volume and composition of mutual deliveries of goods for yearly as well as longer periods and other conditions ensuring uninterrupted and increasing trade turnover between both countries in accordance with the requirements for developing the national economy of each of them.

ARTICLE II. The contracting parties shall grant each other the right to reciprocal most-favoured nation treatment with respect to all matters relating to commerce and navigation between two countries, as well as with regard to the activity of physical and juridical persons of one contracting party, on the territory of the other party.

ARTICLE III. The contracting parties shall in every way promote and consolidate the relations established between them in the fields of culture, science and art.

Accordingly, the Governments of the contracting parties shall enter into negotiations with the object of concluding corresponding agreements. In so doing both Governments shall be guided by their aspirations further to consolidate these relations.

ARTICLE IV. The contracting parties shall facilitate the exchange between both countries of experience in the field of industry and agriculture through the dispatch of experts, the rendering of technical aid, the organization of exhibitions, the exchange of specimens of seeds and plants, as well as in other ways.

ARTICLE V. The present agreement is concluded for a period of ten years.

The agreement shall be ratified in the shortest possible time and shall come into force as from the day of the exchange of ratification instruments, which shall be effected in Pyong-Yang.

Unless either of the contracting parties gives notice in writing one year prior to the expiration of the said ten-year term of its intention to renounce the agreement, the latter will remain in force for one year as from the day when the agreement may be renounced by either of the contracting parties.

In witness whereof the plenipotentiary representatives of both contracting parties have signed the present agreement and affixed their seals thereto.

Done in Moscow on March 17, 1949, in two copies in the Russian and Korean languages, both texts being equally valid.

Upon the authorization of the Presidium of the Supreme Soviet of the Union of Soviet Socialist Republics, A.Y. Vyshinsky.

Upon the authorization of the Presidium of the Supreme National Assembly of the Korean People's Democratic Republic, Kim Ir Sen.

From: Soviet News, London, March 21, 1949.

\#   \#   \#

June 7, 1949

PRESIDENT TRUMAN'S MESSAGE TO CONGRESS ON KOREAN AID

To the Congress of the United States:

I recommend that the Congress authorize the continuation of economic assistance to the Republic of Korea for the fiscal year ending June 30, 1950.

The United States is now providing relief and a small amount of assistance in rehabilitation to the Republic of Korea under Public Law 793--Eightieth Congress. The continuation of that assistance is of great importance to the successful achievement of the foreign policy aims of the United States. The authority of the present act extends only until June 30, 1949. For this reason legislation is urgently needed and I am hopeful that the Congress may give it early consideration.

The people of the United States have long had sympathetic feelings for the Korean people. American missionaries, supported by American churches of many denominations, brought spiritual guidance, education and

medical aid to the Korean people during their forty years of Japanese
bondage. All Americans who have come to know the Korean people appreciate their fierce passion for freedom and their keen desire to become
an independent nation.

Early in the war with Japan, it was resolved that Korea should be
liberated. In the Cairo Declaration of December, 1943, the United States
joined with the United Kingdom and China to express their determination
that in due course Korea should become free and independent. This pledge
was reaffirmed in the Potsdam Declaration of July 26, 1945, with which
the Soviet Union associated itself upon its entrance into the war against
Japan in the following month.

With our victory over Japan, it was hoped that the Korean nation
would be reborn. Unfortunately, however, only the people south of the
Thirty-Eighth Degree Parallel have thus far attained their freedom and
independence.

The present division of Korea along the Thirty-Eighth Parallel was
never intended by the United States. The sole purpose of this line a-
long the Thirty-Eighth Degree Parallel was to facilitate acceptance by
the Soviet and United States forces of the surrender of Japanese troops
north and south of that line. Immediately after the completion of the
Japanese surrender, the United States through direct negotiations with
the Soviet Union sought to restore the unity of Korea.

For two years these efforts were rendered unavailing by the attitude
of the Soviet Union. When it became apparent that further delay would
be injurious to the interests of the Korean people, the United States
submitted the matter to the General Assembly of the United Nations, in
the hope that the United Nations could assist the people of Korea to
assume their rightful place as an independent, democratic nation.

By vote of an overwhelming majority, the General Assembly adopted
a resolution on November 14, 1947, calling for an election, under the
observation of a United Nations temporary commission on Korea, to choose
a representative national assembly for the purpose of drafting a democratic constitution and establishing a national government.

The Soviet Union refused to permit the United Nations Commission
to enter its zone. Consequently, the right of the Korean people to
participate in a free election to establish a free government was confined to South Korea. As a result of this election, the Government of
the Republic of Korea was inaugurated August 15, 1948.

The General Assembly of the United Nations at its next session considered the report of its commission and in December, 1948, adopted a
resolution holding the Government of the Republic of Korea to be the
validly elected, lawful government of the area in which elections were
held under the commission's observation - and the only such government
in Korea. The General Assembly established a reconstituted commission
to consult with the occupying powers on the withdrawal of their forces
and to continue to work for the unification of Korea under representative
government.

The United States terminated its military government in Korea upon the inauguration of the Government of the Republic of Korea and recognized the new Government on New Year's Day, 1949.

The December, 1948, resolution of the General Assembly called on the occupying powers to withdraw their forces as soon as practicable. The United States has thus far retained a small number of troops in Korea at the request of the Government of the republic to give the republic an opportunity to establish forces adequate to protect itself against internal disturbances and external attacks short of an aggressive war supported by a major power. A military advisory group requested by the Korean Government for training purposes will be retained in Korea after the withdrawal of United States troops.

The debilitated state in which the Korean economy was left by the Japanese has been accentuated by the separation of the hydroelectric power, coal and metal and fertilizer industries of the north from the agricultural and textile industries of the south and by the effects of continuing Communist agitation.

The United States has furnished the people of South Korea with basic relief during the period of military government. Despite such assistance however, the republic is still far short of being able to support itself, even at the present modest standard of living of its people. It is in urgent need of further assistance in the difficult period ahead until it can stand on its own feet economically.

The aid now being provided to Korea is essentially for basic relief. Without the continuation of such relief, its economy would collapse - inevitably and rapidly. Bare relief alone, however, would not make it possible for the republic to become self-supporting. The republic would remain dependent upon the continuation of relief from the United States at a costly level into the indefinite future - and subject to the same inevitable collapse at any time the relief should be withdrawn. For these reasons the aid granted should be not for mere relief but for recovery. The kind of program which is needed is the kind which the Congress has authorized for the countries of Western Europe and under which those countries have achieved such rapid progress toward recovery during the past year.

Full advantage should be taken of the broad and successful experience in Western Europe by continuing responsibility for the administration of the Korean aid program in the Economic Cooperation Administration, which has been administering aid to Korea since January 1 of this year.

Prior to January 1 of this year, aid to Korea was administered by the Army as a part of its program for government and relief in occupied areas. The budget which I submitted to the Congress in January contemplated that economic assistance to Korea would be continued outside of the Army's program for government and relief in occupied areas.

The needs of the Republic of Korea for economic assistance have been carefully studied in the light of the latest available information.

I am convinced that the sum of $150,000,000 is the minimum aid essential during the coming year for progress toward economic recovery.

Such a recovery program will cost only a relatively small amount more than a bare relief program. Yet a recovery program - and only a recovery program - will enable the Republic of Korea to commence building up the coal production, electric power capacity and fertilizer production which are fundamental to the establishment of a self-supporting economy and to the termination of the need for aid from the United States. Aid in the restoration of the Korean economy should be less costly to the United States in the end than a continued program of relief.

The recovery program which is recommended is not only the soundest course economically but also the most effective from the standpoint of helping to achieve the objectives of peaceful and democratic conditions in the Far East.

Korea has become a testing ground in which the validity and practical value of the ideals and principles of democracy which the republic is putting into practice are being matched against the practices of communism which have been imposed upon the people of North Korea. The survival and progress of the republic toward a self-supporting, stable economy will have an immense and far-reaching influence on the people of Asia.

Such progress by the young republic will encourage the people of Southern and Southeastern Asia and the islands of the Pacific to resist and reject the Communist propaganda with which they are besieged. Moreover, the Korean Republic, by demonstrating the success and tenacity of democracy in resisting communism, will stand as a beacon to the people of Northern Asia in resisting the control of the Communist forces which have overrun them.

The Republic of Korea, and the freedom-seeking people of North Korea held under Soviet domination, seek for themselves a united, self-governing and sovereign country, independent of foreign control and support and with membership in the United Nations. In their desire for unity and independence, they are supported by the United Nations.

The United States has a deep interest in the continuing progress of the Korean people toward these objectives. The most effective, practical aid which the United States can give toward reaching them will be to assist the republic to move toward self-support at a decent standard of living. In the absence of such assistance, there can be no real hope of achieving a unified, free and democratic Korea.

If we are faithful to our ideals and mindful of our interest in establishing peaceful and prosperous conditions in the world, we will not fail to provide the aid which is so essential to Korea at this critical time.

The White House   HARRY S. TRUMAN
June 7, 1949

From: <u>Department of State Bulletin</u>, Washington, D.C.,
June 19, 1949, pp.781-783.

(In connection with the question of US Economic Aid to Korea,
the following official US Government Reports are important:
viz., <u>Economic Assistance to Certain Areas in the Far East</u>,
House Report No. 1571, Government Printing Office, Washington,
D.C., 1950; <u>Aid to the Republic of Korea</u>, Report of the Senate
Committee on Foreign Relations, No. 748, Washington, D.C.,
July 22, 1949; and <u>Aid to Korea</u>, Report of the House Committee on Foreign Affairs, No. 962, Washington, D.C., July 1,
1949.)

#   #   #

July 28, 1949

<u>CONCLUSIONS OF THE UNITED NATIONS COMMISSION ON KOREA</u>

The people of Korea are remarkably homogeneous. Ethnically and
culturally they are one. They have a passionate longing for unity and
independence and have a profound desire for the peaceful unification of
their country.

The division of Korea has resulted in adverse economic consequences
in the south, the only part of Korea to which the Commission has had ac-
cess. The aftermath of the Second World War would have made the need for
outside aid urgent in any case. But if the country were united, the
south would not require such aid in the same degree and would be able
to stabilize its economy more easily and at a higher level.

The division of Korea has caused bitterness, frustration and mutual
distrust among its people. The frequent raids along the 38th parallel
have further accentuated these feelings. The division of Korea was
caused by the exigencies of the Second World War. There is no justification for the continued separation of the two parts of the country.

The Republic of Korea looks to the United Nations for the solution
of many of its problems, for it feels that the Republic is in some sense
a creation of the United Nations. In the opinion of the Government, as
evidenced by its request that the stay of the Commission in Korea be
prolonged for another year, the presence of the Commission has been a
stabilizing factor in the situation.

Bearing in mind these fundamental considerations underlying the
Korean problem, the United Nations Commission on Korea has reached the
following conclusions:

(1) The embittered propaganda and hostile activities which now mark
the relations between the two parts of Korea render the prospect of unification more and more remote.

(2) As long as the opposition of the Union of Soviet Socialist Republics to the efforts of the United Nations Commission to achieve the objectives of the General Assembly resolution of 12 December 1948 continues, neither a relaxation of hostile propaganda nor any measure can facilitate to a substantial degree the achievement of unification.

(3) The world-wide antagonism between the Union of Soviet Socialist Republics and the United States of America continues to be, as it was when the Temporary Commission was in Korea, one of the basic factors underlying the present difficulties. Without a new effort by those Powers to reach agreement on the question of Korea, no substantial progress toward the achievement of unification on the basis of the principles approved by the General Assembly can be made.

(4) From its very inception, the newly formed Republic of Korea has been confronted with many difficulties. It faced insurgent uprisings from within and was menaced by continuous clashes on the 38th parallel. While making due allowance for these factors, the Commission believes that a broadening of the Government's political base would allow it to meet these difficulties more successfully and so enable it to play a more effective part in achieving unification.

(5) The present Commission, like its predecessor, must place on record an acknowledgment that the situation in Korea is now no better than it was at the beginning, and that it has not been able to facilitate the achievement of the objectives set by the General Assembly.

From: General Assembly Official Records, Fourth Session, Supplement No. 9, Report of the U.N. Commission on Korea, Lake Success, 1949, Volume I, Document A/936, Part D, "Conclusions", p.34.

\#   \#   \#

March 24, 1950

MANIFESTO OF WORKERS' PARTY OF SOUTH KOREA

HEROIC STRUGGLE OF THE PEOPLE OF SOUTH KOREA FOR
UNITY AND INDEPENDENCE OF THE COUNTRY

Pak Hen En (Pok Heun Yung)
Deputy Chairman, Central Committee, Workers' Party of South Korea

The Korean people were liberated from the yoke of Japanese imperialism by the forces of the glorious Soviet Army which played the decisive role in smashing the fascist aggressors both in the West and in the East.

Thanks to the Soviet Union, which consistently fights for genuine democracy and upholds the independence, freedom and sovereignty of large and small nations, the way to a free and happy life, to rehabilitation and development of their national state opened before the 27 million people of Korea.

This great change in the life of Korea awakened the creative forces of the Korean people, forces what had been crushed under the heel of Japanese militarism, and the people resolutely embarked upon the realisation of their age-old aspiration: the creation of an independent democratic Korea. Barely a month after their liberation the Koreans established people's committees - genuine democratic organs of power - in every corner of the country, and proclaimed the formation of their sovereign state, the Korean People's Republic. The people's committees which took power into their hands utterly destroyed the colonial apparatus of government set up by the Japanese invaders, and, without delay, introduced a new, democratic order.

In the vanguard of the patriotic struggle of the Korean people marched the Communist Party - the consistent champion of the national interests of the Korea people and organiser of their struggle for the complete independence and democratic development of the country. Led by the Communist Party, the Korean people rallied around the people's committees while the enemies of the people - pro-Japanese elements, traitors to the country - trembled for their fate before this formidable people's power.

With the formation of the Korean People's Republic decisive democratic transformations were placed on the order of the day: Land reform; nationalisation of basic industries; progressive labour legislation; freedom of speech, press, assembly and organisation; equal rights for women; the spreading of popular education and regeneration of the national culture.

Entering North Korea in August 1945 for the purpose of crushing the Japanese invaders, the great Soviet Army not only supported the patriotic aspirations and democratic demands of the Korean people, it also rendered them all-round disinterested assistance to help them achieve these demands. During its stay on Korean territory the Soviet Army revealed itself to the Korean people as the true standard bearer of the great principles of the Lenin-Stalin foreign policy - the policy of respect for the sovereignty of large and small nations. The Korean people saw for themselves that the Soviet Army pursued no other aim than that of restoring their independence and their democratic development. They welcomed the Soviet Army as their liberator and best friend, and, on its departure, bade farewell to it in the same spirit.

Due to the friendly assistance of the Soviet Union, the aspirations of the Korean people were, after the liberation, fully realised in North Korea. As a result, it is precisely in North Korea that the firm foundation of unity, freedom and independence of the Korean people has now been laid.

There is no doubt whatever that if the American imperialists had not interfered in the internal affairs of Korea and trampled under foot the will of its people, the Korean people would long ago have realised on a national scale the democratic transformations which, so far, have been effected only in North Korea; people's power would also have been established in South Korea, and all Korea would have become a united and independent, democratic state.

I.

Unfortunately for the Korean people, American imperialism appeared on the scene with the same colonising appetite that our people had bitterly experienced under Japanese domination. The Americans, from the first day of the occupation of South Korea, displayed their real aims and designs. The American military authorities in Korea began with repressions against the people and by dispersing the people's committees.

Above all, the Americans attempted to kill the hope of the Koreans for the restoration of their national sovereignty. General Arnold, Chief of the American Military Administration, cynically declared on October 10, 1945, that sovereignty in South Korea belonged not to the Korean people but to the American Military Administration. This statement was immediately confirmed by military measures aimed at suppressing the will of the Korean people. The Americans declared the Korean People's Republic illegal and began to persecute its leaders. This, in effect, was a declaration of war against the Korean people, a forcible abrogation of the sovereignty which was rightfully theirs after the expulsion of the Japanese invaders. The Americans mobilised all their forces to suppress the people's committees.

In place of the people's committees, the administrative apparatus which functioned under the Japanese, an apparatus detested by the people, was restored. Pro-Japanese elements who had waxed rich on the exploitation and oppression of the people in collaboration with the Japanese invaders, once again appeared on the scene, having recovered from their premature fright and having now seen for themselves that a change of masters did not in the least threaten their well-being. Having won the protection of the American colonisers, these traitors gained heart and began to foster and rally the reactionary forces. In collaboration with reactionaries the Americans introduced in South Korea a terrorist, police regime, aimed at suppressing the activities of the democratic parties and public organisations, and at depriving the people of political liberties.

The American aim was to prevent the unification of the democratic forces under the leadership of the Communist Party and to divide the nation. With this in view the American mercenary, Syngman Rhee, nurtured by the Americans, was brought forward and placed at the head of a clique of pro-Japanese elements.

As for American measures in the economic sphere, no Japanese property was handed over to the Korean people; everything was grabbed by the Americans. The carrying through of land reform on the principle of confiscating the land of landlords and traitors and of distributing this land free among the peasants was categorically rejected. The peasant in South Korea remained in the grip of exploitation and oppression as before. The law concerning the eight-hour day remained a dead letter.

Anger and indignation among the Korean people mounted when the Americans deliberately frustrated the carrying out of the decision of the Moscow Conference of Foreign Ministers which provided for the formation of a democratic, united government in Korea. The abandonment by the U.S. Government of the decisions of the Moscow Conference and its blocking of the work of the joint Soviet-American Commission - appointed to carry out this decision - deepened the division in Korea and resulted in new sufferings for the Korea people.

Despite undertakings given concerning freedom of democratic activities, the American Military Administration issued an order for the arrest of the leaders of the Korean Communist Party and arrested and threw into prison, without having grounds for this action, many patriotic leaders who for years had fought selflessly against the Japanese invaders.

The colonisation policy of the Americans in Korea was then openly revealed. To secure a sale for their so-called army surpluses, the Americans imposed a 26 million dollar "credit" on the Koreans. They forcibly requisitioned and exported to Japan rice and other crops, thereby reducing the population of South Korea to a starvation level.

This violence of the Americans, and their colonisation measures evoked throughout South Korea an angry outburst on the part of the mass, people's resistance movement.

The first expression of this large-scale movement was the strike of 40,000 workers in South Korea in October 1946, which in some places developed into an armed uprising.

During this struggle the Americans and their hirelings killed more than 300 patriotic figures; over 2,600 people were wounded, more than 3,600 people were listed as missing (actually most of them were killed) and more than 25,000 were arrested. But despite the killings and bloodshed, over two million workers, peasants, student youth and even urban petty-bourgeoisie took part in this people's action.

This heroic October action of the people of South Korea, under the leadership of the working class, initiated the organised mass struggle of Korean patriots against the American policy of enslaving our country. Since then this struggle has extended and continues to develop, revealing the boundless courage, unity and selflessness of Korean patriots. Today the heroic struggle of the people of South Korea to save their country has developed into a formidable, irresistible force which, in the words of Syngman Rhee himself, is like a forest "fire." This fire will consume all reactionary forces striving to prevent the unification and freedom of Korea.

II.

The October 1946 movement, the general strike of March 22, 1947, the mass struggle of the people of South Korea for a successful outcome of the work of the joint Soviet-American commission in 1947, the nation-wide struggle to secure the realisation of the Soviet proposal for simul-

taneous withdrawal of American and Soviet troops from Korea and to confer on the Korean people the right to form a united government - all
this convinced the Americans that their direct domination in South
Korea was impossible.

The Americans then began to look for methods of deceiving the Korean
people in a way that would enable them, while remaining behind the
scenes, not only to interfere without hindrance in the domestic affairs
of Korea but also completely to dismember the country and turn it into
their colony. To this end they forced a discussion of the Korean question in the U.N. General Assembly, and the adoption of an unlawful decision concerning separate elections in South Korea under the supervision of a so-called U.N. Commission. By means of these elections
the Americans sought to impose their mercenary Syngman Rhee clique on
the people of Korea. This foul scheme was designed to conceal the American policy of enslaving Korea behind the screen of U.N.

But the American imperialists failed to deceive the Korean people;
they failed, as the Korean fable has it, "to steal the bells by turning
a deaf ear". The Korean people realised full well that the formation of
a separate government of American puppets in South Korea would further
deepen the division in Korea, make life even worse for the people in the
South of the country, intensify the terror and police despotism, and
that it would strengthen American domination in the South.

The moment the so-called U.N. Commission arrived in South Korea,
workers in Seoul began a protest movement against its arrival. A general
strike of workers in South Korea began on February 7, 1948. This was
followed by a mass heroic struggle to save the country, a struggle waged
under the slogans: "Down with the U.N. Commission!" "Give the Korean
people the right to form their own united government!" At that time
1,300,000 people took part in strikes and demonstrations against the U.N.
Commission.

The movement against this Commission developed under conditions of
sanguinary terror, when patriots participating in demonstrations risked
their lives. Many heroes of the people fell at the hand of the American
Army and the venal clique of Syngman Rhee. Nevertheless, the movement
acquired a very large scale which testified to the resolute will of the
Korean people to resist the new attempts to enslave their country. Not
infrequently this struggle took the form of armed resistance by the
people.

On April 3, 1948, the flames of the people's partisan struggle
flared up on Chyei-jyu island, off the South Coast of the country. Even
the U.N. Commission could not cover up the conditions which forced the
people of the island to rise against the imposition of this new colonial
yoke. Reporting to the Fourth Session of the General Assembly the Commission pointed out that the affair began with attacks and beatings by
police and members of the North-West Youth Union (a reactionary terrorist organisation.--Author) against persons suspected of Communist Party
membership. Raging against the inhabitants of Chyei-jyu - who wanted
unity and freedom - the reactionary police force, formed by the Americans, arrested more than 10,000 people and tortured to death several

hundred others. Unable to stand the despotism of the police, the people took to arms and rose against their new enemies.

Despite the unfavourable geographic situation of an isolated island, and despite insufficient arms and the cruel scorched earth policy of the enemy who was well armed and supplied with everything necessary, the heroic islanders were able to prevent the separate elections scheduled for their territory on May 10, 1948. No elections were held on the island.

The Syngman Rhee authorities threw against the islanders strong military forces which attacked the patriots with savage brutality. Even the U.N. Commission could not conceal the atrocities of the Syngman Rhee's bandits against the people of Chyei-jyu. The report to the Fourth Session of the General Assembly pointed out: "With the aim of suppression, the government sent large forces of troops to this island, but the disorders did not die down until the beginning of 1949. Military operations had not ended in May 1949. Villages were reduced to ashes, and the damage to buildings, cattle and crops amount to billions of vons."

The armed struggle of the people on Chyei-jyu island led to an intensification in the struggle of all the people in South Korea, a struggle which had begun with the October 1946 action.

The ever growing struggle of all the Korean people against the U.S. colonisation policy prompted leaders of Korean political parties and public organisations of various parties and public organisations of various trends to unite their efforts against attempts to make permanent the temporary dismemberment of Korea. A Congress of representatives of political parties and public organisations from the South and the North, which opened in Pyong-yang on April 29, 1948, called upon all Korean people, in the name of freedom and unification of the country to boycott the separate elections scheduled by the Syngman Rhee clique for May 10.

Rallying to the call of the Congress, the people in South Korea, despite deception, threats and terror, rose in struggle against the separate elections. In many towns and villages in South Korea the "ballot boxes" and "polling booths" were wrecked by the people. On the eve of the elections, hundreds of thousands of people took to the woods and hills, to avoid voting. The notorious "elections" were an ignominious failure. Less than 30 percent of the total electorate voted. As for those who did vote it is common knowledge that most of them voted under pressure, by means of compulsion and deception.

The Americans and their agents in the U.N. Commission had to resort to forgery to declare the elections successful and to install the Syngman Rhee clique in the puppet government of South Korea.

The establishment of the anti-popular puppet regime of Syngman Rhee in the South, confronted the Korean patriots fighting for the unity and the democratisation of their country with the task of creating a real central people's Government of Korea. The Conference of Political Parties and Public Organisations of the North and South, held in June 1948,

decided to hold general democratic elections throughout the country in
August of that year. The Syngman Rhee clique spared no effort to prevent the elections from being held in the South. Two hundred and ninety
one people fell victims of Syngman Rhee's terror and 9,081 were arrested.
Despite this, 6,712,407 out of a total electorate of 8,607,746, i.e.,
77.52 per cent, took part in the secret elections in the South. In
North Korea, where all democratic rights are guaranteed, 99.98 per cent
of the electorate voted. The election results showed the unparalleled
political activity of the masses and the remarkable unanimity of the
Korean people. As a result of these elections the Korean People's
Democratic Republic was proclaimed and the Central Government of Korea
established, headed by Kim Ir Sen, the national hero of the Korean
people.

The Government of the Korean People's Democratic Republic was
formed from an equal number of representatives from both South and North
including representatives of various political trends and social strata
of Korea. The formation of the Central Government is one of the greatest victories of the Korean people in the struggle for unity and freedom.

III.

The treacherous Syngman Rhee clique was placed in power with the
aid of American arms. Without American interference its very existence
would have been unthinkable. The Syngman Rhee clique is isolated from
the people who detest it. Perfectly aware of this universal hatred on
the part of the people, Syngman Rhee and his henchmen see their salvation in perpetual violence and brutal terror against the patriots. But
these anti-popular means which enable the Syngman Rhee clique temporarily
to maintain its rotten regime actually accelerate its doom. The fate
of the Syngman Rhee regime is already sealed.

The constant ministerial chaos, the contradictions in the "National
Assembly" and, the entire policy of the Syngman Rhee Government all testify to the instability and rottenness of the anti-popular puppet regime
in South Korea.

Conscious of its precarious position, the Syngman Rhee clique has,
above all, devoted its efforts to keeping the American occupation army
in our country. It was prepared to yield to the Americans all the wealth
of the country and its freedom if only the clique could receive armed
protection against the people roused to indignation by its policy.

At its first session, the Supreme People's Assembly of the Korean
People's Democratic Republic, expressing the will of the Korean people,
addressed itself to the Governments of the U.S.S.R. and the U.S.A. with
a request that the Soviet proposal be carried out and that the troops
be withdrawn from Korean territory. The Soviet Government immediately
responded to this request of the Supreme People's Assembly of Korea, and
in accord with the national interests of the Korean people withdrew its
troops from North Korea in December 1948. This act of the Soviet Government was an event of historic significance for Korea.

On the occasion of the withdrawal of the units of the great Soviet

140.

Army, the Korean people addressed a letter of gratitude to the leader of the peoples, to the saviour of Korea - Generalissimo Stalin, which letter was signed by 9,900,000 people in South Korea alone.

The rejection of the Soviet proposal by the U.S. Government completely exposed the aggressive designs of the American imperialists who wish to continue the occupation of South Korea with a view to converting it into a U.S. colony and military base. The decision of the Soviet Government to withdraw its troops from Korea and the intensified struggle of the Korean people for the removal of the American occupation forces from Korea, struck fear in the Syngman Rhee clique and made the situation very difficult both for it and for its American masters. In this connection there followed a number of military agreements between the U.S. and the Syngman Rhee clique, while in the "national Assembly" of South Korea threats and provocations were used in order hastily to stage the American-inspired comedy of imploring the U.S. to prolong the stay of American troops in South Korea. The Syngman Rhee clique tries to break the will of the people by a reign of terror unparalleled in scale and brutality.

Beginning with Seoul, Syngman Rhee introduced throughout Southern Korea the so-called mutual responsibility system. This is an unprecedented system of persecution. Every three or five neighbouring houses form a link in this mutual responsibility system. All the occupants of given groups of houses are forced to shadow each other's movements and report immediately to the police or to the "security detachments" any suspicious action or the visit of any strangers to their homes. Should the occupants of these houses fail to comply with these regulations they are subject to arrest, torture, confiscation of their property and exile. And in the event of it becoming known that a suspect had visited one of the houses, the family which received him is physically destroyed.

In districts where partisans are active, the local inhabitants are driven from the area. This is done with such brute force that even the reactionary members of the South Korean "National Assembly" have expressed their concern. Thus Chou Khan En of the "Khang People's Party" (the Korean Kuomintang) stated on October 8, 1949: "There are altogether eight districts in the Bonghva region, North Kengsang province. With the exception of 36 villages (a quarter of the entire district) all the inhabitants were ordered by the military authorities to clear out between October 3 and October 8. The inhabitants do not know where to go."

Compulsory evacuation is being carried out in the districts of Tabyaksan and Chirisang, southern sector of the province of South Chyolla; in the districts of Odesang and Unmusang, in the central mountain districts of the province of North Kengsang, in the districts of Sobiaksang and in other places. The total number of people of South Korea affected by this brutal order is now at least four million. These four million peaceful inhabitants, deprived of their homes, their property, livestock and crops were given five days in which to clear out and live the life of homeless beggars. Such are the monstrous measures adopted by the Syngman Rhee "Government".

When the people resist eviction, the Syngman Rhee forces resort to arms. Kim Kwan Djun, member of the "National Assembly" told the Assembly on October 8, 1949: "If the inhabitants defy eviction now enforced by the military authorities in various districts, they render themselves liable to severe punishment including shooting, as reactionary elements." ("Seoul Sinmun", October 9, 1949.)

Not a trace remains of the promised democratic liberties. Terror and despotic police rule prevail in South Korea. Here is a summary of the activities of the bearers of American "democracy" and their henchmen in South Korea. In 1945, 15 Koreans were killed; in 1946, more than 4,200; in 1947, 3,800; in 1948, over 32,000 and by the end of July 1949, 53,000. Altogether more than 93,000 Korean patriots have been killed. At the same time, over 478,000 people had been arrested by the end of July, 1949. At present the prisons hold 154,000 people. Even the notorious "U.N. Commission" could not close its eyes to the arbitrary rule of the bloodthirsty Syngman Rhee. In its report it points out that under the "State Security Law" which provides for long-term imprisonment and the death penalty for democratic activities "89,710 people had been arrested between September 4th 1948 and April 30, 1949". It is not surprising, therefore, that in these circumstances there is a shortage of prisons in South Korea. The "Government" of Syngman Rhee is hastily building new prisons and extending the old ones. Despite the fact that all likely premises, including factory warehouses in South Korea are used as prisons, they contain 6 to 8 prisoners to every 3.3 square metres in the prisons of South Korea, reported the legal Commission.

IV.

In addition to rampant police terror, the people of South Korea have also to bear the heavy burden of economic ruin. The loudly boosted American "aid" has not improved the economic position of South Korea. On the contrary, deliberate economic disruption continues, and South Korea is becoming more and more dependent on the U.S. Describing the situation in industry in South Korea, the Syngman Rhee paper "Enhab Sinmun" wrote on June 1, 1949:

"If we are to describe how the vital artery of our industry functions we shall have to admit that the situation is indeed very grave. In the industrial centre of Endopo, which can be regarded as the heart of the Khangi state (the ancient name of Korea used by reactionaries), which has a dense network of more than 200 mills and factories, large and small, not more than 55 are in operation, and of these only ten provide a fixed wage, regular hours and pay their employees in cash." Consequently, nor more than five per cent of the industrial enterprises in Endopo are functioning normally.

Such are the benefits accruing to South Korea from the economic "aid" rendered by its American "benefactors".

Hundreds of thousands of people have been thrown out of work and condemned to unemployment as a result of industrial collapse.

The conditions of the unemployed are unbearable. Casual workers live in appalling conditions. This same paper "Enhab Sinmun" writes: "The living conditions of the workers in the major branches of industry are indescribable....Workers are in a terrible state and it is hard to see how they can survive."

The life of the peasants who, denied agrarian reform and who are still groaning under the yoke of the landowners, is equally bad. On June 16th "Enhab Sinmun" wrote: "Increased agricultural production is out of the question. The peasants still continue to till their tiny plots only to prolong life a little more, prolong it simply because it is difficult to die, they pawn everything that it is possible to pawn, borrow money on which they are charged interests as high as 10 to 20 percent". Such is the life of the peasantry; such is the state of agriculture in South Korea. Even the Syngman Rhee organ cannot conceal the horrible conditions of the mass of the people in South Korea groaning under the yoke of American imperialism and domestic reaction.

The people of South Korea are faced with the historic task of ridding themselves of the Syngman Rhee gang, of expelling the American imperialists, and in this way, achieving the speedy unification of the country and the creation of an independent Korean democratic State.

The programme of peaceful unification of the country, advanced by the United Democratic Fatherland Front which unites the best patriotic forces in Korea, expressed the lawful strivings of all our people for unity and independence. This programme was welcomed by all Korean people both in the North and South. On July 20, 1949, the workers in South Korea organized a general two hour strike in support of the United Democratic Fatherland Front programme for peaceful unification. Workers in all branches of industry in South Korea participated while peasants, students and petty bourgeoisie in the towns responded with a mighty movement which rallied several million people.

Afraid of losing its power, the Syngman Rhee clique rejected the proposal for the peaceful unification of the country, and having intensified the terror against the patriots, is openly preparing a numerically strong army equipped and trained by Americans for a campaign against the North. The Syngman Rhee clique wants to embroil Korea in civil war. Pursuing this aim it is constantly provoking incidents in the region of the 38th parallel, the dividing line between North and South Korea, and is sending gangs of spies and saboteurs to the North.

V.

Against this Syngman Rhee policy of treachery and bloodshed, the Korean people are consolidating and activising their ranks, waging an ever more relentless and determined struggle for freedom and independence.

A vivid expression of their selfless patriotism is the armed partisan struggle in South Korea, which, merging with the mass movement of the workers, peasants and petty bourgeoisie, is developing on an ever increasing scale.

On October 20, 1948 the 14th Regiment of Syngman Rhee's army mutinied. It was billeted at Port Losy, through which army units were transported to Chyei-jyu island. When this regiment joined forces with the partisans, the partisans struggle in the South developed on a still wider scale. The regions in which the partisans were most active at that time were the Chirisang mountains in the province of South Choyl-la, the southern maritime district and on Chyei-jyu island. The Syngman Rhee "Government" employed strong army units and invited American officers to act as advisers to suppress the partisans.

Early in 1949, the Syngman Rhee "Government", on the instruction of the U.S. Ambassador Muccio, launched the so-called March and April military campaigns in an attempt to suppress completely the partisans by the spring. As pointed out in the U.N. Commission's report these army campaigns of Syngman Rhee in the province of South Choyl-la "affected" over 23,000 people. Moreover, "all the villages on Chyei-jyu island were reduced to ashes." But this savagery did not deter the patriots. Syngman Rhee failed to extinguish the flames of the people's struggle.

Prior to the summer of 1949 partisan activities were directed mainly to attacks on police posts and on Syngman Rhee officials in populated areas. The partisans operated in small detachments of 50-100 men. They were poorly armed: a light machine-gun was a rare weapon.

The mass people's movement, which developed as a result of the general two-hour strike of South Korean workers on July 20th 1949 in support of the United Democratic Fatherland Front for the peaceful unification of the country, gave the partisan struggle a fresh impetus. From then on it became better organised and more powerful. The partisan detachments are gaining in strength from day to day.

Partisan units, each 400-500 strong, are already operating in the hills of Chirisang, in the southern section of South Choyl-la province, in the Tebyaksang mountains, in the southern sector of North Kensang province and in the Odesang mountains which are the central regions of partisan activities. They have already attacked district administrative centres, police departments and the central depots of Syngman Rhee's army. Successfully engaging the enemy, partisans seize considerable quantities of equipment including mortars, heavy machine-guns and artillery and thus arm themselves at the expense of the Syngman Rhee's army.

In August 1949, more than 44,000 partisans fought 759 actions. They attacked nine district centres and six police depots capturing 523 heavy and light machine-guns and 17,000 rounds of ammunition.

In September, the number of partisans engaging the enemy increased to 77,000 and they fought 1,184 actions.

In partisan areas, the peasants are themselves carrying out agrarian reform. They divide the land confiscated from the landlords. The movement for the revival of the people's committees, which the American military administration dissolved, is spreading.

144.

The partisan movement, the powerful armed force of the people in South Korea, is delivering ever more telling blows against the Syngman Rhee puppet regime.

Suffering from megalomania, Syngman Rhee cannot conceal his great fear of the partisans. In a recent interview with the vice-president of "United Press" he complained that the partisans are a headache and that in view of this he needs arms. ("Seoul Sinmun", October 8, 1949)

At a press conference on October 21, Syngman Rhee actually admitted the failure of his punitive expeditions against the partisans, declaring that it is "difficult to clear the country of partisans with only the army and the police" (Seoul Agency "Hanguk", October 22, 1949). This admission is by no means fortuitous.

The struggle of the heroic partisans in South Korea for the freedom and unity of the country is gaining strength, and reaction can do nothing to suppress it for the Korean partisans are imbued with a sense of lofty patriotism; coming from the ranks of the people the partisans defend the interests of the people and enjoy their support and boundless love. These selfless fighters in South Korea are also inspired by the successes of democratic construction in North Korea where a sound political and economic base is laid for the independence of democratic Korea.

Peaceful, democratic construction in the North, political work among the masses and armed struggle against the colonisers in the South; these are phases in the struggle of the people for achieving the one aim of creating a united independent democratic Korea. Rallied round the Government of the People's Democratic Republic, the Korean people will, at all cost, achieve their cherished aim – and that will be their best contribution to the cause of universal peace and democracy.

From: For a Lasting Peace, for a People's Democracy! Bucharest. Organ of the Information Bureau of the Communist and Workers' Parties -- No. 12 (72) (March 24, 1950) pp.3-4.

(This document gives an authoritative expression of the ideological position of the workers' movement in South Korea which is organized under the direction of Korean Communist Party. The founding of the Korean Communist Party goes back to 1925. Pak Heun Yung, one of the founders, was General-Secretary of the party after V-J Day. See: Washburn, J.N., "Soviet Russia and the Korean Communist Party", in Pacific Affairs, March 1950, p.59-65.)

\#   \#   \#

April 7, 1950

SECRETARY ACHESON'S AIDE-MÉMOIRE TO THE KOREAN AMBASSADOR

The Secretary of State wishes to take this opportunity to express to His Excellency the Ambassador of the Republic of Korea, prior to the latter's return to Seoul, the deep concern of this Government over the mounting inflation in Korea. The Secretary of State wishes His Excellency to convey to the President of the Republic of Korea the view of this Government that the communication of March 4, 1950, from the Korean Prime Minister to the Chief of the Economic Cooperation Mission in Korea, in which the view was expressed that there is no serious problem of inflation in Korea, but rather a threat of deflation, indicates a lack of comprehension on the part of the Korean Government of the seriousness of the problem and an unwillingness to take the drastic measures required to curb the growing inflation.

It is the judgment of this Government that the financial situation in Korea has already reached critical proportions and that, unless this progressive inflation is curbed in the none too distant future, it cannot but seriously impair Korea's ability to utilize effectively the economic assistance provided by the Economic Cooperation Administration. Government expenditures have been vastly expanded by bank overdrafts without reference to limits set by an approved budget. Tax collections have not been increased, aid goods have been underpriced, and governmental subsidies have been expanded. The dangerous practice of voluntary contributions has been used as an inefficient substitute for a sound taxation system. These uneconomic practices have, in turn, served to expand the currency in circulation, unbalance the Korean national budget, and cause a sharp rise in wholesale and retail prices, thereby strengthening the growing forces of inflation.

The Secretary of State must inform His Excellency that, unless the Korean Government is able to take satisfactory and effective measures to counter these inflationary forces, it will be necessary to reexamine, and perhaps to make adjustments in, the Economic Cooperation Administration's assistance program in Korea.

The Secretary of State wishes to inform His Excellency in this connection that the American Ambassador in Seoul is being recalled for consultation within the next few days regarding the critical problems arising our of the growing inflation in Korea.

Of equal concern to this Government are the reported intentions of the Korean Government, as proposed by the President of the Republic of Korea in a message to the National Assembly on March 31, to postpone the general elections from the coming May until sometime in November. The Secretary of State wishes to draw to His Excellency's attention the fact that United States aid, both military and economic, to the Republic of Korea has been predicated upon the existence and growth of democratic institutions within the Republic. Free, popular elections, in accordance with the constitution and other basic laws of the Republic, are the foundation of those democratic institutions. The holding of the elections as scheduled and provided for by the basic laws of the Republic appears to this Government as equally urgent with the taking of necessary measures for countering of the inflationary forces already discussed.

From: Dept. of State Bulletin, Washington, D.C.,
April 17, 1950, p.602.

(Underlining not in original text.)

(This aide-mémoire reflects the concern of the U.S. Government
over economic and political conditions in South Korea under
President Rhee. As early as August 2, 1947, conditions in
South Korea were criticized by Roger N. Baldwin, former Direc-
tor of the Civil Liberties Union, in an article in the Nation
on his return from an officially authorized visit to Korea.
Several months previous to Secretary Acheson's aide-mémoire
given above, the New York Times printed a series of critical
articles on conditions in South Korea by its correspondent,
Mr. Walter Sullivan, in its issues of January 31, 1950,
February 1, 1950, and February 2, 1950. The underlined section of Secretary Acheson's aide-mémoire above refers to the
election for the National Assembly which was finally held on
May 30, 1950.)

#   #   #

June 7, 1950

APPEAL FOR UNIFICATION BY THE DEMOCRATIC FRONT (NORTH)

Members of all democratic political parties and social organizations
throughout Southern Korea!

Our dear compatriots!

In June 1949 the Democratic Front for Unification of the Fatherland
brought forward measures for peaceful unification of our Fatherland. Up
to now, however, these measures still remain to be realized. Five years
have already elapsed since the Soviet army liberated our Korean people
from a long Japanese imperialist rule, but our country still remains to
be unified. Still she is divided.

Who are, then, obstructing the unification of our Fatherland?

For whose interest is this division going on?

As everyone knows, Traitor Rhee Syngman and his gang, in obeisance
to the will of the imperialists, have resorted to every sort of vicious
intrigue to obstruct peaceful unification of our Fatherland - an universal desire of the entire Korean people. And they are obstructing it.

How are they obstructing the unification of the Fatherland?

They are attempting to prevent the Korean people from participating
in the administration of the State. These reactionary traitors fear

their own people. That is why they are frantic in their attempt to maintain and preserve a police state of the reactionary pro-Japanese blood suckers which is hated by the entire people in the southern half area of our Fatherland.

In obeisance to the will of the imperialists and in betrayal of the interests of the Korean people they are attempting to perpetuate the Thirty-Eighth Parallel. For their greedy interests they are selling out our Fatherland as a colony and our people as a slave.

Had not Traitor Rhee Syngman and his gang opposed the Moscow Decision on Korea, Korea already would have been unified several years ago as a democratic independent state.

Had not the imperialists and their running dogs - Traitor Rhee Syngman and his gang - obstructed those measures for peaceful unification of the Fatherland which were brought forward by the Democratic Front for Unification of the Fatherland, our Fatherland would have been unified lastyear.

Therefore, the imperialists and the gang of Traitor Rhee Syngman are solely and entirely responsible for the existing division of our Fatherland.

What has the so-called "United Nations Commission on Korea" done since its arrival in Korea?

It has completely failed in Korea, because its activity has been not for the interests of the Korean people, but for the interests of the imperialists. Turning deaf ears to the earnest aspirations of the Korean people, it is carrying on its activity in close connection with the gang of Traitor Rhee Syngman and the pro-Japanese collaborators. As a matter of fact, it is openly supporting beastly suppression of progressive people, democratic political parties and social organizations; indiscriminate wholesale massacres of people; and punitive expedition against the people's movement - the crimes which are being committed by the gang of Traitor Rhee Syngman.

Therefore, the entire Korean people are resenting the activity of the "United Nations Commission on Korea." And that is why the entire Korean people are carrying on their national struggle as they demand immediate withdrawal of the Commission from Korea.

Our dear compatriots!

Division of our Fatherland across the Thirty-Eighth Parallel is retarding and hindering the development of Korean economy. In the northern half area of our Fatherland electric power, coal, fertilizer, metals, and industrial products are being abundantly produced, and the productivity is growing up and developing every day. But these natural resources cannot be utilized by the people in the southern half area of our Fatherland, because our Fatherland is still divided.

In the southern half area of our Fatherland production is at a standstill; almost all factories and plants are shut down; there are more than 1,500,000 unemployed; peasants are still landless; and people are wandering amid starvation.

It goes without saying that this state of affairs is mainly attributed to crimes committed by the gang of Traitor Rhee Syngman and the imperialists.

The imperialists have on purpose destroyed industries in Southern Korea, and are taking away rice, tungsten, black lead, and numerous other natural resources for cheap prices, all of which are needed by our country.

In the northern half area of our Fatherland the people's committees were established by the creative will of the people, with the result that democratic freedom for the people is fully guaranteed. And from bottom up the people's regime has twice held elections.

Furthermore, the central administrative agency was elected on the basis of the outcome of a general election, held throughout Southern and Northern Korea. This general election was held by secret ballots in accordance with the principles of universal, equal, and direct election. In this democratic election were participated by the entire people representing all walks of life with the exception of the former pro-Japanese collaborators and national traitors.

On the contrary, in the southern half area of our Fatherland there is no regime which has been elected by the people. For there still exists the administrative system of Japanese imperialism which ruled over the Korean people in the past. On May 10, 1948, a separate election, ruinous to our country, was held in Southern Korea, and on the basis of the outcome of this election the so-called "National Assembly" was manufactured. This "National Assembly" is composed of only faithful servants of Traitor Rhee Syngman. In fact, all the assemblymen are the big landowners and reactionaries; there being no single representative of workers and peasants.

Despite this, Traitor Rhee Syngman arrested and jailed several tens of the assemblymen, including Cho Il Whan, Lee Moon Won and Kim Yak Soo.

Not only that. The country-selling election, held on May 30, 1950, in Southern Korea, is by no means a free election. For many candidates who were considered to be unfavorable to Rhee Syngman and who tried to freely speak out their minds, were arrested and imprisoned without exception.

Thus, the "National Assembly" is monopolized by an absolute majority of those assemblymen who were elected thanks to Rhee Syngman's intimidation, lying, arrests and terrorism.

Therefore, the present "National Assembly" is nothing different from the previous one; it is not a people's representative organ.

The gang of Traitor Rhee Syngman, having established a police state in the southern half area of our Fatherland, are suppressing and massacring innumerous patriotic fighters struggling for unification and democratization of our Fatherland.

In 1947 Lyu Woon Hyung, a great patriot of the Korean people, was assassinated, which was followed by the assassination of Kim Koo, a rightist leader, for the reason that he had participated in the South-North Joint Conference, held in Pyongyang in May and June 1948, and that he had advocated peaceful unification of our Fatherland. And for the same reason Kimm Kiusic was kicked out of the political arena.

In 1950 Kim Sam Ryong and Lee Choo Ha, the two superior patriotic fighters of our Fatherland, were arrested and thrown into prison. Besides them, an enormous number of patriots are now groaning in jail; they were arrested by the gang of Traitor Rhee Syngman while fighting for peaceful unification of the Fatherland. And the number of our superior sons and daughters who have been massacred without trial is shocking, indeed.

Such being the actual state of affairs, conscientious elements, and those who are concerned about their country, and even some of the reactionary camp in the southern half area of our Fatherland are praying for the elimination of Rhee Syngman, and are looking for an opportunity of removing him. But the people are resenting such a cowardly attitude of these elements. If they were true patriots, how could they be more faithful to their own safety than to the interests of the people?

How can we fear persecution and look at the Righteousness with folded arms?

Our dear brothers and sisters!

Traitor Rhee Syngman and his gang are enslaving our Fatherland to a foreign country for the filthy selfish interests of their masters and of their own.

For the past five years the entire Korean people have painfully experienced what misfortune and disaster the artificial division of the territory of our country has brought to them.

We do not recognize the Thirty-Eighth Parallel as our frontier, nor can we do so whatever.

The people in the southern half area of our Fatherland are eagerly and ardently desiring the unification of our Fatherland. They hope to live under a unified state - economically and politically.

And also the people in the southern half area of our Fatherland are desiring to celebrate the coming August 15 - the fifth anniversary of the liberation of our Fatherland - with the unification of our Fatherland. It is the hope of the people in the northern half area of our Fatherland, too.

From this standpoint the Central Committee of THE DEMOCRATIC FRONT FOR THE UNIFICATION OF THE FATHERLAND, with the object of realizing peaceful unification of our Fatherland as speedily as possible, hereby propose and appeal to all democratic political parties and social organizations, as well as to the entire patriotic people as follows:

1. A general election shall be held throughout Southern and Northern Korea for four days from August 5 through 8 so that a united supreme legislative organ may be brought into being.

2. On August 15 - the fifth anniversary of the liberation of our Fatherland - the session of the supreme legislative organ, elected by the general election, shall be convened in Seoul.

3. Between June 15 and 17 a consultative Conference of the representatives of the entire political parties and social organizations throughout Southern and Northern Korea who desire peaceful unification of the Fatherland shall be convened either in Haiju or in Kaisung.

(a) All conditions for peaceful unification of the Fatherland.

(b) Procedures for the general election to elect the supreme Korean legislative organ.

(c) Establishment of the Central Guiding Committee, the purpose of which is to direct the general election.

4. The Central Committee of THE DEMOCRATIC FRONT FOR UNIFICATION OF THE FATHERLAND submit the following conditions for participation in the consultative conference of the representatives of the democratic political parties and social organizations throughout Southern and Northern Korea.

(a) The following criminals and traitors who have obstructed peaceful unification of the Fatherland should be excluded from the consultative conference of the representatives of the democratic political parties and social organizations throughout Korea: Rhee Syngman, Lee Bum Suk, Kim Sung Soo, Shin Sung Mo, Cho Byung Ok, Tsai Byung Duk, Pack Sung Wook, Yun Chi Young, and Cynn Heung Woo.

(b) With the work of unifying the Fatherland the United Nations Commission on Korea should not be permitted to interfere, for the Korean people must solve the issue of unifying their Fatherland with their own resources.

5. During the period the consultative conference of the representatives of all the political parties and social organizations throughout Southern and Northern Korea carries on its work and during the period the general election is held, the administrative authorities of both Southern and Northern Korea should hold themselves responsible for guaranteeing and preserving order.

We, the Central Committee of THE DEMOCRATIC FRONT FOR UNIFICATION OF THE FATHERLAND, are firmly convinced that all the democratic political parties and social organizations and their members, as well as the entire Korean people who prize the interests of the Fatherland, will enthusiastically support our proposals.

Long live a democratic unified Korea!

Long live the united Korean people!

In the city of Pyongyang, June 7, 1950.	THE CENTRAL COMMITTEE OF THE DEMOCRATIC FRONT FOR UNIFICATION OF THE FATHERLAND

From: <u>Korean Independence</u>, Los Angeles, July 5, 1950, pp.1-2.

("The Democratic Front for the Unification of the Fatherland" was organized in North Korea on June 25, 1949, as a merger of all "democratic" political organizations in North and South Korea. This organization issued the above document on June 7, 1950, following the U.N.-observed election of May 30, 1950, at which time some 130 candidates out of 210 were elected to the Legislative Assembly of the Republic of Korea ((South)) on an Independent ticket. This new Assembly reconvened on June 19, 1950. The above appeal was delivered to the U.N. Commission on Korea at the 38° parallel border on June 10, 1950. On the next day the three bearers of the appeal were arrested by the police authorities of South Korea. See U.S. Policy in the Korean Crisis, Department of State Publication, No. 3922, July 1950, p.19.)

\#   \#   \#

June 16, 1950

RESOLUTION ON UNITY BY THE DEMOCRATIC FRONT (NORTH)

The Central Committee of the Democratic Front for Unification of the Fatherland, having listened to Mr. Hur Hun's report on the execution of the appeal proposing to speed up peaceful unification of the Fatherland as proposed by the Democratic Front, have reached a decision as follows:

The wide mass movement supporting the proposals submitted by the Democratic Front for Unification of the Fatherland has been expressed through a series of meetings in factories and of mass rallies, many thousands or tens of thousands in number; through resolutions adopted by the central committees of various social organizations; and through statements and appeals made by prominent persons representing all walks of life by means of radio and publications.

But Traitor Syngman Rhee and his traitorous gang are frantically

attempting to incite an internecine civil war for the interests of the
imperialists and of their own. They are opposing peaceful unification
of our Fatherland.

Therefore, these traitors under direct command of the imperialists left no stone unturned in obstructing the realization of measures
for peaceful unification of the Fatherland which were brought forward
by the Democratic Front for Unification of the Fatherland in June
1949. Not only they disrupted the realization of peaceful unification, but also they are now making a desperate attempt to disrupt the
execution of the appeal issued by the Fatherland Front to speed up
the peaceful unification of the Fatherland.

As a matter of fact, Traitor Syngman Rhee and his traitorous gang
are endeavoring to maintain and preserve their anti-popular police
state in Southern Korea under the aegis of guns and swords of the imperialists but across the dead bodies of our compatriots. With the
object of once more disrupting the proposals of the Fatherland Front,
these traitors are enforcing an order for emergency guard along the
border across the Thirty-Eighth Parallel and throughout Southern
Korea. Thus, the representatives of all political parties and social
organizations as well as other patriotic individuals are prohibited
from participating in the proposed South-North Joint Conference, while
those political parties and social organizations as well as patriotic
individuals are being subjected to barbarous suppression and persecution. Furthermore, these traitors, having arrested the peace envoys
of the Fatherland Front who were on their way to Seoul to convey the
Front's appeal to all political parties and social organizations and
patriotic leaders in Southern Korea, are subjecting them to barbarous
tortures.

As the result of such a barbarous outrage committed by the gang
of Traitor Syngman Rhee, the proposed South-North Joint Conference of
the representatives of all political parties and social organizations
both in Southern and Northern Korea, which was scheduled to be held
either in Haiju, or in Kaisung, between June 15 and 17, has been
disrupted.

Once more this discloses the fact that Traitor Syngman Rhee and
his traitorous gang are completely isolated from the Korean people,
that they fear the Korean people, that they are opposed to the universal aspiration of the entire Korean people for peaceful unification of our Fatherland.

On the basis of the aforesaid facts, the Central Committee of the
Democratic Front for Unification of the Fatherland have arrived at the
following decisions:

1. The Democratic Front for Unification of the Fatherland, with
the object of eliminating Traitor Syngman Rhee and his traitorous
gang disrupting the proposal to speed up peaceful unification of the
Fatherland, should strengthen its struggle. For this purpose it
should make efforts to arouse the entire people all the more intensely.

On the other hand, all the political parties and social organizations in the southern half area of our Fatherland should launch a wide
systematic work among the masses of the people for the purpose of
speeding up the realization of peaceful unification of the Fatherland.
At the same time all sorts of struggle against the gang of Traitor
Syngman Rhee should be carried on all the more extensively.

2. Departing from the prevailing conditions created in our country, the Central Committee of the Democratic Front for Unification of
the Fatherland hereby request the Standing Committee of the Supreme
People's Assembly of the Korean People's Democratic Republic to discuss the issue on the possibility of measures for peaceful unification
of the Fatherland being worked out by the sovereign organ of the State.

3. A nation-wide people's struggle should be launched for release of Messrs. Lee In Kyu and Kim Tai Hong, the peace envoys of the
Fatherland Front, who have been arrested on their way to Seoul to
convey the appeal to the political parties and social organizations
as well as to the people in Southern Korea.

June 16, 1950
In the City of Pyongyang

THE CENTRAL COMMITTEE OF
THE DEMOCRATIC FRONT FOR UNIFICATION
OF THE FATHERLAND

From: Korean Independence, Los Angeles,
July 12, 1950.

(This resolution issued close to the day when hostilities
broke out sets forth further suggestions for the implementation of the plans of the Democratic Front for the
unification of Korea. The final plans were set forth in
the resolution of the Supreme People's Assembly ((North))
of June 19, 1950, reproduced on a later page.)

\#   \#   \#

June 19, 1950

SPEECH BY JOHN FOSTER DULLES IN SEOUL

The American people salute the Korean Nation. We honor the valiant
struggle you are making for liberty - human liberty and national liberty.

The American people enlisted in that struggle 175 years ago. We
were then few, poor, divided and menaced. There were only about three
million of us. We were living precariously off the soil and the seas.
We had been divided by loyalties to thirteen rival sovereign states.
We were closely pressed by the great military powers of that time -
Spain to the south, England and France to the north, and Russia which
had moved into our continent in the west. Nevertheless, our founders
saw that Providence had given our people a unique opportunity to show

154.

that a free society could develop a spiritual, intellectual and material
richness which could not be matched by a society of dictatorship, and
that, if we took advantage of that opportunity, our example would
stimulate men elsewhere to cast off the shackles of despotism. From
its beginning, our effort was consciously related to the general welfare of mankind.

We went through many dark days and long nights. But our experiment succeeded. Our conduct and example, despite many faults, did
help to show the infinite possibilities of free men and it encouraged
men everywhere to pry loose the grip of despotism and to take command
of their own destiny. The 19th century was, in most of the world,
an era of human liberation.

But the battle between liberty and despotism is never-ending. It
has no limits either in space or in time. It is part of the constant
struggle between good and evil, a struggle that seems to have been or-
dained for the testing of man.

Despotism, thrown onto the defensive in the 19th Century has resumed the offensive in the 20th Century. Already the United States
has twice intervened with armed might in defense of freedom when it
was hard pressed by unprovoked military aggression. We were not bound
by any treaty to do this. We did so because the American people are
faithful to the cause of human freedom and loyal to those everywhere
who honorably support it.

Today, the Korean people are in the front line of freedom, under
conditions that are both dangerous and exciting. You emerged from
over 40 years spent under Japanese militarism. But you have not
emerged into conditions of placid ease. Instead you encounter a new
menace, that of Soviet Communism. It denies the spritual worth and
dignity of the individual human being. It insists that all men should
be regimented into a pattern of conduct made for them in Moscow. It
seeks to impose that degrading concept upon all men everywhere.

Taking advantage of Japanese surrender terms, Soviet Communism
has seized in its cruel embrace the Korean people to the north of the
38th parallel and from that nearby base it seeks, by terrorism,
fraudulent propaganda, infiltration and incitement to civil unrest,
to enfeeble and discredit your new Republic, hoping no doubt, that
the people might, in despair, accept the iron discipline of the Soviet
Communist Party.

Some observers felt that your task was a hopeless one. You have
proved them to be wrong. Your faith and your works have confounded the
skeptics. You have already held two general elections in an atmosphere
free of terrorism and a very high percentage of all eligible voters
have participated. Out of your electoral processes has come a stable
and representative government. You have developed a strong, disciplined
and loyal defense establishment. Through hard work, you are steadily
improving your country's economic condition.

There is solid ground for encouragement. No doubt there are difficult days ahead and many problems yet unsolved, some internal, some external. But what has already happened shows that it lies within your power to achieve the goal of a Korea that is strong and free. Nothing can prevent that if you persist in your resolute will to be free and if each of you individually exercises the self-controls that are required for the general good. A free society is always a society of diversity. That is the secret of its richness. But also it is a society in which men must voluntarily curb their individualism to the extent needed to enable the nation as a whole to avoid frustration and to achieve creation.

As you establish here in South Korea a wholesome society of steadily expanding well-being, you will set up peaceful influences which will disintegrate the hold of Soviet Communism on your fellows to the north and irresistibly draw them into unity with you. Never for a minute do we concede that Soviet Communists will hold permanently their unwilling captives. No iron curtain can indefinitely block off the attracting force of what you do, if you persist in the way you have been going.

You are conducting what may go down in history as the Great Korean Experiment, an experiment which, in its way, can exert a moral influence in the 20th Century as profound as that which, in the 19th Century, was exerted by what was then called the Great American Experiment. That is why the eyes of the free world are fixed upon you. You carry the hopes and aspirations of multitudes.

The American people give you their support, both moral and material, consistent with your own self-respect and your primary dependence on your own efforts.

We look on you as, spiritually, a part of the United Nations which has acted with near unanimity to advance your political freedom, which seeks your unity with the north and which, even though you are technically deprived of formal membership, nevertheless requires all nations to refrain from any threat or use of force against your territorial integrity or political independence.

The American people welcome you as an equal partner in the great company of those who comprise the Free World, a world which commands vast moral and material power and resolution that is unswerving. Those conditions assure that any despotism which wages aggressive war dooms itself to unutterable disaster.

The Free World has no written Charter, but it is no less real for that. Membership depends on the conduct of a nation itself; there is no veto. Its compulsions to common action are powerful, because they flow from a profound sense of common destiny.

You are not alone. You will never be alone so long as you continue to play worthily your part in the great design of human freedom.

From: U.S. Department of State Press Release,
June 19, 1950.

(This Speech by the Honorable John Foster Dulles, was given
before the National Assembly of the Republic of Korea, Seoul,
in the presence of the Diplomatic Corps and United Nations
Officials, at 3:00 P.M., Korea Time, June 19. ((1:00 A.M.,
E.D.T., Monday, June 19, 1950.)) This was six days before
June 25, 1950, the date of the outbreak of hostilities on
the 38° parallel. On May 30, 1950, an election had been held
for the election of members of the Legislative Assembly of
the Republic of Korea ((South)), the results of which were
an overwhelming victory for the Independent candidates. The
new Assembly convened on June 19, 1950 - the date of the above
speech - and subsequent sessions were marked by severe cri-
ticisms of the Rhee regime.)

#   #   #

June 19, 1950

RESOLUTION ON UNITY BY THE SUPREME PEOPLE'S ASSEMBLY (NORTH KOREA)

Traitor Syngman Rhee and his traitorous gang are strictly forbid-
ding the political parties and social organizations in Southern Korea
from participating in the South-North Joint Conference which has been
proposed by the Democratic Front for Unification of the Fatherland for
the purpose of discussing the speediest realization of peaceful unification of the Fatherland. Thus, these traitors once more are obstructing peaceful unification of our Fatherland. And once more these
traitors have demonstrated that they are betraying the interests of the
Korean people, but that they are acting and moving solely for their
greedy self-interests and for the interests of the alien plunderers.

Therefore, the Standing Committee of the Supreme People's Assembly of the Korean People's Democratic Republic, in accordance with an
indomitable will of the Korean people for unification, independence,
and development of the Fatherland and in accordance with the desire
of all the democratic political parties and social organizations, have
decided to submit to the Southern Korea National Assembly the following proposals:

1. As a measure to merge as a single Korean legislative organ
the Supreme People's Assembly of the Korean People's Democratic
Republic with the Southern Korea National Assembly, the peaceful unification of the Fatherland should be put into execution.

2. The All-Korea Legislative Organ thus established should
adopt the Constitution of the Republic and bring into being the Government of the Republic.

3. On the basis of the Constitution of the Republic thus adopted,
a general election for the All-Korean Legislative Organ should be held.

4. In order to create conditions necessary for peaceful unification of the Fatherland and for the regular activity of the All-Korea Legislative Organ

a. The following arch-criminals and enemies of the Korean people who are obstructing peaceful unification of the Fatherland should be arrested: SYNGMAN RHEE, KIM SUNG SOO, LEE BUM SUK, SHIN SUNG MO, TSAI BYUNG DUK, PACK SUNG WOOK, CHO BYUNG OK, YUN CHI YOUNG, and CYNN HEUNG WOO. They are the national traitors.

b. Freedom of speech, press, assemblage, demonstration, and mass rally should be guaranteed.

c. Suppression of the democratic parties and social organizations as well as of their activists should be stopped. All the political prisoners should be released. Freedom of the activity of the entire democratic political parties and social organizations should be fully guaranteed.

5. The Government to be brought into being by the Legislative Organ should reorganize as a single army and police the existing armies and police or the security strength both in Southern and Northern Korea. The organizations should be carried out on the basis of democratic principles.

6. The United Nations Commission on Korea should be requested to withdraw from the soil of our Fatherland as speedily as possible, for it is being utilized as a tool of the policy to divide and enslave our Fatherland.

The Korean people should solve the problem of peacefully unifying our Fatherland without interference from the outside, but with their own resources.

7. All measures pertaining to the peaceful unification of the Fatherland should be completely put into execution by August 15, 1950 - the fifth anniversary of the liberation of our Fatherland from the Japanese yoke.

8. If the Southern Korea National Assembly agrees with the aforesaid proposals, the Standing Committee of the Supreme People's Assembly of the Korean People's Democratic Republic are ready to send its representatives to Seoul on June 21, 1950, to negotiate with the Southern Korea National Assembly, or to receive in Pyongyang the representatives of the Southern Korea National Assembly for the same purpose. The Southern Korea National Assembly should guarantee inviolability and safety of the representatives of the Supreme People's Assembly of the Korean People's Democratic Republic. At the same time the Standing Committee of the Supreme People's Democratic Republic will guarantee inviolability and safety of the representatives of the Southern Korea National Assembly.

KIM DOO BONG, Chairman
The Standing Committee of the Supreme
    People's Assembly of the Korean
    People's Democratic Republic.

June 19, 1950
In the City of Pyongyang

KANG RYAN WOOK, General Secretary
The Standing Committee of the Supreme
    People's Assembly of the Korean
    People's Democratic Republic.

From: <u>Korean Independence</u>, Los Angeles, July 12,
1950.

(Underlining not in original text.)

(This document, issued on the same day that the newly-elected
National Assembly of the Republic of Korea ((South)) reconvened
in Seoul, reveals the plans for negotiation between the Northern and Southern legislatures for the unification of Korea
worked out under the direction of the Korean Communist Party.
These plans were not consummated, and hostilities broke out
in six days.)

#   #   #

PART IV. THE KOREAN CRISIS OF 1950

June 25, 1950

FIRST RESOLUTION OF SECURITY COUNCIL ON KOREAN CRISIS

Recalling the finding of the General Assembly in its resolution of 21 October 1949 that the Government of the Republic of Korea is a lawfully established government "having effective control and jurisdiction over that part of Korea where the United Nations Temporary Commission on Korea was able to observe and consult and in which the great majority of the people of Korea reside; and that this Government is based on elections which were a valid expression of the free will of the electorate of that part of Korea and which were observed by the Temporary Commission; and that this is the only such Government in Korea":

Mindful of the concern expressed by the General Assembly in its resolutions of 12 December 1948 and 21 October 1949 of the consequences which might follow unless Member States refrained from acts derogatory to the results sought to be achieved by the United Nations in bringing about the complete independence and unity of Korea; and the concern expressed that the situation described by the United Nations Commission on Korea in its report menaces the safety and well being of the Republic of Korea and of the people of Korea and might lead to open military conflict there;

Noting with grave concern the armed attack upon the Republic of Korea by forces from North Korea,

Determines that this action constitutes a breach of the peace,

I. Calls for the Immediate cessation of hostilities; and

Calls upon the authorities of North Korea to withdraw forthwith with their armed forces to the thirty-eighth parallel;

II. Requests the United Nations Commission on Korea

(a) To communicate its fully considered recommendations on the situation with the least possible delay;

(b) To observe the withdrawal of the North Korean forces to the thirty-eighth parallel; and

(c) To keep the Security Council informed on the execution of this resolution;

III. Calls Upon all Members to render every assistance to the United Nations in the execution of this resolution and to refrain from giving assistance to the North Korean authorities.

From: U.S. Policy in the Korean Crisis, Department of State Publication No. 3922, July 1950, p.16 (U.N. Document S/1501).

\#   \#   \#

June 26, 1950

FIRST STATEMENT BY PRESIDENT TRUMAN ON KOREAN CRISIS

I conferred Sunday evening with the Secretaries of State and Defense, their senior advisers and the Joint Chiefs of Staff about the situation in the Far East created by unprovoked aggression against the Republic of Korea.

The Government of the United States is pleased with the speed and determination with which the United Nations Security Council acted to order a withdrawal of the invading forces to positions north of the Thirty-Eighth Parallel. In accordance with the resolution of the Security Council, the United States will vigorously support the effort of the Council to terminate this serious breach of the peace.

Our concern over the lawless action taken by the forces from North Korea, and our sympathy and support for the people of Korea in this situation, are being demonstrated by the cooperative action of American personnel in Korea, as well as by steps taken to expedite and augment assistance of the type being furnished under the Mutual Defense Assistance Program.

Those responsible for this act of aggression must realize how seriously the Government of the United States views such threats to the peace of the world. Willful disregard of the obligation to keep the peace cannot be tolerated by nations that support the United Nations Charter.

> From: U.S. Policy in the Korean Crisis, Department of State Publication No. 3922, July 1950, pp.16-17.

#   #   #

June 27, 1950

SECOND STATEMENT BY PRESIDENT TRUMAN ON KOREAN CRISIS

In Korea the government forces, which were armed to prevent border raids and to preserve internal security, were attacked by invading forces from North Korea.

The Security Council of the United States called upon the invading troops to cease hostilities and to withdraw to the 38th parallel.

This they have not done, but on the contrary have pressed the attack.

The Security Council called upon all members of the United Nations to render every assistance to the United Nations in the execution of this resolution.

The attack upon Korea makes it plain beyond all doubt that communism has passed beyond the use of subversion to conquer independent nations and will use armed invasion and war.

It has defied the orders of the Security Council of the United Nations issued to preserve international peace and security.

In these circumstances the occupation of Formosa by Communist forces would be a direct threat to the security of the Pacific area and to United States forces performing their lawful and necessary functions in that area.

Accordingly, I have ordered the 7th Fleet to prevent any attack on Formosa.

As a corollary of this action, I am calling upon the Chinese government on Formosa to cease all air and sea operations against the mainland.

The 7th Fleet will see that this is done.

The determination of the future status of Formosa must await the restoration of security in the Pacific, a peace settlement with Japan, or consideration by the United Nations.

I have also directed that United States forces in the Philippines be strengthened and that military assistance to the Philippine government be accelerated.

I have similar directed acceleration in the furnishing of military assistance to the forces of France and the associated states in Indo-China and the dispatch of a military mission to provide close-working relations with those forces.

I know that all members of the United States will consider carefully the consequences of this aggression in Korea in defiance of the charter of the United Nations.

A return to the rule of force in international affairs would have far-reaching effects.

The United States will continue to uphold the rule of law.

I have instructed Ambassador Austin, as representative of the United States to the Security Council, to report these steps to the Council.

From: U.S. Policy in the Korean Crisis, Department of State Publication No. 3922, July 1950, p.18.

\#   \#   \#

June 27, 1950

SECOND RESOLUTION OF SECURITY COUNCIL ON KOREAN CRISIS

Having determined that the armed attack upon the Republic of Korea by forces from North Korea constitutes a breach of the peace,

Having called for an immediate cessation of hostilities, and

Having called up the authorities of North Korea to withdraw forthwith their armed forces to the 38th parallel, and

Having noted from the report of the United Nations Commission for Korea that the authorities in North Korea have neither ceased hostilities nor withdrawn their armed forces to the 38th parallel and that urgent military measures are required to restore international peace and security, and

Having noted the appeal from the Republic of Korea to the United Nations for immediate and effective steps to secure peace and security,

Recommends that the Members of the United Nations furnish such assistance to the Republic of Korea as may be necessary to repel the armed attack and to restore international peace and security in the area.

From: U.S. Policy in the Korean Crisis, Department of State Publication No. 3922, July 1950, p.24. (U.N. Document S/1511)

\#   \#   \#

June 29, 1950

SOVIET REPLY TO U.S. ON KOREAN CRISIS

On June 27, the Ambassador of the United States of America, Mr. A. Kirk, sent to the Deputy Foreign Minister, A.A. Gromyko, a memorandum containing a declaration of the United States Government of the following contents:

"My Government has instructed me to draw your attention to the fact that the North Korean troops have crossed the Thirty-eighth Parallel and have invaded the territory of the Republic of Korea at several points with large forces.

"The refusal of the Soviet representative to take part in the meeting of the Security Council of the U.N. on June 25, despite the clear threat to the peace and the obligation which the Charter places on a member of the Security Council, compels the United

States Government to draw the attention of the Government of the U.S.S.R. to this question directly.

"In view of the generally known fact of the close relations between the U.S.S.R. and the North Korean regime, the United States Government asks for an assurance that the U.S.S.R. will not take upon itself the responsibility for this unprovoked and unjustified attack and that it will use its influence with the North Korean authorities toward immediate withdrawal of their invading forces."

On June 29, on the instruction of the Soviet Government, A.A. Gromyko made to Mr. A. Kirk the following declaration:

"In connection with the declaration of the U.S. Government which you handed over on June 27, the Soviet Government has instructed me to declare the following:

"According to reliable data of the Soviet Government, the events which are going on in Korea were provoked by the attack of the troops of the South Korean authorities on the frontier areas of Northern Korea. Therefore, the responsibility of these events lies with the South Korean authorities and with those who stand behind them.

"As is known, the Soviet Government withdrew its troops from Korea earlier than did the U.S. Government and thereby confirmed its traditional principle of non-interference in the internal affairs of other states. The Soviet Government holds now also to the principle of the inadmissibility of the interference of foreign powers in the internal affairs of Korea.

"It is not true that the Soviet Government refused to take part in the meetings of the Security Council; however much it desires it, it was impossible to the Soviet Government to take part in the meetings of the Security Council since by virtue of the attitude of the U.S. Government, the permanent members of the Security Council - China - was not admitted to the council, which made it impossible for the Security Council to take decisions which have legal force."

From: The New York Times, June 30, 1950.

#   #   #

June 30, 1950

PRESS RELEASE ON KOREAN CRISIS BY THE WHITE HOUSE

At a meeting with Congressional leaders at the White House this morning, the President, together with the Secretary of Defense, the Secretary of State, and the Joint Chiefs of Staff, reviewed with them the latest developments of the situation in Korea.

The Congressional leaders were given a full review of the intensified military activities.

In keeping with the United Nations Security Council's request for support to the Republic of Korea in repelling the North Korean invaders and restoring peace in Korea, the President announced that he had authorized the United States Air Force to conduct missions on specific military targets in Northern Korea wherever militarily necessary and had ordered a Naval blockade of the entire Korean coast.

General MacArthur has been authorized to use certain supporting ground troops.

> From: U.S. Policy in the Korean Crisis, Department of State Publication No. 3922, July 1950, pp.24-25.

#   #   #

July 2, 1950

NORTH KOREAN PROTEST TO THE U.N.

I have the honor to request you to bring to the notice of all members of United Nations the declaration made by me on the instructions of the Government of the Korean People's Democratic Republic on 1 July 1950.

In reply to the declaration of the Foreign Minister of the Korean People's Democratic Republic of 27 June, the President of the United States, Mr. Truman, declared that he had ordered the air and naval forces of the United States to intervene in the military operations in Korea on the side of the South Korean puppet regime, which has unleashed civil war in our country at the behest of the American imperialists.

On 30 June, Mr. Truman announced that American land forces had been sent to South Korea. American aircraft are brutally bombing our peaceful population and flying over Pyongyang and other points in North Korea and the liberated cities of South Korea, attacking units of the People's Army with the purpose of hindering their victorious advance southward. The policy pursued by the American imperialists of enslaving the Korean people and turning Korea into a colony of the United States has now developed into open armed intervention against the Korean People's Democratic Republic.

American imperialists have long dreamed of establishing their domination in the Far East. Previously, however, they had to reckon with the imperialistic interests of Great Britain, Japan and other powers and expand their position in the Far East by making deals with those powers at the cost of enslaving the peoples of Asia. The Korean people will not forget in particular the fact that in 1905 the United States,

with a view to reinforcing their domination over the Philippines, negotiated a treacherous deal with Japan and joined in setting up a Japanese
protectorate over Korea.

After the Second World War, which resulted in the defeat of Japan
and the weakening of Great Britain, American imperialists decided to
occupy their place in the countries of the Far East, endeavoring to
transform the Pacific Ocean into an American sea and the peoples of
the Pacific Ocean countries into the slaves of American monopoly. The
strengthening of the forces of the democratic camp, however, the advance of the national liberation movement in the countries of Asia,
and particularly the great victory won by the Chinese people, utterly
destroyed the base designs of the American imperialists. The Korean
people has personally experienced the whole weight of the colonialist
policy of American imperialists. Having rid itself of the hateful
yoke of the Japanese, it again finds itself threatened with enslavement.

The American imperialists, in their anxiety to keep a grip of
South Korea, stubbornly resisted the unification of the Korean people.
They disrupted the formation of a single democratic government based on
the Moscow decision of the Foreign Ministers of the U.S.SR., U.S.A.,
and U.K. They refused to remove their troops from Korea before they
had transformed Southern Korea into their own colony with the assistance
of the puppet government of Syngman Rhee created by them. It is now
clear to every Korean that, even after the withdrawal of American
troops, South Korea was governed by the American imperialists. It is
they who, together with the Syngman Rhee clique, bear full responsibility for the crimes of the military police regime which they have set
up in South Korea, for the executions and murders of tens of thousands
of the sons of the Korean people destroyed by the Syngman Rhee clique
on the orders of their American masters, for the tortures inflicted on
hundreds of thousands of patriots thrown into prison and brutally tortured, for all the sufferings of the people of South Korea. But they
did not succeed in enslaving the Korean people, the main hindrance to
this being the democratic regime established in North Korea.

North Korea has become a powerful base for the fight of the Korean
people for unity, independence, and freedom. Its successes in peaceful
reconstruction, which have shown the superiority of democracy as com-
pared with the anti-popular military and police regime of South Korea,
have inspired the Korean people to fight against the efforts of American imperialists to reduce Korea to a colony, have convinced the people
of ultimate victory.

That is why the American imperialists and their South Korean
lackeys, in their hatred of the Korean People's Democratic Republic,
have long been cherishing plans to throttle it by military force. They
obstructed the realization of the proposals for the peaceful unification
of Korea, which were frequently put forward by the parties and social
organizations and also by the Government of the People's Democratic
Republic.

With the support of the United States, the Government of Syngman
Rhee has for two years past openly prepared for an attack on the North,

boasting that its army could occupy Pyongyang in a single day, and that it was merely awaiting the order to advance, having secured the promise of military support from the U.S.A. At the behest of its American masters, the Syngman Rhee Government on 25 June began civil war in Korea.

In provoking this war the American imperialist intended by means of armed intervention to destroy the Korean Democratic Republic and take possession of all Korea. Civil war in Korea was also necessary to the American imperialists in order to create a pretext for aggression against China and Vietnam also, to throttle the national liberation movement of the peoples of the Orient.

The United States is trying to cover its intervention in Korea with the name of the United Nations, but everyone knows that the American imperialists have placed the United Nations before a fait accompli by undertaking armed intervention; it calculated that it will succeed by means of the votes of countries dependent on the U.S.A., using the name of the United Nations to cover any unlawful action whatsoever, even after it has been penetrated.

The American-dictated resolution of the Security Council based on one-sided, fabricated information, is invalid and contrary to the United Nations Charter, since it was adopted without the participation of representatives of the Government of the Korean People's Democratic Republic and also without the participation of representatives of two great powers, permanent members of the Security Council, the U.S.S.R. and the Chinese People's Republic.

Members of the Security Council who voted in favor of this resolution have once again shown that they are prepared to put their signatures to any document dictated to them by the United States, regardless of the rights and interests of the peoples.

In this connection, it is worthy of remark that the pro-American majority in the United Nations, which has now shown such a feverish readiness to save the bankrupt Syngman Rhee regime, ignored the repeated applications of the Korean People's Democratic Republic and social organizations of Korea made in U.N. organs regarding the atrocities and military provocation committed by the Syngman Rhee regime. It also ignored numerous requests made by Korean social organizations with concrete propoals for the peaceful unification of Korea, thus encouraging the adventurist actions of the U.S.A. and their South Korean vassals to stir up civil war in Korea.

The American imperialists and their South Korean proteges committed a desperate mistake in unleashing civil war in Korea. The troops of Syngman Rhee have met with fitting resistance and under the blows of the People's Army, which has counter-attacked, are fleeing in disorder to the south. The gallant People's Army, in defense of the freedom and independence of the Korean people, is continuing to pursue the enemy. In the military operations of the past week, the People's Army cleared the enemy out of a large area of the southern half of the republic and liberated Seoul, the national capital.

The population is everywhere welcoming its army, which has liberated it from the terrors of the Syngman Rhee regime, and it is giving it active assistance in the liberation of the country. The heroic partisans in South Korea have carried out military operations on the enemy's communications and have cut the main railway line from the harbor of Pusan; in collaboration with the insurgent population they have freed a number of towns in South Korea. The flight of the Syngman Rhee Army and the popular rising in its rear are futher evidence of the rottennes and failure of the anti-popular regime of the South Korean puppets of the U.S.A.

The complete bankruptcy of the Syngman Rhee regime has today become obvious. Seeing the collapse of their plans for the colonization of Korea, the American imperialists are reinforcing their armed intervention against the Korean people. They want to drown the freedom of Korea in the blood of its patriots, but they will not frighten the freedom-loving Korean people.

In reply to the bare-faced aggression of the United States, the Korean people will gather even more closely under the banner of the Korean People's Democratic Republic and strengthen their holy war for the freedom, unity and independence of their native land. The Government of the Korean People's Democratic Republic and the whole Korean nation resolutely protest against American armed intervention in Korea, against the barbarous bombardments of Korean towns and villages, against the inhuman slaughter of peaceful citizens.

We are convinced that all honorable people in the world will indignantly condemn the aggression of the American imperialists against the freedom-loving people of Korea.

We are certain that our just cause will meet with warm sympathy in the hearts of all people.

From: The New York Times, July 3, 1950.

(The above is a translation from a message in Russian, dated July 2, 1950, to Secretary General Trygve Lie from Pak Hen Nen, Foreign Minister of the Korean People's Democratic Republic, Pyongyang.)

#   #   #

July 4, 1950

SOVIET STATEMENT CHARGING U.S. AGGRESSION IN KOREA

The events occurring in Korea arose on June 26 as a result of a provocative attack of the troops of the South Korean authorities on border areas of the Korean People's Democratic Republic.

That attack was the result of a plan prepared in advance.

That the South Korean clique of Syngman Rhee had such a plan has been disclosed from time to time as well by Syngman Rhee himself as by other representatives of the South Korean authorities.

As long ago as October 7, 1949, Syngman Rhee in an interview granted to a United Press correspondent boasted about the success of the preparation of his army.

He openly stated that the South Korean Army could take Pyongyang in three days.

The Minister of Defense of Syngman Rhee's Government, Sin Sen Mo, on October 31, 1949, also stated to the press that the South Korean forces are sufficiently strong to act and take Pyongyang in a few days.

Only a week before the provocative attack on the border districts of the Korean People's Republic, Syngman Rhee, speaking on June 19 in the so-called National Assembly, said in the presence of the adviser to the American Department of State, Mr. (John Foster) Dulles, "We are not able to defend democracy in a cold war. We shall reach victory in a hot war."

It is not difficult to understand that such statements of the representatives of the South Korean authorities could be made only feeling behind their backs American support.

Even one month before the events which started in Korea on May 19 of this year, the head of the American administration of help to Korea, Johnson, stated in the Commission of Appropriations of the United States House of Representatives, that 100,000 soldiers and officers of the South Korean Army, fitted with American equipment and trained by the American military mission, had finished their preparations and could start war at any moment.

It is known that only a few days before the events in Korea, the War Minister of the U.S.A., (Louis) Johnson; the Chief of Staff of the armed forces of the U.S.A., General Bradley, and the adviser of the State Department, Dulles, arrived in Japan and held there a special conference with General MacArthur, and that Dulles after that visited South Korea and journeyed to the border areas on the Thirty-eighth parallel.

Only one week before the events, on June 19, Dulles stated in the "National Assembly" of South Korea mentioned above that the United States was ready to give all necessary moral and material help to South Korea, which is fighting against communism.

These facts are sufficiently eloquent by themselves and do not require comments.

But the first days have already shown that the events were not taking a turn favorable to the authorities of South Korea.

The Korean People's Republic achieved a series of successes against the South Korean forces directed by the American military advisers.

When it became clear that the terrorist regime of Syngman Rhee, which has never enjoyed the support of the Korean people, would fall, the Government of the United States passed openly to intervention in Korea, ordering air, naval, and then also its land forces to enter in action on the side of the South Korean authorities against the Korean people.

Doing that, the Government of the United States passed from a policy of preparing an aggression to the policy of open interference in the internal affairs of Korea, to the policy of armed intervention in Korea.

Choosing that road, the Government of the United States infringed peace, showing that not only does it not tend to consolidate peace but on the contrary is an enemy of peace.

Facts show that the Government of the Unites States is disclosing its aggressive plans in Korea only step by step.

At the beginning the United States Government stated that the intervention of the United States in Korea would be limited only to the dispatch of military and other equipment.

After that it was announced that air and naval forces, but not ground forces would be sent.

After that it was announced that ground forces of the United States would also be sent to Korea.

It is known also that at the beginning the Government of the United States announced that American forces would be used only in operations taking place on the territory of southern Korea.

But after scarcely a few days the American air forces shifted their operations to North Korean territory and attacked Pyongyang and other cities.

All that shows that the Government of the United States is dragging the United States into war, but being compelled to consider the fact that the American people do not wish to be entangled in a new war adventure, it gradually pushes the country step by step toward open war.

The Government of the United States of America is attempting to justify the intervention against Korea by contending that the intervention was allegedly started on the directive of the Security Council.

The hypocrisy of that assertion is quite evident.

What happened in reality?

It is known that the Government of the United States began to intervene with arms in Korea before the session of the Security Council had been called on June 27, without considering what the decision of the Security Council would be.

Thus the United States Government confronted the United Nations organization with a "fait accompli," with the violation of peace.

Only after the accomplished fact did the Security Council set the seal on the resolution proposed by the United States Government, approving the aggressive actions undertaken by that Government.

The American resolution was accepted by the Security Council by a gross infringement of the Charter of the United Nations.

According to Article 27 of the Charter of the United Nations, the decisions of the Security Council in important matters must be taken by not less than seven votes, including in that the votes of all five permanent members of the Security Council, namely: the U.S.S.R., China, Great Britain, the United States and France.

In reality the American resolution approving the military intervention of the United States in Korea was taken by six votes only, those of the United States, Great Britain, France, Norway, Cuba and Ecuador.

The vote of the Kuomingtanite, Tsiang Ting-fu, who unlawfully takes China's seat in the Security Council, was counted as the seventh vote for that resolution.

Furthermore, at the meeting of the Security Council on June 27 only three of the five permanent members of the Council were present; the United States, Britain, and France.

Two other permanent members of the Security Council, the U.S.S.R. and China, were not present at the Council's meeting because the United States Government's hostile attitude towards the Chinese people deprives China of the opportunity of having her own representative in the Security Council and this fact has made it impossible for the Soviet Union to take part in the conferences of the Security Council.

Thus, neither of these two requirements of the Charter of the United Nations concerning the procedure for taking decisions was complied with at the session of the Council of June 27, which deprives the resolution adopted at that session of any legal force.

It is also known that the Charter of the United Nations provides for intervention of the Security Council only in cases which concern events of an international nature and not of an internal character.

In this respect the Charter directly forbids the intervention of the organization of the United Nations in the affairs of any country when there is an internal conflict between two groups in a state.

Thus the Security Council in their resolution of June 27 also infringed this most important principle of the organization of the United Nations.

The facts stated above prove that the resolution which the United

States Government is using as a cover for its armed intervention in Korea was illegally put through the Security Council, while the Charter of the organization of the United Nations has been grossly infringed.

That has been made possible only owing to great pressure by the United States Government on the members of the Security Council which has transformed the United Nations organization into a kind of branch of the State Department of the United States, into an obedient tool for the policy of the American ruling circles, who have acted as violators of peace.

Having the duty, owing to his function, of watching the correct implementation of the Charter of the United Nations, the Secretary General, while the Korean question was discussed in the Security Council, not only did not accomplish his direct obligations, but, on the contrary in an officious way helped the United States Government and other members of the Security Council to infringe grossly the Charter.

At a press conference on June 29, President Truman denied that the United States, having started military action in Korea, was in a state of war. He stated that that was just police action, in support of the United Nations, and that allegedly that action was directed against a group of bandits from northern Korea.

It is easy to see that such an assertion is unwarranted.

The illegal resolution of June 27, adopted by the Security Council under pressure from the United States Government, shows that the Security Council is acting, not as a body invested with the main responsibility for the maintenance of peace, but as an instrument employed by the United States ruling circles with the object of unleashing war.

This resolution of the Security Council represents a hostile act against peace.

Had the Security Council valued the cause of peace, it should have attempted to reconcile the fighting sides in Korea before it adopted such a scandalous resolution.

Only the Security Council and the United Nations Secretary General could have done this. They failed to make that attempt, however, being obviously aware that such an action is contrary to the aggressors' plans.

The military action of General MacArthur, started in Korea by the order of the United States Government, can be considered a "police action" to support the United Nations organization just as much as the war started in 1937 against China by the Japanese militarists could be considered an "incident to maintain peace in the East."

The operations of the armed forces in Korea are led, as is known, not under the orders of some police officer, but under the orders of General MacArthur.

But it would be absurd to admit that the Commander in Chief of the

United States forces in Japan, MacArthur, directs in Korea not military operations but some "police action."

Who will believe that MacArthur's armed forces, which include air forces up to "Flying Fortresses" and jet aircraft attacking the civil population and the peaceful towns of Korea, which include the Navy with its cruisers and aircraft carriers and also ground forces, have been called for a "police action" against a group of "bandits"?

Perhaps even the most credulous people will not believe it.

What are the real aims of the American armed intervention in Korea?

It appears that the aggressive circles of the United States have violated peace in order to grab not only southern but also northern Korea.

The intrusion of the American forces into Korea represents an open war against the Korean people.

The aim is to deprive Korea of national independence, to prevent the creation of a single democratic Korean state, and to establish by violence in Korea an anti-national regime which would allow the ruling circles of the United States to transform that country into their colony and to use Korean territory as a military base in the Far East.

Ordering the armed forces of the United States to attack Korea, President Truman at the same time announced that he has given the American Navy orders to "prevent an attack on Formosa," which means the occupation by American armed forces of that territory belonging to China.

That step of the United States Government is a direct aggression against China.

That step of the United States Government is moreover a gross infringement of the international agreements of Cairo and Potsdam on Formosa as belonging to China, signed by the United States.

It is also an infringment of President Truman's statement by which on January 25 last he announced that the American Government would not interfere in the affairs of Formosa.

President Truman has announced that he ordered the reinforcement of the American armed forces on the Philippine Islands, which was aimed at interfering in the internal affairs of the Philippine state and at kindling internal strife.

That act of the United States Government shows that it continues to consider the Philippines as its colony and not as an independent state which, furthermore, is a member of the United Nations.

President Truman also stated that he had ordered the acceleration of the so-called military aid to France in Indo-China

That statement of Truman shows that the United States Government has adopted the policy of kindling war against the Vietnamese people for the sake of supporting the colonial regime in Indo-China - thus proving that the United States Government is assuming the role of gendarme of the peoples of Asia.

President Truman's statement of June 27 means thus that the Government of the United States has violated peace and has passed from a policy of preparation for aggression to direct act of aggression, and above that at the same time in a number of countries of Asia.

In doing so the United States Government has trampled underfoot its obligations toward the United Nations organization for the consolidation of peace in the whole world and has appeared as a violator of peace.

The Soviet Government has already expressed its attitude in respect of the policy of gross interference in the internal affairs of Korea led by the Government of the United States in its reply of June 29 to the announcement of the United States Government of June 27.

The Soviet Government is persisting without change in the policy of consolidation of peace in the whole world and of its traditional principle of non-intervention in the internal affairs of other states.

The Soviet Government considers that the Koreans have the same right to organize according to their wishes their internal national affairs in the matter of the unification of the South and North of Korea into one state as that right which belonged to and was used by the North Americans in the Sixties of the last century, when they unified the South and the North of America into one national state.

From all that it is to be deduced that the United States Government has committed an act of hostility against peace and the responsibility for the results of the armed aggression committed by that Government are falling on it.

The United Nations will accomplish its obligations concerning the maintenance of peace only if the Security Council will demand the absolute cessation of the American military intervention and the immediate evacuation of the American armed forces from Korea.

From: The New York Times, July 5, 1950.

(The above is the text of a statement made in Moscow by Andrei A. Gromyko, Soviet Deputy Foreign Minister, and distributed in London on July 4, 1950 by the Soviet news agency Tass.)

#　　　　　#　　　　　#

July 7, 1950

THIRD RESOLUTION OF SECURITY COUNCIL ON KOREAN CRISIS

The Security Council,

Having determined that the armed attack upon the Republic of Korea by forces from North Korea constitutes a breach of the peace,

Having recommended that Members of the United Nations furnish such assistance to the Republic of Korea as may be necessary to repel the armed attack and to restore international peace and security in the area,

1. Welcomes the prompt and vigorous support which governments and peoples of the United Nations have given to its Resolutions of 25 and 27 June 1950 to assist the Republic of Korea in defending itself against armed attack and thus to restore international peace and security in the area.

2. Notes that Members of the United Nations have transmitted to the United Nations offers of assistance for the Republic of Korea;

3. Recommends that all Members providing military forces and other assistance pursuant to the aforesaid Security Council resolutions make such forces and other assistance available to a unified command under the United States;

4. Requests the United States to designate the commander of such forces;

5. Authorizes the unified command at its discretion to use the United Nations flag in the course of operations against North Korean forces concurrently with the flags of the various nations participating.

6. Requests the United States to provide the Security Council with reports as appropriate on the course of action taken under the unified command.

From: U.S. Policy in the Korean Crisis, Department of State Publication No.3922, July 1950, pp.66-67.

\#   \#   \#

July 8, 1950

THIRD STATEMENT BY PRESIDENT TRUMAN ON KOREAN CRISIS

The Security Council of the United Nations in its resolution of July 7, 1950, has recommended that all members providing military forces and other assistance pursuant to the Security Council resolutions of

June 25 and 27, make such forces and other assistance available to a unified command under the United States.

The Security Council resolution also requests that the United States designate the commander of such forces, and authorizes the unified command at its discretion to use the United Nations flag in the course of operations against the North Korean forces concurrently with the flags of the various nations participating.

I am responding to the recommendation of the Security Council and have designated General Douglas MacArthur as the commanding general of the military forces which the members of the United Nations place under the States pursuant to the United Nations' assistance to the Republic of Korea in repelling the unprovoked armed attack against it.

I am directing General MacArthur, pursuant to the Security Council resolution, to use the United Nations flag in the course of operations against the North Korean forces concurrently with the flags of the various nations participating.

From: U.S. Policy in the Korean Crisis, Department of State Publication No. 3922, July 1950, p.67.

\#   \#   \#

July 11, 1950

SOVIET REPLY TO U.N. SECRETARY-GENERAL ON KOREAN CRISIS

The Soviet Government has received your telegram citing the text of the Security Council resolution of 7 July, which calls for the provision of military forces and other assistance to the so-called "unified command under the United States", requests the United States to designate the commander of such forces and authorizes the use of the United Nations flag in the course of operations in Korea. The Soviet Government considers that the adoption of this resolution constitutes the same flagrant violations of the United Nations Charter as the Security Council resolution of 27 June on the Korean question. The resolution was adopted in the absence of two Permanent Members of the Security Council - the Union of Soviet Socialist Republics and China - and received only six votes, the seventh vote being that of the Kuomintang representative, who has no legal right to represent China. In these circumstances this Security Council resolution also can clearly have no legal force. It must be emphasized that the aim of the Security Council resolution referred to is to permit the illegal use of the United Nations flag as a cloak for United States military operations in Korea, which are a direct aggression by the United States against the Korean people. All this gives the Soviet Government grounds for declaring that the Security Council resolution of 7 July, firstly, is illegal and,

176.

secondly, constitutes direct act of assistance to armed aggression against the Korean people.

From: <u>U.S. Policy in the Korean Crisis</u>, Department of State Publication No. 3922, July 1950, pp.67-68.

(This statement was signed by A.A. Gromyko, Deputy Minister of Foreign Affairs of the U.S.S.R.)

#   #   #

July 19, 1950

<u>PRESIDENT TRUMAN'S MESSAGE TO CONGRESS ON KOREAN CRISIS</u>

To the Congress of the United States:

I am reporting to the Congress on the situation which has been created in Korea and on the actions which this nation has taken, as a member of the United Nations, to meet this situation. I am also laying before the Congress my views concerning the significance of these events for this nation and the world and certain recommendations for legislative action which I believe should be taken at this time.

At 4:00 o'clock in the morning, Sunday, June 25, Korean time, armed forces from north of the Thirty-eighth Parallel invaded the Republic of Korea.

The Republic of Korea was established as an independent nation in August, 1948, after a free election held under the auspices of the United Nations. This election, which was originally intended to cover all of Korea, was held only in the part of the Korean peninsula south of the Thirty-eighth Parallel, because the Soviet Government, which occupied the peninsula north of that parallel, refused to allow the election to be held in the area under its control.

The United States, and a majority of the other members of the United Nations, have recognized the Republic of Korea. The admission of Korea to the United Nations has been blocked by the Soviet veto.

In December, 1948, the Soviet Government stated that it had withdrawn its occupation troops from Northern Korea, and that a local regime had been established there. The authorities in Northern Korea continued to refuse to permit United Nations observers to pass the Thirty-eighth Parallel to supervise or observe a free election, or to verify the withdrawal of Soviet troops.

Nevertheless, the United Nations continued tis efforts to obtain a freely elected government for all of Korea and, at the time of the attack, a United Nations Commission, made up of representatives of seven nations

- Australia, China, El Salvador, France, India, the Philippines and Turkey - was in the Republic of Korea.

Just one day before the attack of June 25, field observers attached to the United Nations Commission on Korea had completed a routine tour, lasting two weeks, of the military positions of the Republic of Korea south of the Thirty-eighth Parallel. The report of these international observers stated that the army of the Republic of Korea was organized entirely for defense. The observers found the parallel guarded on the south side by small bodies of troops in scattered outposts, with roving patrols. The found no concentration of troops and no preparation to attack. The observers concluded that the absence of armor, air support, heavy artillery and military supplies precluded any offensive action by the forces of the Republic of Korea.

On June 25, within a few hours after the invasion was launched from the North, the Commission reported to the United Nations that the attack had come without warning and without provocation.

The reports from the Commission make it unmistakably clear that the attack was naked, deliberate, unprovoked aggression, without a shadow of justification.

This outright breach of the peace, in violation of the United Nations Charter, created a real and present danger to the security of every nation. This attack was, in addition, a demonstration of contempt for the United Nations, since it was an attempt to settle, by military aggression, a question which the United Nations had been working to settle by peaceful means.

The attack on the Republic of Korea, therefore, was a clear challenge to the basic principles of the United Nations Charter and to the specific actions taken by the United Nations in Korea. If this challenge had not been met squarely, the effectiveness of the United Nations would have been all but ended, and the hope of mankind that the United Nations would develop into an institution of world order would have been shattered.

Prompt action was imperative. The Security Council of the United Nations met, at the request of the United States, in New York at 2 o'clock in the afternoon, Sunday, June 25, Eastern Daylight Time. Since there is a fourteen-hour difference in time between Korea and New York, this meant that the Council convened just twenty-four hours after the attack began.

At this meeting the Security Council passed a resolution which called for the immediate cessation of hostilities and for the withdrawal of the invading troops to the Thirty-eighth Parallel, and which requested the members of the United Nations to refrain from giving aid to the Northern aggressors and to assist in the execution of this resolution. The representative of the Soviet Union to the Security Council stayed away from the meeting, and the Soviet Government has refused to support the Council's resolution.

The attack launched on June 25 moved ahead rapidly. The tactical surprise gained by the aggressors and their superiority in planes, tanks and artillery, forced the lightly armed defenders to retreat. The speed, the scale, and the coordination of the attack left no doubt that it had been plotted long in advnace.

When the attack came, our Ambassador to Korea, John J. Muccio, began the immediate evacuation of American women and children from the danger zone. To protect this evacuation, air cover and sea cover were provided by the Commander in Chief of United States Forces in the Far East, General of the Army Douglas MacArthur. In response to urgent appeals from the Government of Korea, General MacArthur was immediately authorized to send supplies of ammunition to the Korean defenders. These supplies were sent by air transport, with fighter protection. The United States Seventh Fleet was ordered north from the Philippines, so that it might be available in the area in case of need.

Throughout Monday, June 26, the invaders continued their attack with no heed to the resolution of the Security Council of the United Nations. Accordingly, in order to support the resolution, and on the unanimous advice of our civil and military authorities, I ordered United States air and sea forces to give the Korean Government troops, cover and support.

On Tuesday, June 27, when the United Nations Commission in Korea had reported that the Northern troops had neither ceased hostilities nor withdrawn to the Thirty-Eighth Parallel, the United Nations Security Council met again and passed a second resolution recommending that members of the United Nations furnish to the Republic of Korea such aid as might be necessary to repel the attack and to restore international peace and security in the area. The representative of the Soviet Union to the Security Council stayed away from this meeting also, and the Soviet Government has refused to support the Council's resolution.

The vigorous and unhesitating actions of the United Nations and the United States in the face of this aggression met with an immediate and overwhelming response throughout the free world. The first blow of aggression had brought dismay and anxiety to the hearts of men the world over. The fateful events of the Nineteen Thirties, when aggression unopposed bred more aggression and eventually war, were fresh in our memory.

But the free nations had learned the lesson of history. Their determined and unified actions uplifted the spirit of free men everywhere. As a result, where there had been dismay there is hope; where there had been anxiety there is firm determination.

Fifty-two of the fity-nine member nations have supported the United Nations action to restore peace in Korea.

A number of member nations have offered military support or other types of assistance for the United Nations action to repel the aggressors in Korea. In a third resolution, passed on July 7, the Security Council requested the United States to designate a commander for all the forces of the members of the United Nations in the Korean operation, and authorized these forces to fly the United Nations flag. In response to this resolution, General MacArthur has been designated as commander of these forces. These are important steps forward in the development of a United Nations system of collective security. Already, aircraft of two nations - Australia and Great Britain - and naval vessels of five nations - Australia, Canada, Great Britain, the Netherlands, and New Zealand - have been made available for operations in the Korean area, along with forces of Korea and the United States, under General MacArthur's command. The other offers of assistance that have been and will continue to be made will be coordinated by the United Nations and by the unified command, in order to support the effort in Korea to maximum advantage.

All the members of the United Nations who have indorsed the action of the Security Council realize the significance of the step that has been taken. This united and resolute action to put down lawless aggression is a milestone toward the establishment of a rule of law among nations.

Only a few countries have failed to support the common action to restore the peace. The most important of these is the Soviet Union. Since the Soviet representative had refused to participate in the meetings of the Security Council which took action regarding Korea, the United States brought the matter directly to the attention of the Soviet Government in Moscow. On June 27, we requested the Soviet Government, in view of its known close relations with the North Korean regime, to use its influence to have the invaders withdraw at once.

The Soviet Government, in its reply on June 29 and in subsequent statements, has taken the position that the attack launched by the North Korean forces was provoked by the Republic of Korea and that the actions of the United Nations Security Council were illegal.

These Soviet claims are flatly disproved by the facts.

The attitude of the Soviet Government toward the aggression against the Republic of Korea is in direct contradiction to its often expressed intention to work with other nations to achieve peace in the world.

For our part, we shall continue to support the United Nations action to restore peace in the Korean area.

As the situation has developed, I have authorized a number of measures to be taken. Within the first week of the fighting, General MacArthur reported, after a visit to the front, that the forces from North Korea were continuing to drive south, and further support to the Republic of Korea was needed. Accordingly, General MacArthur was authorized to use United States army troops in Korea, and to use United States aircraft of the Air Force and the Navy to conduct missions against specific military targets in Korea north of the Thirty-eighth Parallel, where necessary to carry out the United Nations resolutions. General MacArthur was also directed to blockade the Korean coast.

The attacking forces from the north have continued to move forward, although their advance has been slowed down. The troops of the Republic of Korea, though initially overwhelmed by the tanks and artillery of the surprise attack by the invaders, have been reorganized and are fighting bravely.

United States forces, as they have arrived in the area, have fought with great valor. The Army troops have been conducting a very difficult delaying operation with skill and determination, outnumbered many times over by attacking troops, spearheaded by tanks. Despite the bad weather of the rainy season, our troops have been valiantly supported by the air and naval forces of both the United States and other members of the United Nations.

In this connection, I think it is important that the nature of our military action in Korea be understood. It should be made perfectly clear that the action was undertaken as a matter of basic moral princi- ple. The United States was going to the aid of a nation established and supported by the United Nations and unjustifiably attacked by an aggressor force. Consequently, we were not deterred by the relative immediate superiority of the attacking forces, by the fact that our base of supplies was 5,000 miles away, or by the further fact that we would have to supply our forces through port facilities that are far from satisfactory.

We are moving as rapidly as possible to bring to bear on the fight- ing front larger forces and heavier equipment and to increase our naval and air superiority. But it will take time, men and material to slow down the forces of aggression, bring these forces to a halt, and throw them back.

Nevertheless, our assistance to the Republic of Korea has pre- vented the invaders from crushing that nation in a few days - as they had evidently expected to do. We are determined to support the United Nations in its effort to restore peace and security to Korea, and its effort to assure the people of Korea an opportunity to choose their own form of government free from coercion, as expressed in the General As- sembly resolutions of November 14, 1947, and December 12, 1948.

In addition to the direct military effort we and other members of the United Nations are making in Korea, the outbreak of aggression there requires us to consider its implications for peace throughout the world. The attack upon the Republic of Korea makes it plain beyond all doubt that the international Communist movement is prepared to use armed invasion to conquer independent nations. We must therefore recog- nize the possibility that armed aggression may take place in other areas.

In view of this, I have already directed the United States forces in support of the Philippines to be strengthened and that military as- sistance be speeded up to the Philippine Government and to the Associa- ted States of Indo-China and to the forces of France in Indo-China. I have also ordered the United States Seventh Fleet to prevent any attack upon Formosa, and I have requested the Chinese Government on Formosa to cease all air and sea operations against the mainland. These steps were at once reported to the United Nations Security Council.

Our action in regard to Formosa was a matter of elementary security. The peace and stability of the Pacific area had been violently disturbed by the attack on Korea. Attacks everywhere in the Pacific area would have enlarged the Korean crisis, thereby rendering much more difficult the carrying out of our obligations to the United Nations in Korea.

In order that there may be no doubt in any quarter about our intentions regarding Formosa, I wish to state that the United States has no territorial ambitions whatever concerning that island, nor do we seek for ourselves any special position or privilege on Formosa. The present military neutralization of Formosa is without prejudice to political questions affecting that island. Our desire is that Formosa not become embroiled in hostilities disturbing to the peace and stability of the Pacific and that all questions affecting Formosa be settled by peaceful means as envisaged in the Charter of the United Nations.

With peace established, even the most complex policitical questions are susceptible of solution. In the presence of brutal and unprovoked aggression, however, some of these questions may have to be held in abeyance in the interest of the essential security of all.

(Section on recommendations for domestic policies omitted.)

The free world has made it clear, through the United Nations, that lawless aggression will be met with force. This is the significance of Korea - and it is a significance whose importance cannot be overestimated.

I shall not attempt to predict the course of events. But I am sure that those who have it in their power to unleash or withhold acts of armed aggression must realize that new recourse to aggression in the world today might well strain to the breaking point the fabric of world peace.

The United States can be proud of the part it has played in the United Nations action in this crisis. We can be proud of the unhesitating support of the American people for the resolute actions taken to halt the aggression in Korea and to support the cause of world peace.

The Congress of the United States, by its strong, bipartisan support of the steps we are taking and by repeated actions in support of international cooperation, has contributed most vitally to the cause of peace. The expressions of support which have been forthcoming from the leaders of both political parties for the actions of our Government and of the United Nations in dealing with the present crisis have buttressed the firm morale of the entire free world in the face of this challenge.

The American people, together with other free peoples, seeks a new era in world affairs. We seek a world where all men may live in peace and freedom, with steadily improving living conditions, under governments of their own free choice.

182.

For ourselves, we seek no territory or domination over others. We are determined to maintain our democratic institutions so that Americans now and in the future can enjoy personal liberty, economic opportunity, and political equality.

We are concerned with advancing our prosperity and our well-being as a nation but we know that our future is inseparably joined with the future of other free peoples.

We will follow the course we have chosen with courage and with faith, because we carry in our hearts the flame of freedom. We are fighting for liberty and for peace - and with God's blessing we shall succeed.

From: Department of State Bulletin, No. 578, July 31, 1950.

\#   \#   \#

July 20, 1950

U.S. "WHITE PAPER" ON KOREAN CRISIS

Foreword

The surprise attack launched against the Republic of Korea in the early morning of June 25 by the Communist regime in North Korea was a brutal blow to the peace of the world. It was directed against a peaceful people ruled by an independent government of their own choosing, brought into being with the participation of the United Nations, and recognized by the majority of the free nations of the world.

The United Nations lost no time in branding the North Korean Communist attack as a breach of the peace, and in recommending to United Nations members that they furnish to the Republic of Korea the assistance necessary to repel the armed attack and restore international peace and security in the area.

The United States, in accordance with its obligations, has supported the action of the United Nations and, in agreement with other free nations of the world, has taken action against the agressor.

It is the Department of State's responsibility to place full and accurate information on such critical events before the people of the United States and the world so that they may reach informed judgments concerning the actions of this government.

The documents bearing on United States policy toward these developments are therefore being published.

Introduction

During World War II the United States, the United Kingdom, and China pledged their determination, in the Cairo Declaration of December, 1943, that Korea would "in due course" become free and independent. This pledge was reaffirmed in the Potsdam Declaration of July 26, 1945, and was subscribed to by the Soviet Union when it declared war against Japan on August 8, 1945. The defeat of Japan made it possible for Korea to look forward to the realization of its desire for independence.

Korea was never formally divided into zones of occupation between the United States and the Soviet Union at any of the high-level wartime conferences. After receipt of the Japanese offer of surrender, with the nearest American troops at Okinawa and with Soviet troops already in Korea, the United States Government, in providing for the surrender of Japanese troops, proposed that Soviet troops accept the surrender of Japanese troops in Korea north of the Thirty-eighth Parallel and that Japanese troops in Korea south of that line surrender to American forces. After this arrangement had been accepted by Generalissimo Stalin, it was incorporated in the first General Order which General MacArthur, as Supreme Commander for the Allied Powers, caused to be issued on September 2, 1945. The United States did not contemplate a lasting division of Korea along this line, which was a fortuitous line resulting from the exigencies of the war.

Soviet forces first entered Korea on August 12, 1945, and proceeded to occupy the Northern half of Korea. American troops landed on September 8 and accepted the surrender of Japanese troops in the southern part of the peninsula on the following day. It soon became apparent that the division of Korea for surrender purposes was to be arbitrarily interpreted by the Soviet occupation authorities as creating a permanent delineation between two military zones, passage between which was possible only by permission of the military commanders. This situation continued despite persistent efforts of the United States Commander to negotiate arrangements with his Soviet counterpart with a view to reestablishing the essential unity of the country.

At Moscow in December 1945 the Foreign Ministers of the United States, the United Kingdom, and the Soviet Union agreed that a provisional Korean democratic government should be set up for all Korea. The Moscow Agreement, to which the Chinese Government subsequently adhered, provided that the United States and Soviet commands in Korea were to form a Joint Commission which, in consultation with Korean democratic parties and social organizations, was to make recommendations to the Four Powers for the organization of a provisional Korean democratic government. Every effort to give effect to this agreement, however, was blocked by Soviet intransigence.

The United States, unwilling to permit this situation to delay further the realization of Korean independence, then laid the question of Korean independence before the United Nations. The General Assembly of the United Nations in November 1947 called for an election, under the observation of the United Nations Temporary Commission on Korea, to choose representatives, not mere appointees of military authorities in Korea, who might be invited to participate in the discussion of the question by the United Nations and who, constituting a National Assembly, should draft a democratic constitution and establish a National Government.

The Soviet Union held that the Korean question, like others connected with the conclusion of peace treaties, did not fall within the jurisdiction of the United Nations. It adopted a "negative attitude" toward the Temporary Commission and refused to allow it even to enter the northern part of Korea. Consequently, the right of the Korean people to participate in a free election and to establish a free government was confined to southern Korea. The election was held on May 10, 1948, under the supervision of the United Nations Temporary Commission on Korea, and the Government of the Republic of Korea was established on August 15, 1948.

The Government of the Republic of Korea was accepted by the United Nations in December 1948 as the validly elected, lawful Government of the area in which elections were permitted - the only such government in Korea. The General Assembly established a reconstituted Commission to continue to work for unification and a representative government for the entire country. The United States recognized the new government on January 1, 1949, and 31 other nations have done likewise. The Soviet Union and its satellites have not recognized the Republic of Korea, whose membership in the United Nations has been blocked by the Soviet use of the veto in the Security Council.

Meanwhile, north of the 38th parallel, which had become a part of the "Iron Curtain," the Soviet Union established a Communist regime. The formal creation of this regime, the so-called "Democratic People's Republic of Korea," claiming jurisdiction over the entire country, was proclaimed on September 9, 1948. This regime has lived, as it was created, in complete defiance of the United Nations.

In pursuance of the recommendations contained in the General Assembly's resolution of December 12, 1948, to the effect that the occupying Powers should "withdraw their occupation forces from Korea as early as practicable" the United States completed the withdrawal of its occupation forces on June 29, 1949. This withdrawal was observed and verified by the United Nations Commission on Korea as recorded in its report dated at Seoul, July 28, 1949. The Soviet Union announced that it had completed withdrawal of its troops in December 1948, but the United Nations Commission has not been permitted to verify this action.

It has been the aim of the United States to provide the people of the Republic of Korea with sufficient assistance and support to enable them to progress through their own efforts toward freedom and independence. The transfer of functions from the United States Military Government to Korean agencies was carried out progressively from the establishment of the Republic. The United States continued to give assistance and support to the Republic both within the framework of the United Nations and directly. The United States has extended economic aid and technical economic aid and technical advice and, in general, has assisted the people of Korea in establishing a democratic political and economic structure responsive to their needs.

The Korean Crisis

The first official report that North Korean forces had launched an all-out offensive across the 38th parallel against the Republic of Korea just before daybreak on Sunday, June 25, 1950 (Korean time), was received from the American Ambassador at Seoul, John J. Muccio. The Ambassador's report was received in the Department of State on Saturday night, June 24, at 9:26 P.M. Eastern Daylight Time.

Considering this assault upon the Republic of Korea as a breach of the peace and an act of aggression, the United States Government brought the matter to the attention of the United Nations at once and at 3 A.M. on June 25 requested an immediate meeting of the Security Council. By the time the Security Council met at Lake Success at 2 P.M. on June 25, that body had before it a report from the United Nations Commission on Korea which confirmed attack on the territory of the Republic and stated:

"Commission wishes to draw attention of Secretary-General to serious situation developing which is assuming character of full-scale war and may endanger the maintenance of international peace and security. It suggests that he consider possibility of bringing matter to notice of Security Council."

At this meeting of the Security Council the Deputy Representative of the United States, Earnest A. Gross, made a statement in which he traced briefly developments in Korea since the end of 1945 and pointed out the part played by the United Nations in the creation of the Republic of Korea. Mr. Gross also introduced a draft resolution for the consideration of the council. After amendment and revision of the United States draft, the Security Council, by a vote of nine to zero, with one abstention and one absence, adopted a resolution which determined that the armed attack upon the Republic of Korea constituted a breach of the peace and called for (1) immediate cessation of hostilities and (2) withdrawal of North Korean forces to the 38th parallel. The resolution also called upon "all Members to render every assistance to the United Nations in the execution of this resolution and to refrain from giving assistance to the North Korean authorities." The resolution requested the United Nations Commission to observe the withdrawal of the North Korean forces and to keep the Security Council informed on the execution of the resolution.

Besides laying the matter before the United Nations, the United States immediately ordered the evacuation of American women and children from Korea and provided air cover for the evacuation. After action by the Security Council the United States considered methods of aiding the Republic of Korea under the terms of the Security Council's resolution. Following a conference on Sunday evening, June 25, attended by the President, the Secretaries of State and Defense, their senior advisers, and the Joint Chiefs of Staff, Gen. Douglas MacArthur was authorized to furnish to the Korean Government additional military supplies and assistance of the type furnished under the Mutual Defense Assistance Program. This action was made public in a presidential press statement on June 26. At this time the President said: "In accordance with the resolution of the Security Council, the United States will vigorously support the effort of the Council to terminate this serious breach of the peace."

By this time the United States Government had received a direct appeal from the Korean National Assembly for "increasing support" and for "effective and timely aid in order to prevent this act of destruction of world peace." The National Assembly had also appealed to the United Nations through its Commission on Korea for "immediate and effective steps to secure peace and security."

The following day, June 27, the President announced at noon that he had "ordered United States air and sea forces to give the Korean Government troops cover and support" in accordance with the Security Council's Resolution of June 25.

When the Security Council met at 3 p.m. on Tuesday, June 27, it had before it a number of cablegrams from the United Nations Commission on Korea (UNCOK). One contained a summary report on the background events preceding the outbreak of hostilities. The Commission also reported that its efforts to make contact with North Korean authorities in the preceding 18 months had "met only with negative response" and stated its conviction that "North Korea will not heed Council resolution nor accept UNCOK good offices." The Commission suggested alternate methods of possible mediation but pointed out the danger that rapid developments might render "academic" the "question of cease-fire and withdrawal" called for in the Security Council's resolution. The Commission further indicated that the aggression was continuing and gave its estimate of the situation as follows:

"Commission's present view...is, first, that judging from actual progress of operations Northern regime is carrying out well-planned, concerted and full-scale invasion of South Korea, second, that South Korea forces were deployed on wholly defensive basis in all sectors of the parallel, and, third, that they were taken completely by surprise as they had no reason to believe from intelligence sources that invasion was imminent."

The Council subsequently received further background information from the Commission in the form of a report of June 24 from United Nations field observers. This report clearly indicated that even before the major attack began the North Korean forces had been "in effective possession of salients" on the south side of the 38th parallel and that the Army of the Republic of Korea was "organized entirely for defense" and was "in no condition to carry out attack on large scale against forces of North."

At the meeting of June 27 Ambassador Warren R. Austin, the United States Representative, stated to the Security Council that the continuing invasion of the Republic of Korea by North Korean authorities in the face of the Council's resolution of June 25 was "an attack on the United Nations itself." Mr. Austin said that it was the "duty of the Security

Council to invoke stringent sanctions to restore international peace," and he introduced a draft resolution for the consideration of the Council. He read the President's announcement of noon of that day, quoted above, and concluded his statement as follows:

"The keynote of the draft resolution and of my statement, and the significant characteristic of the action taken by the President, is support of the United Nations' purposes and principles - in a word: 'peace'."

The resolution which the Security Council adopted at this meeting by a vote of seven to one, with two abstentions and one absence recommended that the "Members of the United Nations furnish such assistance to the Republic of Korea as may be necessary to repel the armed attack and to restore international peace and security in the area."

On June 30 the President announced that in keeping with the Security Council's resolution "he had authorized the United States Air Force to conduct missions on specific military targets in Northern Korea" and had ordered "a Naval blockade of the entire Korean coast." He also announced that General MacArthur had been "authorized to use certain supporting units." In a speech at the Security Council meeting on the same day Mr. Austin called attention to the President's announcement and stressed the historic significance of the action of the Security Council in coming to the aid of the Republic of Korea. The Foreign Minister of the Republic on July 4 thanked the United Nations for its action and added that the people of Korea were "deeply moved by the promptness and vigour with which Members of the United Nations in honourable fulfilment of their obligations under the Charter have acted to repel the aggression and to restore peace in Korea."

The response of the members of the United Nations to the Security Council's resolution of June 27 and to the Secretary-General's communication of June 29, asking to be advised of the type of assistance the members were prepared to furnish, has been prompt and overwhelmingly favorable. Of all those Nations which have communicated their views to the Secretary-General in writing, only three - The Soviet Union, Czechoslovakia, and Poland - opposed the Council's resolution. The great majority of the others promised either their material or moral support. A considerable number promised special types of assistance in accordance with their particular abilities. Thailand has indicated that it would furnish foodstuffs, such as rice, to the Republic of Korea; Denmark has offered medicinal supplies; Norway has offered tonnage for transportation; Chile will cooperate by "ensuring regular and adequate supplies of copper, saltpetre, and other strategic materials to countries responsible for operations"; the Philippines is prepared to contribute "such amounts of copra, cocoanut oil, soap, rice, and anti-cholera, typhoid, dysentery vaccines; also smallpox virus that may help facilitate the implementation of the resolution"; and Nicaragua has stated that it is prepared to assist with foodstuffs, raw materials such as rubber, and even personnel when deemed advisable. Australian aircraft and naval vessels are participating in operations in Korea; Canada, New Zealand, and the Netherlands have dispatched naval vessels for operations in Korean waters; and the United Kingdom has placed its naval forces in Japanese waters at the dis-

posal of the United States authorities to be operated on behalf of the
Security Council in support of the Republic of Korea. The Chinese Government offered three divisions of troops, together with 20 transport
planes and "a moderate amount of naval escort," if the latter should be
required. In addition to these offers of implementation of the Security Council's resolution of June 27, the Council of the Organization of
American States adopted a resolution at its meeting on June 28 in support of the action of the Security Council.

The United States informed the Secretary-General on June 30 and
July 6 of the measures which it had taken in implementation of the
Security Council's resolutions of June 25 and 27. It likewise advised the Chinese Government that in its view it would be desirable for
representatives of General MacArthur's headquarters to hold discussions
with the Chinese military authorities prior to any final decision on the
use of Chinese troops.

The Soviet Union, Czechoslovakia, and Poland, in communications to
the Secretary-General of the United Nations, attacked the legality of
the Security Council's resolutions regarding Korea on the ground that
the Soviet Union, a permanent member of the Council, had not participated in the voting and that China had been represented by the Chinese
Nationalist delegate rather than by a representative of the Chinese
Communist regime. The Soviet cable stated that the Security Council's
resolution of June 27 "was adopted by six votes, the seventh vote being
that of the Kuomintang representative Dr. Tingfu F. Tsiang who had no
legal right to represent China," and that the resolution "was passed in
the absence of two permanent members of the Security Council, the Union
of Soviet Socialist Republics and China." It also stated that, according to the provisions of the United Nations Charter, "a decision of the
Security Council on an important matter can only be made with the concurring votes of all five permanent members of the council."

The Department of State analyzed the Soviet charges of illegality
of the Security Council's action in the form of a press statement of
June 30. With respect to the Soviet claim concerning the Chinese vote
the Department stated that the "Rules of Procedure of the Security
Council provide the machinery for the seating of an accredited representative of the Security Council" and added that the "credentials of
the representative of the National Government of China were approved by
the Council and the Soviet attempt at a later date to withdraw this approval was defeated." As regards the Charter provisions on voting in
the Security Council the Department agreed that Article 27 provides that
"substantive questions be decided by an affirmative vote of seven members including the concurring votes of the permanent members," but added:

"By a long series of precedents, however, dating back to 1946, the
practice has been established whereby abstention by permanent members
of the Council does not constitute a veto,

"In short, prior to the Soviet allegations, every member of the
United Nations, including the U.S.S.R. accepted as legal and binding decisions of the Security Council made without the concurrence, as expressed through an affirmative vote, of all permanent members of the
Council."

The Department then cited a number of instances where one or more permanent members of the Security Council, and frequently the Soviet Union itself, had abstained from voting on substantive matters under consideration and where the legality of the Council's action had not been questioned. The Department also pointed to three instances in which the Soviet Union had voted with the majority, with other permanent members of the Council abstaining, and in which the Soviet Union had never questioned the legality of the resulting Security Council action. The Department concluded:

"The voluntary absence of a permanent member from the Security Council is clearly analogous to abstention.

"Furthermore Article 28 of the Charter provides that the Security Council shall be organized as to be able to function continuously. This injunction is defeated if the absence of a representative of a permanent member is construed to have the effect of preventing all substantive action by the Council.

"No one of the 10 members of the Council participating in the meetings of June 25 and 27 raised any question regarding the legality of the action - not even the member who dissented on June 27."

Despite the fact that the Soviet Union was not participating in the work of the United Nations, the United States sought Soviet cooperation in the restoration of peace in Korea. In a note to the Soviet Foreign Minister dated June 27 the United States called attention to the violation of the territory of the Republic of Korea by the North Korean forces and to the Security Council resolution of June 25. In view of the close relations between the Soviet Union and the North Korean regime, the United States asked for assurances that the Soviet Union "disavows responsibility for this unprovoked and unwarranted attack" and requested the Soviet Government to "use its influence with the North Korean authorities to withdraw their invading forces immediately." The Soviet reply, read to the American Ambassador at Moscow on June 29, accused the authorities of the Republic of Korea of starting hostilities and stated that as the Soviet Union adhered to the "principle of non-interference in the internal affairs of other states," it would not interfere in the internal affairs of Korea. The Soviet Government also denied the legality of the action of the Security Council.

Under instructions from the Department of State the American Ambassador at Moscow on July 4 informed the Soviet Foreign Minister of the President's order establishing a naval blockade of the Korean coast in keeping with the Security Council's request for support of the Republic of Korea in repelling the North Korean invaders and restoring peace. The Soviet reply, in the form of a note dated July 6, again denied the legality of the Security Council's action regarding Korea and characterized the naval blockade of Korea as "a new act of aggression.... just as incompatible with the principles of the United Nations as is the entire armed intervention of the United States in Korea." It concluded that the "Soviet Government will consider the Government of the United States of America responsible for all the consequences of this act and for the entire damage which may be caused to the interests of the Soviet

190.

Union in connection with the conduct of the blockade mentioned." A similar position was taken by the Polish Government, which was likewise notified of the naval blockade, as were all other Governments with which the United States maintains diplomatic relations.

In order better to utilize the various offers of assistance and to unify the operations in defense of the Republic of Korea, the Security Council adopted, on July 7, 1950, by a vote of seven to zero, with three abstentions and one absence, a resolution requesting the nations supplying forces and other assistance for this police action to put them under a unified command headed by the United States. The resolution also requested the United States to designate the commander of such forces and authorized the unified command at its discretion to use the United Nations flag in the operations against North Korean forces concurrently with the flags of the various nations participating. In addition the resolution requested the United States to provide the Council with reports on the acts of the unified command. Mr. Austin informed the Council that the United States would accept the responsibilities and obligations placed upon it by the Council. The next day, July 8, the President complied with the Security Council's resolution. The President designated General MacArthur as commanding general of the forces operating in Korea in accordance with the Security Council's decisions and directed him to use the United Nations flag pursuant to the Security Council's resolution.

From: New York Times, July 22, 1950.

(The full text of the so-called "White Paper on Korea", entitled U.S. Policy in the Korean Crisis, Department of State Publication No. 3922, July 1950, Washington, D.C., gives 101 diplomatic documents following the text of the sections entitled Foreword, Introduction, and Korean Crisis, reproduced above.)

\#   \#   \#